WEBER'S
NEW REAL GRILLING

JAMIE PURVIANCE

PHOTOGRAPHY BY TIM TURNER

TABLE OF CONTENTS

foreword

BY MIKE KEMPSTER

I was born in the early wave of baby boomers. It was the early 1950s, not long after our troops returned home from World War II. It was a time when the American dream really took root and people began settling into new homes and optimistic new lives. Back then, you knew you were doing well if you had a car with gigantic fins parked in front of a new home, a lush lawn, and a backyard patio decked out with a barbecue grill and picnic table. Life was good. Dads everywhere were stepping up to the grill, and a passion for grilling was beginning to burn across the land.

I grew up watching my dad use some of the first grills that were mass-produced for homeowners. Little did I know back then that grilling would become such an integral part of my adult life.

The year was 1952. George Stephen, a metalworker and father of twelve, loved to barbecue, but grills on the market at the time were far from ideal. Most were open braziers, making it impossible to control flare-ups. George thought that a lid with vents might help control airflow, prevent flare-ups, and keep the ashes and the elements at bay.

It's been said that necessity is the mother of invention, and that was certainly true when George invented the Weber® kettle. He was working at his father's company, Weber Brothers Metal Works, at the time, welding metal spheres into buoys. He was just about to weld two sphere halves together when it hit him: he could make a grill out of the two halves. So he did just that, and the classic Weber kettle was born. Over the next two decades, George grew

his invention from a curiosity into a backyard staple.

I started selling Weber® grills when I was a teenager working in a Kansas City hardware store. I never imagined that I would be hired by George Stephen and go on to become a lifelong Weber salesman and barbecue fanatic. In the early 1970s, growing the business meant hauling grills around from store to store conducting grilling demonstrations. We even published little paper pamphlets that we sold for fifty cents. Each had a dozen or so recipes and grilling tips, and boy, were they popular. So we decided to go a little bigger.

We published our first hardcover cookbook, *Barbecuing the Weber® Covered Way*, in 1972. Some of the recipes and ingredients wouldn't stand a

Mike Kempster and
George Stephen
circa 1974

chance now, but we had fun reminiscing and thought we'd share some with you.

As the years have passed, traditional barbecued meals have evolved. Grilling enthusiasts are more adventuresome, and their palates expect to be treated to the wide range of food and flavors that were not popular or didn't even exist ten or twenty years ago.

It's my pleasure to introduce you to *Weber's New Real Grilling*™. Decades of hands-on grilling, answering grilling questions, and feeding the fire are behind every word and photo. I think you will enjoy this book as much as we have enjoyed bringing it to life.

Mike Kempster

WHAT'S OLD IS NEW AGAIN

Once upon a charcoal grill, there was a tiny chef named Topper. With his little apron and his big smile, he introduced America to the concept of covered cooking as part of the original red and gold "Weber Bar-B-Q Kettle" logo in the 1950s.

Our logo has evolved over the years, but Topper makes a comeback in this book. Whenever you see our hatted mascot next to a recipe, you'll know that the recipe is part of our "Recipe Remix: Then and Now," a timeless grilling favorite reimagined for how we eat today. We found all sorts of these golden oldies in our first cookbook, *Barbecuing the Weber® Covered Way*, published in 1972. This was also the first cookbook with instructions on how to use something very new—a Weber® gas grill.

Our grills are now sold around the globe, and our cookbooks have become international best sellers. No matter the country, grilling enthusiasts have shown their excitement for great recipes and for becoming better outdoor grillers.

introduction

BY JAMIE PURVIANCE

In the beginning there was fire. Then we threw some burgers and hot dogs on it, and there was dinner.

When I was a boy in suburban New Jersey in the 1960s, this is how my family grilled. Those were the days when meat came off the grill, and pretty much everything else came out of the kitchen. Americans were still reveling in post-war, modern conveniences like Jell-O® salads, instant rice, orange juice powders, and boxed cake mixes that were "ready in a jiffy."

As the decades came and went, so did many food trends, including our passing interests in things like nouvelle cuisine and east-west fusion foods. If nothing else, these trends brought some great ingredients to ordinary supermarkets.

Remember that back in the 1980s, items such as real balsamic vinegar, chipotle chile peppers, and *panko* bread crumbs were "ethnic" foods that you could only find in specialty shops, if at all. Now they are supermarket staples and, as a result, grilling staples.

Weber's New Real Grilling™ is a collection of delicious but doable recipes built on today's supermarket staples. Trust us, we get it. We know you have better things to do than going on a crazed hunt for rare groceries. We all want to be at home, enjoying our downtime with good food, family, and friends. In this era of financial uncertainty, market upheavals, and debt crises, the home is a safe haven. The backyard is our oasis. The grill is our hearth. This is where memories are made. This is what is real.

In these pages you'll find many classic dishes that have been popular for years, but we gave each one a twist. Nothing crazy, just riffs on popular themes— think Cheeseburgers with Mango-Chile Salsa, Coffee-Rubbed Rib Eye Steaks with Stout Glaze, and Shrimp Kabobs with Pistachio-Tarragon Pesto. Also, in the spirit of retro fun, we reprinted some grilling recipes from days long gone and paired each with a "remixed" version that reflects today's tastes and ingredients.

Grilling tools and cookware have come a long way, too. It used to be that all the food went right on the cooking grate and we moved them with one of two items: tongs or a spatula. Now we have more accessories and, therefore, much more fun. Have you ever used your grill to make cioppino in a wok or a loaf of

bread on a pizza stone? This ingenuity, this old-meets-new ethic—this is the new American grilling. Welcome to the party.

Grilling is more a part of the American ideal than it's ever been. We've been cooking this way since the beginning of time, but how we see it now—as a gateway to the good life, as a tasty means to our contented end—has evolved. Grilling is how we entertain, how we relax, and how we reconnect with what means most. This book captures all those contemporary elements of grilling while staying focused on what really never changes. It's fun, and it's delicious. That's why we grilled back then, and that's why we grill today.

Jamie Purviance

ABOUT THE AUTHOR

Jamie Purviance graduated from the Culinary Institute of America and Stanford University before earning a reputation as one of America's top grilling experts.

He is the author of all of Weber's cookbooks, with millions of copies sold, and his articles have appeared in numerous publications, such as *Bon Appétit*, *Better Homes and Gardens*, *Cooking Light*, *EatingWell*, *Town & Country*, and the *Los Angeles Times*.

One of his recent books, *Weber's Way to Grill*™, was a finalist for a James Beard Award, and two of his cookbooks have been *New York Times* best sellers. Purviance teaches grilling at schools and resorts all over America and has appeared on many national television shows: *Today*, *The Early Show*, *Good Morning America*, and *The Oprah Winfrey Show* as well as on PBS, CNN, and the Food Network.

1

GRILLING EVOLVED

the evolution
OF FIRE

What began with a spark turned into flames . . . and then the flames sparked some clever designs.

CHARCOAL GRILLS

Our classic kettle is a purist griller's dream, but for those who dream even bigger, along came a few bells and whistles. To some charcoal grills we added the convenience of gas-assisted ignition and plenty of grill-side charcoal storage. A large work surface on some recent models answers the ever-present "where do I put my tongs?" call, and a lid holder provides a safe place for the lid while you tend to your fire.

GAS GRILLS

Back before we introduced the Genesis® grill in the mid-'80s, predecessor gas grills used lava rocks to distribute heat. While, um, groovy in theory, they were a little too hotheaded in practice, causing volcanic flare-ups and torching food beyond recognition. The gas grill market was booming and just starting to outpace charcoal grill sales, as busy folks everywhere sought convenient options. Riding that wave—but steering clear of the lava thing—we engineered the Genesis grill with a set of precisely angled bars set over the flames. These Flavorizer® bars channel juices falling from the cooking grates down onto the heating element where they sizzle and smoke, creating that coveted grill flavor all the while deterring flare-ups.

That first Genesis model was a runaway hit, but it keeps on getting better. For instance, a Sear Station® allows you to cook food at extremely high temperatures—a must for that perfect steak. A tank scale provides an accurate reading of how much gas is available, which is nice to avoid panicked propane runs. Side burner technology rivals the kitchen stove with the ability to cook at super low or super high temperatures.

SOME OF WEBER'S MORE MEMORABLE HITS AND MISSES OVER THE LAST 60+ YEARS.

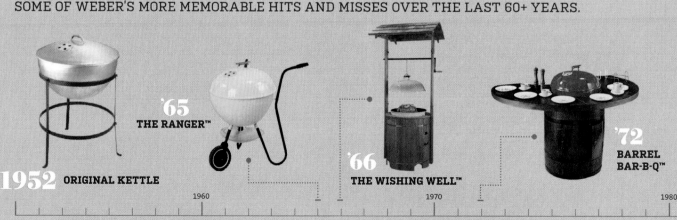

'65
THE RANGER™

'66
THE WISHING WELL™

'72
BARREL BAR-B-Q™

1952 **ORIGINAL KETTLE**

1960   1970   1980

SMOKERS

Where the kettle leaves off, the smoker picks up, and that is at the next level of low-and-slow grilling intensity. The first smokers were fashioned out of old oil drums cut in half and rigged with a cooking grate. Like any good idea, it was taken in all sorts of directions—vertical smokers, water smokers, electric smokers—that all did pretty much the same thing: cook food at a low temperature for a very long time. The Smokey Mountain Cooker™ smoker is designed simply but smartly, enabling consistent temperatures using a spot-on thermometer and vents to control airflow.

ELECTRIC GRILLS

Apartment dwellers, campers, and the otherwise space-challenged need love, too. Enter: the portable and compact Q® electric grill. Having a tiny footprint is great, but not when you can't get the thing hot enough using a standard 110-volt household current. Innovations to grill design, however, have yielded searing hot results. The Q grill produces food that tastes just like it was grilled on a standard-sized grill.

CHARCOAL VERSUS GAS
The debate has left many a house divided, but it's finally been settled. Which is better? Both.

Before you slam this book shut, hear us out: charcoal and gas allegiances have less to do with one fuel's superiority than his or her personal taste and lifestyle. If it's mostly weeknight burgers and chicken breasts on the docket, then you may be partial to the flick-of-a-switch ease of a gas grill. Perhaps you're more of a low-and-slow type, relishing the smoke and strategy behind coals in a kettle—then charcoal it is. Gas gets a bad rap for being too mild in smoke flavor, but juicy meat plus fire equals smoke every time, regardless of the grill type. And if all else fails, there's always the smoker box.

Charcoal's many varieties, from no-frills briquettes to the knock-your-socks-off smokiness of lump coals, give us good options. Each type uniquely flavors food and impacts how much hands-on time and money go in to grilling it (pricier charcoals tend to burn hotter—and faster). For these reasons, cost isn't always a good argument for charcoal versus gas because of all the variables attached to your style and frequency of grilling. When in doubt, embrace both. There's no need for rivalry talk when everybody wins.

'85 GENESIS®

'90 PERFORMER®

'00 ONE-TOUCH®

SUMMIT®

TODAY

1990

2000

2010

USING A
wok

Wok cooking on your grill may sound like
newfangled fusion cuisine, but in fact it's steeped in
tradition. For thousands of years, the focal point in a typical
Chinese kitchen was a round hole over a firebox of burning
wood and embers with a wok fit snugly inside the hole,
making efficient use of a small amount of expensive fuel.
And you can replicate the ancient art of stir-frying over live
fire by using a grill-proof wok on your backyard barbecue.

TRY THESE WOK RECIPES:

Five-Minute Pepper Steak Stir-Fry, page 99

Chicken and Broccoli Stir-Fry with Peanuts
and Scallions, page 186

1 Prep everything first. Then cook.
Stir-frying happens in a short burst of time. Once it starts, you won't have time to slice or dice anything, so arrange all your chopped ingredients, sauces, and even serving platters near the grill first. Chop all the ingredients into cubes or strips of about the same size (no bigger than bite size) so they cook evenly.

2 Get the wok hot. Smoking hot.
It's pretty simple, really. Light 50 to 75 briquettes and let them burn until they are lightly coated with ash. Arrange the charcoal one or two layers deep in the center of the charcoal grate. Put in place the cooking grate with a hole in the center. Set the wok in the hole and close the lid. Let the wok get smoking hot for about 10 minutes. When you flick a few drops of water into the wok, they should dance vigorously and disappear within just a second.

3 To stir or not to stir? That is the question. Stir-fry masters have a keen sense for when to stir with zeal and when to exercise patience. In most cases, when you add meat or other protein to a wok, you should quickly spread out the pieces to get as many of them as possible in direct contact with the hot wok surface. Then wait for 20 to 30 seconds so the food has a chance to sear.

4 Scoop and toss. Next, scoop to the bottom of the wok with two wok spatulas to lift the ingredients into the air and let them tumble back down repeatedly until the outside is evenly browned. Move the meat up the cooler sides of the wok to finish cooking it, and then add the vegetables to the blazing hot bottom of the wok. Again, let the new ingredients sear for a matter of seconds, and then toss them with your spatulas.

USING A
pizza stone

It's a long fall from the culinary heights of the Italian masterpiece known as pizza to the lows of the American convenience food made of frozen, lifeless dough covered in icy toppings. Why take that fall when nowadays many supermarkets carry the components that used to take us so long to make? When you can buy fresh dough, good tomato sauce, and grated cheese, a pizza worthy of its authentic roots is really only about 30 minutes away. The key is using the impressive heat retained by a solid stone slab to fill each pizza with light, doughy air pockets and to toast the bottom with a golden brown crust.

TRY THESE PIZZA STONE RECIPES:

Grilled Pizzas with Sausage, Peppers, and Herbs, page 146

Spinach and Ricotta Calzones, page 286

Beer and Cheddar Bread, page 290

Chocolate Chip and Peanut Butter Cookies, page 313

1 Preheat the pizza stone first. Prepare your gas or charcoal grill for direct cooking over high heat, and preheat the stone for at least 15 minutes. The temperature of the grill should rise to at least 500°F. Meanwhile, roll the dough and prepare your other ingredients.

2 Roll the dough on a lightly floured surface. Turn the ball of dough in the flour a few times so it is not so sticky. Flatten into a disc and use a rolling pin to roll to a thickness of about $1/3$ inch, flipping the dough over once or twice to make sure it's not sticking.

3 Lightly coat a pizza peel with flour, too. Then slide the peel completely under the dough. Spread a thin layer of sauce almost all the way to the outer edge of the crust. Don't use too much sauce; otherwise, the dough will soak it up and turn soggy.

4 Scatter the toppings over the sauce. Don't use any toppings (like raw meat) that would not be safe to eat after only 10 minutes of cooking. Make sure the pizza can slide a little on the peel. If any areas of the dough are sticking, lift them up and flick a large pinch of flour underneath.

WHAT YOU'LL NEED

▸ GAS OR CHARCOAL GRILL
▸ PIZZA STONE
▸ ROLLING PIN
▸ WOOD OR METAL PIZZA PEEL

5 Slide the pizza onto the hot stone. Tilt the peel so that the pizza slides easily away from you and the edge of the crust lands near the part of the stone farthest from you. Then slowly pull the peel toward you and lay the rest of the pizza on the stone. Close the lid and let the pizza cook for 4 to 5 minutes.

6 Rotate the pizza once or twice. Slide the peel or a large spatula underneath and rotate the pizza a half turn for even cooking. You will know it is ready when the underside of the crust is golden brown in spots and the cheese is completely melted.

USING A
griddle

Is there anything that appears as ordinary as a black slab of metal? You might be surprised to learn that there is also probably no other accessory that opens up as many cooking possibilities on the grill. For example, what if your vegetables are cut so small that they might fall through the cooking grates? What if a fish is too thin or delicate to put right on an open grate? What if you need a hot, flat surface to toast panini crust evenly? What if you feel like making breakfast with eggs, bacon, and pancakes on the grill? A griddle handles all these jobs and more easily.

TRY THESE GRIDDLE RECIPES:

Cheesesteaks with the Works, page 85

Black Forest Ham, Brie, and Pear Panini, page 156

Griddled Cod with Sweet Pickle Tartar Sauce, page 257

French Toast with Grilled Peaches and Blueberry Syrup, page 305

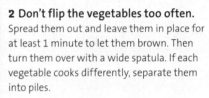

1 **Preheat a grill-proof griddle for at least 10 minutes.** It takes that long for the thick metal to get hot. Cut any vegetables small enough so that they cook in less than 10 minutes, and coat them with oil before sliding them onto the griddle.

2 **Don't flip the vegetables too often.** Spread them out and leave them in place for at least 1 minute to let them brown. Then turn them over with a wide spatula. If each vegetable cooks differently, separate them into piles.

3 **Remember to toast the bread.** Brush the cut sides with oil or butter and lay them flat on the griddle. Meanwhile, you can grill the meat right on the cooking grate.

4 **Bring it all together.** As a final touch, warm the sandwiches on the griddle until the outsides are crusty. If you like, flatten the sandwiches with a grill press.

WHAT YOU'LL NEED

▸ **GAS OR CHARCOAL GRILL**

▸ **GRILL-PROOF GRIDDLE**
Make sure it fits your grill's dimensions.

▸ **LONG-HANDLED SPATULA OR TONGS**

▸ **GRILL PRESS**
Use one you can hold in your hand for good control when toasting grilled cheese sandwiches, flattening bacon, and crisping chicken skin.

braising

Grilling can dazzle us with its flickering, sparkling flames. Its dry, searing heat creates charred crusts and smoky aromas to admire—but don't overlook what a grill can also do with moist, gentle heat. Those same flames can simmer a flavorful liquid for braising and tenderizing meats and vegetables of many kinds, even the toughest of all, like beef brisket. By combining both dry and moist heat, you can develop layers of flavors and textures that one kind of heat alone could not achieve. In the kielbasa recipe shown here, the sausages benefit first from the char of a sizzling hot cooking grate. Then they are submerged in a savory stew of red onions, sauerkraut, and beer. What happens next is close to magic, as all those ingredients blend into something much greater than the sum of their individual flavors.

TRY THESE BRAISING RECIPES:

Braised and Glazed Short Ribs, page 117

Kielbasa Submarine Sandwiches with Beer-Braised Onions, page 150

1 Use a heavy, grill-proof pan. In a large cast-iron skillet braise the onions in simmering sauerkraut and beer. This softens the onions and builds a rich base of flavors for braising the sausages later.

2 Sear the meat on the side. While the onions are braising, brown the sausages over direct heat. Cutting each sausage in half lengthwise exposes more surface area for browning and charring right on the hot cooking grate.

3 Combine the meat and vegetables. Chop the browned sausages into bite-sized pieces and push them into the braising pool. Nestle the sausages into the liquid and let them simmer in the juices.

WHAT YOU'LL NEED

▸ **GAS OR CHARCOAL GRILL**

▸ **LARGE CAST-IRON SKILLET**

▸ **DISPOSABLE FOIL PAN**

▸ **HEAVY-DUTY ALUMINUM FOIL**
When you want to simmer the liquid without much of it evaporating, it's good to cover the pan tightly with aluminum foil.

4 Move the pan for the right heat level. To slow down the cooking, slide the skillet over indirect heat and close the grill lid. Your food will stay warm and moist for at least 30 minutes. When you are ready to eat, toast some buns over direct heat and pile them high with sausages and onions.

USING A
rotisserie

Rotisseries may conjure up images of medieval knights cranking a spit by hand to slow cook a wild beast over a bed of embers, but so much has changed since the days of King Arthur. For one thing, we cook in a covered grill now, which means that the meats are surrounded by circulating heat to cook them more quickly and evenly. Rotisserie cooking today is much more like oven-roasting large cuts of meat and whole birds in midair, with the significant advantage that as the food turns (with a motor, by the way), its juices are slowly redistributed to baste the food inside and outside.

ADAPTING RECIPES FOR THE ROTISSERIE

Almost any recipe that calls for indirect heat does really well on the rotisserie. As long as the meat can be evenly balanced on the spit, it's a prime candidate for the rotisserie. For example, try one of these recipes:

Leg of Lamb with Apricot and Chickpea Couscous, page 118
Summer Herb-Roasted Chicken, page 206
Beer-Brined Turkey, page 210

1 Truss any unwieldy meats. If you are cooking something that holds together naturally, such as a beef rib roast, there is no need to truss it. But if it could fall apart or flop around and cook unevenly on the revolving spit, such as these pork loins, you must truss.

2 Secure the food with forks. Run the spit right down the center and insert the forked tongs into each end. If necessary, first turn the spit so that the tongs are inserted into a dense section of the meat that will hold the tongs in place.

3 Press the tongs all the way into the meat. The meat will shrink as it cooks and could potentially slide off the tongs, so begin with the tongs pressed in as deep as possible.

4 Center the roast. There should be an equal distance of metal on each side. Tighten the screws on the tongs.

WHAT YOU'LL NEED

▸ **GAS OR CHARCOAL GRILL THAT ACCOMMODATES A ROTISSERIE**

▸ **ELECTRICAL OUTLET AND AN EXTENSION CORD**

▸ **INSULATED BARBECUE MITTS**

▸ **BUTCHER'S TWINE**

5 Put the roast on the grill. Place the tip of the spit into the mount of the rotisserie motor, and then lower the other end of the spit into place.

6 Catch the drippings with a disposable foil pan. To make room for the pan, you may need to remove the cooking grates first.

GETTING STARTED

2

STARTING
your grill

STARTING A CHARCOAL FIRE

The time required to fire up a charcoal grill can be as little as fifteen to twenty minutes, if you use the right equipment.

1 The easiest method is to use a chimney starter, an upright metal cylinder with two handles on the outside and a wire rack inside. Simply fill the space under the wire rack with wadded-up newspaper or a few paraffin cubes, then fill the space above with charcoal briquettes.

2 Once you light the newspaper or the paraffin cubes, some impressive thermodynamics channel the heat evenly throughout the briquettes.

3 When the briquettes are lightly covered with white ash, put on two insulated barbecue mitts and grab hold of the two handles on the chimney starter. The swinging handle is there to help you lift the chimney starter and safely aim the coals just where you want them.

HEAT CONFIGURATIONS

The most flexible charcoal configuration is a two-zone fire. That means the coals are spread out on one side of the charcoal grate. This allows you to cook with both direct and indirect heat.

There are times when you might prefer a three-zone split fire, where the coals are separated into two equal piles on opposite sides of the charcoal grate. This gives you two zones for direct heat and one zone between them for indirect heat. This works well for cooking a roast over indirect heat, because you have the same level of heat on both sides of the roast.

After the coals are fully lit, put the cooking grate in place, put the lid on the grill, and wait for about ten minutes until the temperature rises to at least 500°F on the lid's thermometer. Your charcoal grill's temperature depends on how much charcoal you use and how long it has been burning. The coals are at their hottest when they are newly lit. Over time they will gradually lose heat.

FUEL CHOICES

Briquettes are inexpensive and available practically everywhere. Most commonly, they are compressed black bundles of sawdust and coal, along with binders and fillers like clay and sodium nitrate. They produce a predictable, even heat over a long period of time. A batch of 80 to 100 briquettes will last for about an hour.

Pure hardwood briquettes are considered the gold standard of charcoal. They have the same pillow shape of standard briquettes, but they burn at higher temperatures and with none of the questionable fillers. They are usually made of crushed hardwoods bound together with nothing but natural starches.

Lump charcoal is made by burning hardwood logs in an oxygen-deprived environment, such as an underground pit or a kiln. This type of charcoal lights faster than briquettes, burns hotter, and burns out faster. It also tends to spark and crackle like real wood. Fortunately, it creates smoky aromas like real wood, too.

STARTING A GAS GRILL

Lighting a gas grill, in most cases, is as simple as lifting the lid, turning on the gas, and igniting the burners. After you have opened the valve on your propane tank all the way (or turned on the gas at the source), wait a minute for the gas to travel through the gas line, and then turn each burner to high, making sure one burner has ignited before turning on the next. Close the lid and preheat the grill for ten to fifteen minutes. For both gas and charcoal grills, this makes the cooking grate much easier to clean, and it improves the grill's ability to sear.

If you smell gas, that might indicate a leak around the connection or in the hose. Turn off all the burners. Close the valve on your propane tank (or natural gas line) and disconnect the hose. Wait five to ten minutes, and then reconnect the hose. Try lighting the grill again. If you still smell gas, shut the grill down and call the manufacturer.

HEAT CONFIGURATIONS

For direct cooking, simply leave all the burners on and adjust them for the heat level you want. For example, if you want to cook with direct medium heat, turn all the burners down to medium and wait until the thermometer indicates that the temperature is in the range of 350° to 450°F. For indirect cooking, you can leave some of the burners on and turn one or two of them off.

GRILL SAFETY

Please read your Owner's Guide and familiarize yourself with and follow all "dangers," "warnings," and "cautions." Also follow the grilling procedures and maintenance requirements listed in your Owner's Guide.

If you cannot locate the Owner's Guide for your grill model, please contact the manufacturer prior to use. If you have any questions concerning the "dangers," "warnings," and "cautions" contained in your Weber® gas, charcoal, or electric grill Owner's Guide, or if you do not have an Owner's Guide for your specific grill model, please contact Weber-Stephen Products LLC Customer Service at 1.800.446.1071 before using your grill. You can also access your Owner's Guide online at www.weber.com.

GAS AND CHARCOAL GRILLS

After preheating the grill, put on an insulated barbecue mitt, and use a long-handled grill brush to scrape off any bits and pieces stuck to the cooking grates. There's no need to oil the grates before grilling; it would just drip into the grill, causing flare-ups. Improve the chances of your food releasing easily by oiling the food, not the grates.

Once your grill is preheated and brushed clean, bring out all the food and other supplies you will need and organize them nearby. If you have everything chopped and measured beforehand, the cooking will go faster, and you won't have to run back into the kitchen. Don't forget clean plates and platters for serving the grilled food.

DIRECT AND INDIRECT
cooking

When it comes to grilling with direct and indirect heat, there's good news and there's bad news. Bad news first: the difference between direct and indirect heat is the most complicated part. Good news: it's not complicated at all.

When a recipe calls for "direct heat," this means that the grill's heat source—be it the hot coals of a charcoal grill or the fired-up burners on your gas grill—is directly underneath your food. This hot blast of energy is what gives it a great caramelized crust and grill marks, all the while cooking your food all the way through. Grilling over direct heat works best with thinner, more tender items that cook quickly: think steak, hamburgers, boneless chicken pieces, fish fillets, shellfish, cut vegetables, and fruit.

And now, we dabble in some more technical talk. Direct heat cooking is the product of both conductive and radiant heat.

The fire from the coals or burners zaps the cooking grates, which conduct the heat directly onto the surface of your food, giving it those distinct, tasty grill marks. The radiant heat is the oven effect that is created when hot air is swirling around food under the grill's closed lid. This brings us to our next point—keeping the lid on. With few exceptions, the lid should be closed as much as possible. The lid keeps air from getting to the fire, which controls flare-ups and allows the food to cook from both the bottom and the top. While food will always cook faster from the bottom (this is why we flip!), a closed lid keeps that radiant heat in play and speeds up cooking times. Quicker cooking means fewer chances of burning or drying out our food. And of course, eating sooner, too.

If you're a charcoal griller, consider setting up a two-zone fire, in which all the coals are pushed to one side. This way, even if you're not planning on needing indirect heat, you have that option if your food begins to cook too fast. For gas

CHARCOAL: DIRECT COOKING

With direct heat, the fire is right below the food. The heat radiates off the charcoal and conducts through the metal of the cooking grate to create those dark, handsome grill marks.

CHARCOAL: INDIRECT COOKING

With indirect heat, the charcoal is arranged to one side of the food, or it is on both sides of the food. A large disposable foil pan catches the drippings underneath.

grillers, the principle is the same. Turn on all the burners to your desired heat level for direct heat. On-the-fly heat adjustments are a little easier on a gas grill, so if you feel that the fire is too hot, you've got the option of either lowering the heat on the burners or turning some off altogether.

This setup also benefits all us steak lovers out there. We like having a two-zone fire for the "sear and slide" grilling method. For thick-cut steaks and chops, a few minutes on each side over direct heat will take care of the sear; then, slide it over to the side without the fire to finish the cooking. This is the secret to that perfectly cooked steak.

In the case of indirect heat, you've probably already figured out what this means. Whereas direct heat puts your food directly above the heat source, indirect heat has it off to the side. This is a good option for larger, tougher cuts of meat that take a while to cook, such as roasts, whole chickens, and racks of ribs. There tend to be fewer overcooking surprises when using indirect heat, as this method uses the grill's slightly gentler, oven-like radiant heat to do the bulk of the work. We still like to start these bigger, tougher items over direct heat, but then send them over to the indirect side to hang out for a while. It's the best of both worlds approach—getting those flavorful grill marks while your meat is still thoroughly cooked, but not overcooked.

GRILL MAINTENANCE
Grill, you had us with the food. But you kept us with the easy upkeep.

In order to get those great grill marks, to keep food from sticking to the grill, and to prevent remnants of yesterday's brisket attaching to today's burgers, the cooking grates should be cleaned before every use. With the lid closed, preheat the grill to about 500°F for 10 minutes. Wearing an insulated barbecue mitt, open the lid and scrape the grates with a long-handled grill brush to loosen charred bits and pieces. That's it. You're done.

Your grill may need a more thorough cleaning every month or so, which is still really easy to do. Always check the instructions in your Owner's Guide first, but start by wiping the outside of the grill down with warm, soapy water. Scrape any accumulated debris from the inside of the lid. Remove the cooking grates, brush the burners, and clean out the bottom of the cooking box and drip pan. For the full upkeep and maintenance treatment, consult your Owner's Guide.

Charcoal grillers, take note: ash contains a small amount of water. All ash sitting at the bottom of the kettle should be removed regularly to prevent rust.

GAS: DIRECT COOKING

To use direct heat on a gas grill, simply light the burners right below the food and adjust the knobs for the temperature level you want.

GAS: INDIRECT COOKING

To use indirect heat on a gas grill, light the burners on the far left and far right of the grill, and cook the food between them. If your grill has just two burners, turn one on and keep one off. Place the food over the unlit burner.

smoking
ON THE GRILL

Barbecue masters and "sultans of smoke" (almost always self-proclaimed) tend to talk a big game and lead you to believe that their smoking techniques are far beyond the understanding of backyard grillers. Don't be intimidated by the bravado and secrecy. Smoking is much simpler than it looks—and it doesn't require a humongous barbecue rig either. Smoking is really just a form of seasoning, like rubbing meat with spices or soaking it in a marinade. Think of smoking as cooking your food in an aromatic cloud of seasonings. The keys, then, are knowing which seasonings (woods) to use and how much of them to use.

FOR A CHARCOAL GRILL

All you need to get started on a charcoal grill is to soak your wood chips in water for at least thirty minutes. Then shake off the excess water, and use tongs to scatter the chips on top of the burning charcoal. Many smoking recipes are true barbecue, taking a few hours or more over indirect low heat to cook, and so they will require some new additions of soaked and drained wood chips (and charcoal) to keep the smoke flowing.

FOR A GAS GRILL

You will need some sort of box for smoking soaked, drained wood chips on a gas grill, whether it's a built-in smoker box inside your grill, a stainless steel smoker box that you place on top of the cooking grate, or a disposable foil pan covered with aluminum foil and poked with holes to allow the smoke to escape. If you need to add more chips to a smoker box, do it while some of the old chips are still burning. The old chips will help to light the new ones.

FOR A WATER SMOKER

Wood chunks are a good choice when using a water smoker. They last much longer than chips, so you won't have to replenish them as often. Another little convenience with chunks is that you don't need to soak them. As dry as they are, they don't flame up the way wood chips do.

WHICH WOOD TO USE

Like herbs and spices, each type of wood has its own strengths or intensities, from mild to moderate to strong. It's a good idea to match the intensity of the smoke to the intensity of your food. This chart provides some of our favorite combinations. We're talking about personal preferences here, so there really is no wrong choice of wood. Well, actually . . . some woods, such as pine and aspen, are so soft and resinous that their smoke is bitter and potentially toxic. Stick with the hardwoods listed below instead.

WOOD TYPE	CHARACTERISTICS
Alder	**Mild:** Delicate flavor **Pairs with:** Pork, poultry, salmon, swordfish, other fish
Apple	**Mild:** Slightly sweet but also dense, fruity smoke flavor **Pairs with:** Beef, pork (particularly ham), poultry, game birds
Hickory	**Moderate:** Pungent, smoky, bacon-like flavor **Pairs with:** Beef, pork, poultry, wild game, cheeses
Oak	**Moderate:** An assertive but pleasing flavor; sometimes a little acidic; blends well with sweeter woods **Pairs with:** Beef (particularly brisket), pork, poultry
Mesquite	**Strong:** In a class by itself—a big, bold smoke bordering on bitter **Pairs with:** Beef and lamb

HOW MUCH WOOD TO USE

The most common rookie mistake is oversmoking food, which is particularly easy to do with seafood and light meats, because they soak up smoke in a matter of minutes. At some point, the smoke creeps over a line and changes from being pleasantly fragrant and woodsy to being aggressively bitter and sooty. To stay clear of that line, add a few handfuls of water-soaked and drained wood chips every hour, but stop smoking your food after the first half of its cooking time so it doesn't get too smoky. That's a good guideline.

knife
SKILLS

Knife skills are to grilling what swinging a bat is to baseball: fundamental. Without getting a handle on those basics, there's no chance of a win. Understanding how to use and to care for your knives, and knowing which knives are right for your cooking task, will make you a better, happier, and more efficient cook . . . with all your fingers intact. A huge knife collection isn't necessary, nor is spending too much on them. But having a few quality tools you enjoy using? That's a home run.

SHARPENING STEEL
A few glides down the sharpening steel before using your knife will grind and realign its edges back to sharpened life.

CHEF'S KNIFE
Above all others, this is the one to have. Slicing, dicing, carving, and cutting, it's the kitchen workhorse.

SERRATED KNIFE
Its saw-like teeth cut through bread without crushing, through tomatoes without squishing, and through meat without toughening.

SANTOKU KNIFE
A little smaller than a chef's knife, this is a good one for smaller (or less sure) hands.

BONING KNIFE
This thin, almost flexible blade allows for more precise work along the edges of bones and in tight spaces.

PARING KNIFE
Use this short, handy little tool for peeling, trimming, and mincing vegetables and fruits.

USING A SHARPENING STEEL

All knives lose their sharp edges when you run them across cutting boards again and again. They dull just from cutting food. If your knives are dull, you'll need to work harder and longer to cut your food, raising the chances that you will slip while exerting too much force. A steel doesn't sharpen a knife as much as it straightens crooked edges. The safest way to do this is with the "butcher's method," shown below. It's an easy, inexpensive way to ensure that your knives remain more of an asset than a liability.

1 Point the narrow end of the steel facing down on a cutting board. Position the heel of your knife at a 15- to 20-degree angle near the handle of the steel.

2 Swipe the blade down one side of the steel, pulling the knife toward you at the same time so that every part of the blade runs along the steel.

3 Repeat the swiping action on the opposite side of the steel.

4 Continue to swipe on both sides of the steel a few times or until the knife can easily cut through a piece of paper.

CHOPPING AN ONION

They're round, they're slippery, and they make us cry: onions aren't doing anyone any chopping favors. But this vegetable, above all others, benefits from a good trip under the knife. Minced, sliced, diced, or rough-chopped, onions do so much of the flavorful heavy lifting in our recipes. Knowing how to properly prep them is integral and will make chopping all other vegetables a walk in the tear-free park.

1 Trim about ½ inch from the stem end, but keep the root end intact; otherwise, the onion will fall apart.

2 Cut the onion in half through the stem and root ends.

3 Peel off the skin and possibly one layer of each half with your fingers or a paring knife.

4 Lay each half, flat side down, on a cutting board. Hold the onion steady with the fingertips of one hand.

5 Using the knife in your other hand, make a series of horizontal cuts, working from the bottom up and from the stem toward the root end, to but not through it.

6 Then make a series of vertical cuts, with the tip of the knife cutting almost but not quite through the root end.

7 Then cut each half crosswise to create an evenly sized dice.

8 The dice size depends on how far apart you make each horizontal, vertical, and crosswise cut.

ESSENTIAL tools

① ② ③ ④ ⑤

True, once you've got a grill, you don't need much else, but in order to prevent burned food, scorched fingers, flare-ups, and flameouts, you're going to really want the following items.

1 BARBECUE MITTS
When it doubt, wear 'em. The good ones are insulated and protect both hand and forearm.

2 THERMOMETER
Small and relatively inexpensive, this gadget is essential for quickly gauging the internal temperature of the meat when grilling.

3 TIMER
Avoid the disappointment of torching your dinner by simply setting a timer. Nothing fancy needed— just one that is reliable and easy to use.

4 DISPOSABLE PANS
Available in a variety of sizes, disposable foil pans offer many conveniences. Use them to move food to and from the grill and to keep food warm on the cooking grates.

5 GRILL BRUSH
A must-use before you even dream of grilling. A quick once-over on hot grates prevents the charred remains of meals past from sticking to your meals present.

6 GRILL PAN
Designed for food that is either too small or too delicate for the cooking grates, a perforated grill pan keeps food right where it ought to be— on the grill, not in it.

7 BRUSH AND MOP
Look for a basting brush with heat-resistant silicone bristles and a long handle, and a mop with long, cotton threads that sop up the thinner, vinegar-based sauces.

8 TONGS
Consider these to be an extension of your hand. The best tongs should have an effortless tension mechanism, comfortable hand grips, and a lock to keep them compact.

9 SPATULA
Look for a long-handled spatula designed with a bent (offset) neck so that the blade is set lower than the handle. This makes it easier to lift food off the cooking grates.

10 CHIMNEY STARTER
Take some briquettes, lighter cubes or crumpled newspapers, and a match, and you've got a safely and quickly lit fire without lighter fluid.

NEW TOOLS AND toys

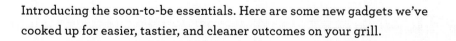

Introducing the soon-to-be essentials. Here are some new gadgets we've cooked up for easier, tastier, and cleaner outcomes on your grill.

1 RIB RACK/ ROAST HOLDER
Small grill and big crowd? No worries. Drop up to five racks of ribs in the plated steel slots, or flip it over and nestle in a whole chicken or roast.

2 BURGER PRESS
A burger press ensures that all patties are uniform in size and thickness, so the grilling process remains quick, efficient, and hockey puck-free.

3 SMOKER BOX
It fits right on the cooking grates and has ample space for your favorite wood chips, lending food a smoke flavor catered to your taste.

4 CEDAR PLANKS
Simple and natural, cedar planks deliver incredible flavor with minimal effort. Be sure to soak them for at least 1 hour before using.

5 PIZZA STONE
A good pizza stone produces an evenly light and crispy crust and guarantees that your creation remains on, not under, the cooking grates.

6 WOK

A cast-iron wok with enamel coating is durable and easy to clean, and it ensures even, consistent heat distribution.

7 POULTRY ROASTER

The grill is as good as an oven, so why not roast in it? A poultry roaster perches the bird upright on the cooking grate, allowing heat to flow evenly around the meat.

8 GRILL PRESS

Sit it atop panini, chicken, and more to add some heft and flavorful char. It can be heated on the cooking grate and then placed on your food to brown from both sides.

9 FISH BASKET

Adjustable, stainless steel wire baskets expose all kinds of fish to the flavors of the grill without ever letting them stick to the cooking grates.

10 GRIDDLE

Breakfast on the grill? They said it couldn't be done. They were wrong. With a griddle, bacon, eggs, and hash browns are as good as grilled.

THE GRILLER'S pantry

EXTRA-VIRGIN OLIVE OIL

You won't be getting far without this stuff. An invaluable ingredient and a handy tool (no more food sticking to the cooking grates), it's always good to have basic extra-virgin olive oil on hand because of its mild, fruity flavor, its health benefits, and its availability just about everywhere.

KOSHER SALT

Alongside extra-virgin olive oil, this is on the "desert island" list. Coarser and purer tasting than standard table salt, and with a larger grain, kosher salt covers more surface area on your food and with fewer additives than the stuff that comes out of a shaker. It also dissolves beautifully.

BLACK PEPPERCORNS

Salt's superhero sidekick, peppercorns give our palate the "pow" we need to properly taste food. Have a stash of whole peppercorns on hand that can be tossed into a pepper mill and coarsely ground. Easier still, throw a handful into a spice grinder and you've got fresh pepper for the week.

HERBS AND SPICES

These are the quickest and easiest routes to serious flavor and are the basis for a good rub. You don't need every kind the grocery store has to offer, but the essentials—thyme, oregano, chile powder, cumin, and paprika (try smoked paprika)—ought to always be stocked on your shelves.

MAYONNAISE

Mayonnaise elevates other ingredients' games while still being great on its own. It makes a delicious spread mixed with garlic or horseradish for grilled steak sandwiches, but it can also be slathered on lean cuts before grilling to lock in moisture. Some styles of barbecue even use it abundantly in sauces.

DIJON MUSTARD

Sophisticated Dijon mustard boasts a creamy, spicy tang and makes a great "glue" to keep rubs and other seasonings on meats. Great for a glaze, in mopping sauces, and in marinades, it's also often that note of creamy complexity found in salad dressings.

SOY SAUCE
Brewed from fermented soybeans, soy sauce is a favorite in marinades for its ability to really sink into food and blast it with flavor. It's a staple in Asian recipes, but it's also great for the pungent "umami" it lends to so much more. Just a teaspoon in a vinaigrette can wake up the other ingredients' flavors.

WORCESTERSHIRE SAUCE
This ranks alongside soy sauce in the "umami" major league. One tiny bottle contains vinegar, spices, herbs, anchovies, and more—the combo of which perks up otherwise bland recipes and even makes meat taste meatier (it's great in burgers). A little goes a long way.

KETCHUP
No self-respecting griller would be caught without this one. This classic topping for burgers and hot dogs is also the main ingredient in homemade barbecue sauces. Store-bought brands are about as good as you can make at home.

SUGAR (GRANULATED AND BROWN)
Thank sugar for that sweet little note you get in the perfect barbecue sauce or in the caramelized crust on your slow-cooked pork shoulder. Brown sugar is used more often than granulated sugar because it has a deep, molasses flavor that complements spicy ingredients.

BALSAMIC VINEGAR
Vinegar is everything oil is not—thin, acidic, pungent—but it so beautifully highlights everything oil is, which is why they're not often apart. Vinegar is a must in marinades, dressings, and mopping sauces. Balsamic and cider vinegars are good choices for both their flavor and their availability.

BARBECUE SAUCE
This can be the griller's be-all and end-all. A good sauce can steal the spotlight, but a better one makes your meat the star. Tangy, spicy, or sweet and spicy, barbecue sauce should have both subtle and intense layers of flavor. Brush it on your meat toward the end of its cooking time, or serve it as a side.

salt,
PEPPER, AND OIL

Good ole salt, pepper, and olive oil. Rare is the recipe that doesn't involve this terrific trio. Why? Well, they're a griller's dream—tasty and practical. Salt is both a natural preservative and a mineral that our bodies require in proper doses (those potato chip cravings are no coincidence). Salt draws moisture out of whatever it is sprinkled onto, concentrating the natural flavors of our food and allowing items, such as meat and fish, to develop a well-seasoned crust on the grill. Pepper, while not exactly life-sustaining, provides a kicky little palate pick-me-up. The slight tickle it leaves on the tongue enables it to be more receptive to flavors—like jumper cables for our taste buds. Olive oil acts as a barrier protecting your food from the intense heat of the grill—no sticking, no burning, and little-to-no effort. Its mild, fruity flavor, availability, and health benefits (olive oil is the ultimate "good" fat) are what make it so indispensable in recipes, from marinades to salad dressings and everything in between.

Kosher salt and freshly ground black pepper have a purer taste and a larger grain than table salt and pre-ground pepper, which covers more surface area and cuts down on the chance of over-seasoning. Kosher salt dissolves easily enough when you whisk it rigorously in water, but it dissolves slowly on meats, making it great for both brining and seasoning. If you prefer to use table salt in a recipe, be sure to cut the amount called for in half—it weighs twice as much as kosher salt and is easy to overdo. Use the easy-to-find, inexpensive extra-virgin olive oils for grilling. The scorching hot temperature of the grill would ruin the nuances of really expensive, cold-pressed olive oils that are made for dressings; however, the less expensive olive oils hold up well on the grill and taste better than flavorless vegetable oils.

top ten
GRILLING DOS AND DON'TS

Do preheat the grill. If your cooking grates aren't hot enough, some food will stick and will never have a decent chance of searing properly or developing handsome grill marks. Even if a recipe calls for medium or low heat, you should preheat the grill on high first. Open the grill's lid, fire up the charcoal or the gas burners, close the lid, and then let the cooking grates get screaming hot for about ten minutes. The grill temperature should reach at least 500°F.

Don't start with dirty grates. Tossing food onto the cooking grates before they have been cleaned is a great way to experience dinner déjà vu—if you're into that sort of thing. Leftover "stuff" on the grates acts like glue, binding both your new food to the old and all of it to the grates. After you have preheated the grill for about ten minutes, brush that stuff off entirely so that whatever you are grilling now has a clean, smooth surface to brown evenly. The best tool for the job is a sturdy, long-handled brush with stiff, stainless steel bristles.

Do get your act together. Bring everything you need near the grill before you actually grill. If you have to run back into the kitchen while your food is cooking, you might miss (that is, overcook or burn) something important. So bring your tools, bring your food that is already oiled and seasoned, bring your glaze or sauce or whatever. Don't forget clean platters for the cooked food. French chefs call this *mise en place* (meaning, "put in place"). We call it getting your act together.

Do give yourself at least two heat zones. If you set up your grill for one type of heat only, your options are limited. What if something is cooking too fast? What if your food is flaring up? What if you are grilling two very different foods at the same time? You should have at least two heat zones: one for direct heat (where the fire is right under the food) and one for indirect heat (where the fire is off to the side of the food). That way, you can move your food from one zone to another whenever you like.

Don't overcrowd the grill. Packing too much food into a tight space on the grill restricts your flexibility. You should leave at least one-quarter of the cooking grates clear, with plenty of space between each food item so that you can get your tongs in there and easily move them around. Sometimes grilling involves split-second decisions and the ability to jockey food from one area to another. So give yourself enough room to work.

Do use the lid. Believe it or not, a grill's lid is for much more than just keeping the rain out. Its more important job is preventing too much air from getting in and too much heat and smoke from getting out. When the lid is closed, the cooking grates are hotter, the grilling times are faster, the smoky tastes are stronger, and the flare-ups are fewer. So put a lid on it. Having said that, don't forget to open the charcoal grill's lid vent at least halfway. Every fire needs a little air to keep on burning.

Don't touch the food so much. We all like food when it is seared to a deep brown color with plenty of beautifully charred bits. The trouble is, many people move their food so often that it doesn't get enough time in one place to reach that desirable level of color and flavor. In nearly all cases, you should turn food just once or twice. If you're fiddling with it more than that, you are probably also opening the lid too much, which causes its own set of problems. Step back and trust the process.

Do take charge of the fire. On its own, a charcoal fire climbs to its hottest temperatures first and then loses heat either quickly or slowly, depending on your type of charcoal and, more importantly, on you. So make some proactive moves like refueling the fire before you lose too much heat, rearranging coals to suit your needs, sweeping away the ashes that could clog the bottom vents, and adjusting the vents on the lid for ideal airflow. A grill master is always in charge.

Don't serve rubbery chicken. When grilling, sometimes the most important thing is knowing when to stop. If you specialize in chicken breasts so overcooked that they bounce, it's time to learn some doneness clues, as in the gently yielding firmness of perfectly grilled chicken when you press the surface with a fingertip. If you want an even more reliable test of doneness, get an instant-read thermometer. This slim little gem will help you pinpoint that critical moment when your food is at its best.

Do use the grill for more than grilling. Back in the 1950s, grilling meant one thing: meat (and only meat) charred over open flames. A true measure of a griller today is the depth and breadth of the menu. That means appetizers through desserts cooked on the grill and, in some cases, that means learning how to braise, roast, smoke, simmer, and even sauté or stir-fry. When you have learned how to harness the heat of the grill to do all this and more, you're officially a master of new American grilling.

3
STARTERS

grill SKILLS:
PERFECT SHELLFISH

Shrimp

Terms like "small," medium," and "large" are used inconsistently where shrimp are sold. The best way to know for sure what you are buying is to look for the number of shrimp per pound. A label that reads "16/20" means that it takes 16 to 20 of those shrimp to make a pound. In the photo above, the shrimp on the far left is an example of what you get when you buy 36/45. Immediately to the right is an example of 31/35. The next one is an example of 21/30. The next is an example of 16/20. And the one on the far right is an example of 11/15. Generally speaking, the three largest sizes are the best choices for grilling because they are easy to peel and they don't dry out as quickly as the smaller shrimp.

When Is It Done?

Shellfish don't flake, but they turn an opaque, pearly white color at the center when they are cooked. The only way to know for sure how the center looks is to cut into it, so plan on sacrificing one or two shellfish. In this photo, the shrimp on the left is underdone, the shrimp on the right is overdone, and the shrimp in the middle is just right.

Scallops

As with shrimp, bigger is usually better because bigger scallops allow for more time on the grill to develop flavors. However, avoid "wet packed" scallops that have been treated with a phosphate-and-water solution that causes them to swell with liquid. Wet scallops tend to steam (and stick) rather than sear on the grill, so look for "dry-packed" scallops instead.

Mussels, Clams, and Oysters

The easiest way to cook any of these bivalves (meaning they have two shells) is to lay them directly over the fire. When they get hot, their briny juices boil and the steam released puts pressure on their shells, causing them to open. When the shells burn just a little, the smoke carries magical aromas.

A tightly closed mussel shell is a good sign of freshness. If any mussel is gaping open a bit, tap it with a finger. If the shell closes immediately, the mussel is alive and fresh.

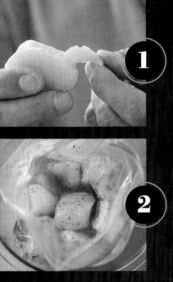

1 Check your scallops for a small, tough muscle along the side. This is the adductor muscle that helps the scallop hold onto its shell. It is quite chewy, so pull it off with your finger and discard it before grilling.

2 Marinate your scallops for extra flavor and moisture, but don't overdo it. If your marinade has a fair amount of acidity, your scallops could turn mushy. One to two hours of marinating is usually a good time frame.

3 Going onto the grill, scallops should be well oiled or buttered, but not dripping wet. Too much liquid causes sticking. If you have used a wet marinade, lightly pat the scallops dry on paper towels.

4 Grill scallops over direct high heat with the flattest side down first. Wait at least two minutes for that side to brown. Turn them over only when you can lift each scallop along its edge with tongs. Don't scrape under a scallop with a spatula and tear it.

5 The sweet succulence of a perfectly grilled scallop is spectacular. When it reaches its ideal doneness, the pearly color is opaque, and the texture is both creamy and wet.

Some mussels come with the added issue of a "beard." To remove the beard, use your thumb and index finger to grasp the beard, and pull sharply, perpendicular to the mussel. Do this shortly before grilling, because once its beard has been removed, a mussel begins to spoil.

Clams and mussels often have some sand and grit inside and outside. The easiest way to clean them is to soak them in salt water ($1\frac{1}{2}$ cups kosher salt to 1 quart of water) for 30 minutes to 1 hour. Then rinse and scrub the outside of the shells with a stiff brush.

Big, juicy oysters do best on the grill. After you have shucked each one and have released the flesh from the shell, grill it with the deeper shell balanced over direct high heat, with or without sauce. As soon as the juices start to bubble, the oysters are done.

SPECIAL EQUIPMENT: clam knife (optional)

36 littleneck clams, scrubbed

TOPPING
4 slices bacon, finely diced
½ cup finely diced red bell pepper
2 medium garlic cloves, minced or pushed through a press
2 tablespoons white wine
1 cup fresh bread crumbs
2 tablespoons finely chopped fresh Italian parsley leaves
1 tablespoon finely chopped fresh oregano leaves
    Kosher salt
    Freshly ground black pepper

1 lemon, cut into wedges

A crumpled sheet or two of aluminum foil inside a sheet pan will hold the clams in place, replacing the rock salt used for this purpose in many shellfish recipes. Nestle the shucked clams in the foil and spoon some of the bacon-and-crumb mixture over each.

1. Shuck the clams: Cover your left hand (if you are right-handed) with a double or triple thickness of kitchen towel. Using the towel, grip one clam so that the thickest edges, or lips, are pointing outward, away from your palm. Holding a clam knife in your right hand, place the sharp edge of the blade (not the tip) between the lips. Slide the blade between the two halves of the shell. (The towel should be positioned so that it will protect your hand in case the knife slips down the side of the shell.) Work the knife blade around the edges of the shell to cut through the adductor muscles, and then give the knife a twist to pry open the shell. Use your fingers to finish opening the shell and gently scrape the clam from both halves of the shell using the tip of the knife. Break off one half of the shell, leaving the clam and its juices in the remaining half. If you are having difficulty opening the clams, you can put three or four clams at a time on a microwave-safe plate and microwave on high for 15 to 25 seconds. This will cause the clams to open slightly, creating an opening so you can insert the knife and proceed as directed above.

2. Prepare the grill for indirect cooking over high heat (450° to 550°F).

3. In a large skillet over high heat, cook the bacon until crisp, 7 to 8 minutes, stirring occasionally. Using a slotted spoon, transfer the bacon to paper towels to drain. Carefully remove about half of the bacon fat from the skillet and discard. Add the bell pepper and cook over high heat until it begins to soften, about 3 minutes. Add the garlic and cook until fragrant, about 1 minute, stirring occasionally. Add the wine and cook for about 10 seconds. Add the bread crumbs, parsley, and oregano and cook until the bread crumbs are lightly toasted, about 4 minutes, stirring often. Remove the skillet from the heat, add the cooked bacon, and mix well. Season with salt and pepper and set aside.

4. Lightly crumple one or two large pieces of aluminum foil and use them to line a large sheet pan or rimmed baking sheet. Nestle the clams in the foil and spoon a generous teaspoon of the topping over each. Grill the clams on the sheet pan over *indirect high heat*, with the lid closed, until the bread crumbs have browned and the juices are bubbling, taking care not to overcook the clams, 6 to 8 minutes. Serve warm with the lemon wedges.

SERVES: 4 | PREP TIME: 15 minutes | GRILLING TIME: 6–8 minutes

SPECIAL EQUIPMENT: 16 cocktail toothpicks

16 large shrimp (21/30 count), peeled and deveined, tails left on
 8 slices bacon, each cut crosswise in half
 2 ounces Monterey Jack cheese, cut into 16 sticks
16 pickled jalapeño pepper rings (from a jar)

Wrapping shrimp in bacon seems like a great idea until you realize that the shrimp are fully cooked before the bacon gets crispy. Solution: precook the bacon slices for a few minutes before wrapping the shrimp. Also, secure both ends of each slice with a cocktail pick so the bacon does not fall off.

1. Soak the toothpicks in water for at least 30 minutes.

2. Butterfly each shrimp by cutting along its curved back from the head end to the tail end, cutting almost all the way through the shrimp. Leave the tail section intact.

3. Prepare the grill for direct cooking over medium heat (350° to 450°F).

4. In a microwave oven on high, cook the bacon until the fat is slightly rendered, 2 to 3 minutes.

5. Place one piece of the cheese and one jalapeño ring inside each butterflied shrimp. Close the shrimp, and then wrap one piece of bacon around each shrimp so that the cheese and the jalapeño are enclosed. Insert a toothpick into the shrimp, pushing it through the exposed end of the bacon strip so that the bacon is held in place and the shrimp is held closed. Grill over *direct medium heat*, with the lid closed, until the shrimp are firm to the touch and just turning opaque at the center and the bacon is crisp, 6 to 8 minutes, turning once. Serve immediately.

SERVES: 4 | PREP TIME: 20 minutes | GRILLING TIME: 12–16 minutes | MARINATING TIME: 1–4 hours

1 poblano chile pepper, about 6 ounces
24 large shrimp (21/30 count), peeled and deveined, tails removed
    Extra-virgin olive oil
2 medium tomatoes, seeded and finely diced (about 1 cup)
1 small Fresno chile pepper, seeded and minced
1 jalapeño chile pepper, seeded and minced
¼ cup finely diced red onion
1 large garlic clove, minced or pushed through a press
3 tablespoons fresh lime juice
½ teaspoon kosher salt
½ teaspoon freshly ground black pepper
¼ cup finely chopped fresh cilantro leaves
    Tortilla chips

Tip

Be sure to take a small taste of the chiles to determine how hot they are, and then adjust the amount you use accordingly.

1. Prepare the grill for direct cooking over medium heat (350° to 450°F).

2. Grill the poblano over *direct medium heat*, with the lid closed, until blackened and blistered all over, 10 to 12 minutes, turning occasionally. Put the poblano in a bowl and cover with plastic wrap to trap the steam. Let stand for about 10 minutes. Peel away and discard the charred skin, cut off and discard the stem and seeds, and then cut the poblano into ¼-inch dice. Put the diced poblano back in the bowl.

3. Increase the temperature of the grill to high heat (450° to 550°F). Lightly brush the shrimp on both sides with oil. Grill over *direct high heat*, with the lid closed, until they are firm to the touch and just turning opaque in the center, 2 to 4 minutes. Cut the shrimp into ¼-inch pieces.

4. To the bowl with the diced poblano, add the shrimp, 1 tablespoon oil, the tomatoes, Fresno and jalapeño chiles, the onion, garlic, lime juice, salt, and pepper; toss to combine. Cover and refrigerate for at least 1 hour or up to 4 hours. Just before serving, stir in the cilantro. Serve the salsa immediately with tortilla chips.

SERVES: 4 | PREP TIME: 30 minutes | GRILLING TIME: 2–4 minutes

SPECIAL EQUIPMENT: perforated grill pan

SAUCE

- 1 cup Asian sweet chili sauce
- 3 tablespoons minced fresh mint leaves
- 1 teaspoon finely grated lime zest
- 4 teaspoons fresh lime juice
- 2 teaspoons peeled, minced fresh ginger
- 1 large garlic clove, minced or pushed through a press

- 1 pound cleaned squid, tubes and tentacles separated, thawed if frozen
- 1 tablespoon vegetable oil
- ½ teaspoon kosher salt
- ¼ teaspoon freshly ground black pepper
- ½ English cucumber
- 8 large leaves butter lettuce
- 2 tablespoons loosely packed fresh mint leaves

Many supermarkets carry squid that has already been cleaned. Often sold frozen, with the tubes and tentacles separated, the squid just needs a little time to thaw before you prepare it.

1. In a medium bowl whisk the sauce ingredients. Transfer ½ cup of the sauce to a large bowl. Set aside the sauce in the medium bowl for serving.

2. Prepare the grill for direct cooking over high heat (450° to 550°F) and preheat a perforated grill pan.

3. Pat the squid dry with paper towels. To the large bowl with the ½ cup sauce, add the squid, oil, salt, and pepper. Stir to coat evenly.

4. Cut the cucumber crosswise into thin slices, and then cut the slices into ½-inch-wide strips. You should have about 1 cup.

5. Lift the squid from the bowl and place in a single layer on the grill pan. Discard the sauce in the large bowl. Grill over *direct high heat*, with the lid closed, until the squid are just turning opaque and no longer look wet, 2 to 4 minutes, turning once. Remove from the grill and cut the tubes crosswise into ½-inch-wide rings. Leave the tentacles whole.

6. Arrange two lettuce leaves on each of four plates. Divide the squid equally among the lettuce leaves and top with the cucumber strips. Drizzle with the reserved sauce from the medium bowl and finish with the mint. Serve immediately.

SERVES: 8–10 (makes 2½ cups) | PREP TIME: 15 minutes | GRILLING TIME: 35–45 minutes | CHILLING TIME: 30 minutes–8 hours

SPECIAL EQUIPMENT: 1 large handful hickory wood chips, large disposable foil pan

2	tablespoons vegetable oil
2	large yellow onions, thinly sliced
1	cup sour cream
½	cup plain low-fat yogurt *or* additional sour cream
2	ounces crumbled blue cheese, at room temperature
	Kosher salt
	Freshly ground black pepper
1	tablespoon finely chopped fresh chives
	Potato chips

1. Soak the wood chips in water for at least 30 minutes.

2. Prepare the grill for indirect cooking over medium heat (350° to 450°F).

3. Pour the oil in a large disposable foil pan and tilt to coat the bottom of the pan. Add the onions and turn to coat in the oil.

4. Drain and add the wood chips to the charcoal or to the smoker box of a gas grill, following manufacturer's instructions, and close the lid. When the wood begins to smoke, cook the pan of onions over *indirect medium heat*, with the lid closed, until they are rich golden brown and some of their edges are just beginning to char, 35 to 45 minutes, stirring occasionally. Remove from the grill and let cool completely. Cut the onions into a small dice.

5. Combine the sour cream, yogurt, and cheese; stir and mash together until the cheese crumbles are about half their original size. Add 1½ cups of the onions and season the dip with salt and pepper, keeping in mind that the potato chips are salty, too. (If you have more than 1½ cups of onions, save the remainder for another use.) Transfer to a serving bowl and top with the chives. Chill the dip for at least 30 minutes or up to 8 hours. Serve with potato chips.

JAM

14   sun-dried tomato halves packed in oil, about 4 ounces total, drained and oil reserved
2   tablespoons oil from the jar of sun-dried tomatoes, plus more as needed
1   teaspoon fresh thyme leaves

6   flour tortillas (8 inches)
    Vegetable oil
12   ounces Monterey Jack or Havarti cheese, grated (about 3 cups)
¼   cup minced red onion
1   large Hass avocado, diced
½   teaspoon kosher salt
¼   teaspoon freshly ground black pepper
½   cup sour cream

1. In a food processor combine the jam ingredients. Process until the mixture has a jam-like consistency, scraping down the sides of the bowl and adding a little more oil, if necessary.

2. Prepare the grill for direct cooking over medium heat (350° to 450°F).

3. Lightly brush one side of each tortilla with vegetable oil. Place the tortillas, oiled side down, on a work surface. Assemble the quesadillas by scattering about ¼ cup of the cheese on one half of each tortilla. Top the cheese with equal amounts of onion, avocado, salt, pepper, and another ¼ cup of the cheese. Fold the empty side of each tortilla over the filling and press down.

4. Grill the quesadillas over *direct medium heat*, with the lid closed, until golden on both sides, 4 to 6 minutes, turning once. Remove from the grill and cut into wedges. Spread each wedge with a little jam and top with sour cream. Serve hot.

TOUR DE TORTILLA

Quesadillas may hail from Mexico, but they're world travelers. Their only necessity is some good melting cheese. Flour tortillas take an Italian turn with pesto, mozzarella, and sun-dried tomatoes. Brie and a smear of fruit preserves are a nod to the French. A dollop of chutney and a pinch of curry powder over grilled veggies and mild cheddar take you to India in an instant. And sliced steak, grilled onions, and blue cheese bring you back stateside. No passport required.

SERVES: 6 | PREP TIME: 25 minutes | GRILLING TIME: 8–10 minutes

1 globe eggplant, 14–16 ounces, ends trimmed, cut crosswise into 12 slices, each about ⅓ inch thick
Extra-virgin olive oil
Kosher salt
Freshly ground black pepper
3 plum tomatoes, each about 3 ounces
2½ tablespoons white balsamic vinegar
2 tablespoons chopped fresh basil leaves
1 tablespoon chopped fresh chives
1 tablespoon chopped fresh dill
1 garlic clove, minced or pushed through a press
2 tomatoes, each about 8 ounces, cut crosswise into 12 slices total, each about ⅓ inch thick
2 balls fresh mozzarella cheese, each about 4 ounces, cut into 12 slices total, each about ⅓ inch thick

1. Prepare the grill for direct cooking over medium heat (350° to 450°F).

2. Brush the eggplant slices on both sides with oil and season evenly with ¾ teaspoon salt and ½ teaspoon pepper.

3. Grill the eggplant slices over *direct medium heat*, with the lid closed, until lightly charred and tender, 8 to 10 minutes, turning once or twice. At the same time, grill the plum tomatoes over *direct medium heat* until the skins begin to

wrinkle and start to brown, 5 to 6 minutes, turning once or twice. Remove from the grill as they are done. When the tomatoes are cool enough to handle, remove and discard the skin and seeds and then finely chop them.

4. To make the vinaigrette: in a small bowl whisk the chopped tomatoes, ¼ cup plus 1 tablespoon oil, the vinegar, basil, chives, dill, garlic, ½ teaspoon salt, and ½ teaspoon pepper.

5. Arrange the eggplant slices, tomato slices, and mozzarella slices on a large platter so that they overlap slightly. Spoon the vinaigrette evenly over the top and serve immediately.

 Tip

Fresh herbs tend to wilt and fade after just a few days, even when refrigerated. You can keep them fresh much longer by storing them in a jar covered with a plastic bag. First, trim off the bottom of the stems. Fill a jar or a cup with about 1 inch of water and place the stem ends of the herbs in the water. Cover the herbs loosely with a plastic bag and store in the refrigerator. If the water discolors after a few days, change it.

SERVES: 6–8 | PREP TIME: 20 minutes | GRILLING TIME: 13–17 minutes

GARLIC OIL

2   garlic cloves, chopped
½   teaspoon kosher salt
¼   cup extra-virgin olive oil
2   tablespoons capers, rinsed, drained, and finely chopped
1   tablespoon finely chopped fresh Italian parsley leaves
¼   teaspoon freshly ground black pepper

4   large bell peppers, preferably 2 red and 2 yellow
    or orange
5   ounces fresh mozzarella cheese, cut into 16 slices,
    each about ¼ inch thick, at room temperature
    Juice of 1 lemon

1. Prepare the grill for direct cooking over medium heat (350° to 450°F).

2. Mince the chopped garlic with the salt, occasionally scraping the mixture against a cutting board with the side of your knife to form a paste. Thoroughly combine the garlic paste with the remaining garlic oil ingredients.

3. Grill the bell peppers over *direct medium heat,* with the lid closed, until blackened and blistered all over, 10 to 12 minutes, turning occasionally. Put the peppers in a bowl and cover with plastic wrap to trap the steam. Let stand for about 10 minutes. Remove the peppers from the bowl and peel away and discard the charred skin and remove the stems. Cut the peppers lengthwise into quarters, and scrape away the veins and seeds.

4. Grill the pepper quarters, smooth side up, over *direct medium heat,* with the lid closed, just to warm them through, 1 to 2 minutes. Turn the peppers over, and top each with a slice of mozzarella. Continue grilling, with the lid closed, until the cheese is beginning to soften and run slightly at the edges, 2 to 3 minutes. Transfer to a large platter and top with the garlic oil and fresh lemon juice. Serve warm or at room temperature.

SERVES: 4–6 | PREP TIME: 30 minutes | GRILLING TIME: 6–8 minutes

1 lemon
    Kosher salt
12 baby artichokes
1 tablespoon extra-virgin olive oil
    Freshly ground black pepper

AIOLI

½ cup mayonnaise
1 tablespoon freshly grated
    Parmigiano-Reggiano® cheese
1 tablespoon finely chopped fresh Italian parsley leaves
1 medium garlic clove, minced or pushed through a press

Unlike mature artichokes, baby artichokes do not have a fully developed choke, so there is no need to remove it.

1. Finely grate 2 teaspoons zest from the lemon and set aside. Cut the lemon in half. Squeeze the juice of one half into a large bowl of water. Juice the other half and set aside to use in the aioli.

2. Snap off the dark green outer leaves of the artichokes to reveal the yellowish leaves with light green tips. Cut off the stem end and the sharp tip of each artichoke. Cut each artichoke in half lengthwise. Pare off the green skin from the base and stem. After each artichoke is trimmed, place in the lemon water.

3. Prepare the grill for direct cooking over medium heat (350° to 450°F).

4. Bring a saucepan of lightly salted water to a boil. Drain the artichokes. Cook them in the boiling water until just tender when pierced with the tip of a knife, 5 to 7 minutes. Drain and rinse them under cold water. Pat dry, transfer to a bowl, toss with the oil, and season with salt and pepper.

5. Whisk the aioli ingredients, including the 2 teaspoons of lemon zest and 1 tablespoon of the reserved lemon juice.

6. Grill the artichokes over *direct medium heat*, with the lid closed, until golden brown, 6 to 8 minutes, turning once or twice. Remove from the grill and serve warm with the aioli.

SERVES: 8 | PREP TIME: 20 minutes | GRILLING TIME: 8–10 minutes

PASTE

¼ cup thinly sliced scallions (white and light green parts only)
1 jalapeño chile pepper, roughly chopped
1 tablespoon peanut oil
1 tablespoon peeled, minced fresh ginger
1 tablespoon packed dark brown sugar
½ teaspoon dried thyme
½ teaspoon ground allspice
½ teaspoon ground cinnamon
½ teaspoon kosher salt

1 large pineapple, peeled, cored, and cut into 16 spears, each about 1 by 5 inches
32 thin slices prosciutto, about 1 pound total

1. Prepare the grill for direct cooking over high heat (450° to 550°F).

2. In a food processor or a blender combine the paste ingredients. Process until a chunky paste forms, scraping down the sides of the bowl at least once.

3. Coat each pineapple spear with about 1 teaspoon of the paste, and then wrap each spear with two prosciutto slices. Grill the spears over *direct high heat,* with the lid closed, until the prosciutto is crisp on all sides, 8 to 10 minutes, turning occasionally. Serve immediately.

HELPFUL KITCHEN EQUIPMENT

The grill is the star of this show, but it's time for the "best supporting appliances" to take a bow. Ladies and gentlemen: the food processor and the blender.

Our favorite kitchen appliances make short work of what can be tedious grill prep. Yes, there is a difference between the two gadgets, and yes, having both is worthwhile. The food processor uniformly minces, chops, grates, and grinds vegetables, herbs, cheese, and even meat so fast you'll wonder why you have knives (okay, you still need knives). The blender needs some liquid in order to work, which is why it is a whiz at whirring up velvety smooth sauces and marinades. Both are speedy, efficient, multitasking additions to our grilling cast of characters—they're winners, without a doubt.

RECIPE REMIX:
Then and Now

Nothing terribly incriminating about something called "Red Apple Salad," right? Wrong. Salads of the '70s were rarely the healthy, crunchy palate pleasers we enjoy today—and they never relied on the grill. That generation favored taking a few fruits and veggies (emphasis on "few") and drenching them in heavy, creamy, sugary sauces and toppings. You'd need a real salad to recover from this salad. Enter our Remix, with its crisp-tender grilled apples and romaine lettuce, toasted walnuts, fresh herbs, and a light, citrusy, yogurt-based dressing. It tastes like a treat, but one you can feel good about eating.

The Original

Red Apple Salad

Recipe from *Barbecuing the Weber® Covered Way,* ©1972

4 cups diced, washed, unpeeled red eating apples
1 cup drained pineapple tidbits
1/3 cup quartered maraschino cherries
1-1/2 cups thinly sliced celery
1/2 cup coarsely chopped walnuts or peanuts
3/4 cup salad dressing
2 tablespoons sugar
1 teaspoon lemon juice
1/8 teaspoon salt
1/2 cup whipping cream, whipped
Crisp salad greens

Combine fruits, celery, and nuts in a bowl. Combine and mix salad dressing, sugar, lemon juice, and salt. Fold in whipped cream. Add to fruit; mix carefully. Chill until ready to serve. Serve on crisp salad greens. Yield: 6 to 8 servings.

GRILLED APPLE AND ROMAINE SALAD
WITH FENNEL, CRANBERRIES, AND WALNUTS

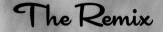
The Remix

SERVES: 6 | PREP TIME: 20 minutes | GRILLING TIME: 7–10 minutes

SPECIAL EQUIPMENT: perforated grill pan or cast-iron skillet

DRESSING
⅓ cup whole-milk Greek yogurt
3 tablespoons extra-virgin olive oil
1 teaspoon finely grated lemon zest
3 tablespoons fresh lemon juice
1 tablespoon roughly chopped fresh tarragon or basil leaves
1 teaspoon kosher salt
½ teaspoon freshly ground black pepper

SALAD
2 small fennel bulbs, root ends and stalks removed
⅔ cup walnut halves
2 large, crisp red apples, such as Fuji, halved, cored, and cut crosswise into ½-inch slices
    Extra-virgin olive oil
3 hearts of romaine, about 1 pound total, each cut lengthwise in half, trimmed
    Kosher salt
    Freshly ground black pepper
⅓ cup sweetened dried cranberries
2 tablespoons roughly chopped fresh tarragon or basil leaves

1. Prepare the grill for direct cooking over medium heat (350° to 450°F) and preheat a perforated grill pan.

2. Whisk the dressing ingredients and set aside.

3. Cut each fennel bulb in half lengthwise and then cut away and remove the thick, triangular core. Cut the fennel lengthwise as thinly as possible.

4. Spread the walnuts in a single layer on the grill pan and grill over *direct medium heat*, with the lid open, until they are golden brown and fragrant, 1 to 2 minutes, stirring occasionally. Remove the walnuts from the grill pan and, when cool enough to handle, coarsely chop them.

5. Drizzle the apple slices with 1 tablespoon oil and toss to coat. Spread the apple slices in a single layer on the grill pan and cook over *direct medium heat*, with the lid closed, until they have grill marks on both sides, 4 to 6 minutes, turning once or twice. Remove the grill pan with the apples from the grill and transfer the apples to a cutting board. When cool enough to handle, cut the apples into ¾-inch pieces. Lightly brush the romaine on both sides with oil and season evenly with salt and pepper. Grill the romaine, cut side down first, over *direct medium heat*, with the lid closed, until slightly wilted, about 2 minutes, turning once. Transfer the romaine to a serving platter cut side up.

6. In a bowl combine the walnuts, apples, fennel, and cranberries. Pour in half of the dressing and toss to combine, adding additional dressing, if desired. Spoon the apple mixture over the romaine. Garnish with the tarragon and serve right away.

SERVES: 4 | PREP TIME: 15 minutes | GRILLING TIME: 2–3 minutes

DRESSING

- 1 anchovy fillet packed in olive oil, drained *or* ½ teaspoon anchovy paste
- 2 tablespoons extra-virgin olive oil
- 1½ tablespoons mayonnaise
- 1½ teaspoons fresh lemon juice
- 1 teaspoon Dijon mustard
- ½ teaspoon Worcestershire sauce
- ½ small garlic clove, minced or pushed through a press
- ¼ teaspoon freshly ground black pepper

- 1 French roll, about 6 inches long, cut lengthwise into quarters
- 1 garlic clove, cut in half
- 3 hearts of romaine, about 1 pound total, each cut lengthwise into quarters
- 2 tablespoons extra-virgin olive oil
- 2 tablespoons freshly grated Parmigiano-Reggiano® cheese

1. Prepare the grill for direct cooking over medium heat (350° to 450°F).

2. Mash the anchovy fillet into a paste. Put all of the dressing ingredients into a bowl and whisk to combine.

3. Grill the bread quarters over *direct medium heat*, with the lid closed, until lightly toasted, 1 to 2 minutes, turning three times. Remove from the grill and rub the cut sides of the bread with the cut side of the garlic clove. Set aside.

4. Brush the romaine all over with the oil and grill over *direct medium heat*, with the lid open, until slightly wilted, about 1 minute (you may not need to turn). Remove from the grill. Top the romaine with the dressing and the cheese, and serve with the toasted bread quarters.

Anchovy paste, sold in tubes next to the whole anchovies packed in olive oil at the grocery store, is a good substitute for anchovy fillets here. Once opened, the tube can be stored in the refrigerator for several months.

SERVES: 6 | PREP TIME: 25 minutes | MARINATING TIME: 10 minutes | GRILLING TIME: 5–7 minutes

2   heads radicchio, about 1¼ pounds total, each
     cut through the core into quarters

MARINADE/VINAIGRETTE
¼   cup plus 1 teaspoon balsamic vinegar, divided
⅓   cup plus 2 tablespoons extra-virgin olive oil, divided
1   large garlic clove, minced or pushed through a press
1½ teaspoons finely chopped fresh rosemary leaves
1   teaspoon kosher salt
½   teaspoon freshly ground black pepper
2   medium shallots, minced

2   cups loosely packed fresh watercress leaves and
     tender stems
1   tablespoon finely grated lemon zest
1   wedge, about 3 ounces, Parmigiano-Reggiano® cheese
3   tablespoons pine nuts, toasted

1. Prepare the grill for direct cooking over medium heat
(350° to 450°F).

2. Rinse the radicchio under cold water and then drain briefly,
cut side down, on paper towels.

3. In a large bowl whisk ¼ cup of the vinegar, ⅓ cup of the oil,
the garlic, rosemary, salt, and pepper. Add the radicchio to the
bowl and turn to coat evenly. Let stand for 10 minutes.

4. Lift the radicchio from the bowl and transfer to a plate,
leaving any excess marinade in the bowl. To make the
vinaigrette, whisk the remaining 1 teaspoon vinegar and the
remaining 2 tablespoons oil into the marinade. Stir in the
shallots and set aside.

5. Grill the radicchio over *direct medium heat*, with the
lid closed, until slightly charred, 3 to 4 minutes. Turn the
radicchio over and grill until the outer layers are browned and
crisp and the inside is still tender and purple, 2 to 3 minutes
more. Remove from the grill. When cool enough to handle,
cut the radicchio crosswise into 1-inch strips. Add to the bowl
with the vinaigrette along with the watercress and the lemon
zest. Toss to coat evenly. Using a vegetable peeler, shave curls
of the cheese over the salad and top with the pine nuts.
Serve immediately.

SERVES: 4 | PREP TIME: 10 minutes | GRILLING TIME: about 8 minutes

4 ounces cream cheese, softened
2 tablespoons granulated sugar
1 tablespoon fresh thyme leaves
4 firm but ripe peaches, each cut in half
8 slices Italian or French bread, each about ½ inch thick
   Extra-virgin olive oil
   Kosher salt
4 ounces crumbled blue cheese (1 cup)
3 tablespoons honey

Apricots or nectarines may be substituted for the peaches.

1. Prepare the grill for direct cooking over medium-low heat (about 350°F).

2. Stir the cream cheese, sugar, and thyme until blended. Set aside. Lightly brush the peach halves and the bread slices on both sides with oil.

3. Grill the peach halves over *direct medium-low heat*, with the lid closed, until lightly charred and beginning to soften, about 8 minutes, turning once. During the last minute of grilling time, toast the bread slices over direct heat, turning once or twice. Remove the peaches and the bread from the grill.

4. Spread each bread slice with an equal amount of the cream cheese mixture.

5. Cut the peach halves into ¼-inch slices. Divide the peach slices among the bread slices, overlapping them slightly. Top with the blue cheese and drizzle with the honey. Serve right away.

SERVES: 6 | PREP TIME: 45 minutes | GRILLING TIME: about 6 minutes

TOPPING

Extra-virgin olive oil
8 ounces sweet Italian sausages, casings removed
1 medium yellow onion, finely chopped
2 medium garlic cloves, minced or pushed through a press
1 can (14½ ounces) diced plum tomatoes in juice
1½ teaspoons Italian herb seasoning
¼ teaspoon crushed red pepper flakes

1 baguette, about 6 ounces, cut crosswise into
   ½- to 1-inch slices
⅓ cup freshly grated Parmigiano-Reggiano® cheese
1½ cups grated mozzarella cheese (6 ounces)

1. In a saucepan over medium-high heat, warm 1 tablespoon oil. Add the sausages and cook until lightly browned, about 5 minutes, breaking up the meat with the side of a spoon. Using a slotted spoon, transfer the sausage to a bowl, leaving the fat in the saucepan.

2. Add the onion to the saucepan and cook until softened, about 3 minutes, stirring occasionally. Add the garlic and cook until fragrant, about 1 minute, stirring often. Add the tomatoes and juice, Italian herb seasoning, and red pepper flakes and stir to combine. Add the sausage and bring the mixture to a boil. Reduce the heat to medium-low and simmer until the liquid is almost completely evaporated, 10 to 15 minutes, stirring occasionally. Remove from the heat.

3. Prepare the grill for direct cooking over medium-low heat (about 350°F).

4. Lightly brush one side of each baguette slice with oil. Toast the baguette slices over *direct medium-low heat*, with the lid closed, for about 1 minute, turning once or twice. Transfer the slices, oiled side up, to a sheet pan or a baking sheet. Top with equal amounts of Parmigiano-Reggiano cheese, the topping, and the mozzarella. Grill the bruschetta on the sheet pan over *direct medium-low heat*, with the lid closed, until the cheese is melted, about 5 minutes. Serve warm.

MEATBALLS

1½ pounds ground turkey, preferably thigh meat
¼ cup finely chopped fresh cilantro leaves
2 scallions (white and light green parts only), minced
1 tablespoon soy sauce
1 tablespoon peeled, grated fresh ginger
2 teaspoons hot chili-garlic sauce, such as Sriracha
2 garlic cloves, minced or pushed through a press
1 teaspoon ground coriander
1 teaspoon kosher salt

SAUCE

½ cup rice vinegar
¼ cup fresh lime juice
¼ cup granulated sugar
1 tablespoon finely chopped fresh cilantro leaves
2 teaspoons minced red jalapeño chile pepper
2 teaspoons peeled, grated fresh ginger
1 teaspoon kosher salt
1 garlic clove, minced or pushed through a press

Vegetable oil

1. Combine the meatball ingredients, gently mixing until the ingredients are evenly distributed. With wet hands, form into equal-sized balls, each about 1½ inches in diameter. Cover with plastic wrap and refrigerate for at least 1 hour.

2. In a saucepan over medium-high heat, combine the vinegar, lime juice, and sugar. Bring to a boil and cook until the sugar dissolves and the liquid is reduced by one-third, about 5 minutes, stirring occasionally. Transfer the mixture to a bowl and stir in the remaining sauce ingredients. Let cool completely.

3. Prepare the grill for direct cooking over medium heat (350° to 450°F).

4. Lightly brush the meatballs with oil. Grill over *direct medium heat,* with the lid closed, until the meat is cooked through, 8 to 10 minutes, turning two or three times. Remove from the grill and serve warm with the sauce.

Be sure to purchase ground turkey made from dark meat rather than white meat. Not only is dark meat turkey more flavorful, but it also holds up better to handling, which is important when you're shaping the meatballs.

SERVES: 4–6 | PREP TIME: 20 minutes | GRILLING TIME: 20–25 minutes

SPECIAL EQUIPMENT: spice mill or mortar and pestle (optional)

GLAZE

¾ cup seedless raspberry jam
¼ cup balsamic vinegar
2 teaspoons finely grated lemon zest
¼ teaspoon crushed red pepper flakes

RUB

1 teaspoon fennel seed
1 teaspoon garlic powder
1 teaspoon dried basil
1 teaspoon kosher salt
½ teaspoon freshly ground black pepper

12 chicken wings, about 3 pounds total, each cut in half at the joint and wing tips removed

1. Prepare the grill for direct and indirect cooking over medium heat (350° to 450°F).

2. Whisk the glaze ingredients.

3. In a spice mill process the fennel seed until coarsely ground (or use the bottom of a heavy pan to crush it). Pour the fennel seed into a large bowl and add the remaining rub ingredients. Add the chicken wings and toss to coat them with the rub.

4. Grill the wings over *direct medium heat*, with the lid closed, until golden brown, 10 to 15 minutes, turning once or twice. Move the wings over *indirect medium heat*, brush with half of the glaze, and continue grilling until the skin is crisp at the edges and the meat is no longer pink at the bone, about 10 minutes more. During the last 5 minutes of grilling time, brush the wings evenly with the remaining glaze, turning once or twice (you may not need all of the glaze). Serve warm.

SERVES: 4–6 | PREP TIME: 30 minutes | GRILLING TIME: about 16 minutes

SAUCE

1	can (8 ounces) tomato sauce
½	cup minced yellow onion
¼	cup tomato paste
3	tablespoons cider vinegar
1½	tablespoons packed golden brown sugar
1½	teaspoons Worcestershire sauce
1	teaspoon fresh lemon juice
¾	teaspoon mustard powder
½	teaspoon celery salt
½	teaspoon kosher salt
1	garlic clove, minced or pushed through a press
¼	teaspoon prepared chili powder
⅛	teaspoon freshly ground black pepper
2	drops hot pepper sauce, or to taste

18	chicken drumettes, about 2 pounds total
	Extra-virgin olive oil
½	teaspoon kosher salt
¼	teaspoon freshly ground black pepper
2	ounces crumbled blue cheese

1. In a saucepan combine the sauce ingredients. Cover and simmer gently over medium heat until thickened, about 15 minutes, stirring occasionally. Remove from the heat and let cool. Pour the sauce through a fine-mesh strainer, and then use the back of a spoon to press on the solids to extract the liquid. Discard the solids. Put about one-third of the sauce in a small bowl for brushing on the drumettes while grilling. Reserve the remaining sauce for serving.

2. Prepare the grill for direct cooking over low heat (250° to 350°F).

3. Lightly brush the drumettes on both sides with oil and season evenly with the salt and pepper.

4. Grill the drumettes over *direct low heat*, with the lid closed, until sizzling and nicely marked, about 8 minutes, turning once. Brush the drumettes with some of the sauce in the small bowl and continue cooking until the juices run clear and the meat is no longer pink at the bone, about 8 minutes more, turning and brushing with sauce once. Remove from the grill. Brush the drumettes with some of the reserved sauce and top with blue cheese. Serve with any remaining reserved sauce.

4

RED MEAT

GRILLING BEEF

CUT	THICKNESS / WEIGHT	APPROXIMATE GRILLING TIME
Steak: New York strip, porterhouse, rib eye, T-bone, and filet mignon (tenderloin)	¾ inch thick	**4–6 minutes** direct high heat
	1 inch thick	**6–8 minutes** direct high heat
	1¼ inches thick	**8–10 minutes** direct high heat
	1½ inches thick	**10–14 minutes:** sear 6–8 minutes direct high heat, grill 4–6 minutes indirect high heat
Beef, ground	¾ inch thick	**8–10 minutes** direct medium-high heat
Flank steak	1½–2 pounds, ¾ inch thick	**8–10 minutes** direct medium heat
Flat iron steak	1 inch thick	**8–10 minutes** direct medium heat
Hanger steak	1 inch thick	**8–10 minutes** direct medium heat
Kabob	1-inch cubes	**4–6 minutes** direct high heat
	1½-inch cubes	**6–7 minutes** direct high heat
Rib roast (prime rib), boneless	5–6 pounds	**1¼–1¾ hours** indirect medium heat
Rib roast (prime rib), with bone	8 pounds	**2–3 hours:** sear 10 minutes direct medium heat, grill 2–3 hours indirect low heat
Skirt steak	¼–½ inch thick	**4–6 minutes** direct high heat
Strip loin roast, boneless	4–5 pounds	**50 minutes–1 hour:** sear 10 minutes direct medium heat, grill 40–50 minutes indirect medium heat
Tenderloin, whole	3½–4 pounds	**35–45 minutes:** sear 15 minutes direct medium heat, grill 20–30 minutes indirect medium heat
Top sirloin	1½ inches thick	**10–14 minutes:** sear 6–8 minutes direct high heat, grill 4–6 minutes indirect high heat
Tri-tip	2–2½ pounds	**30–40 minutes:** sear 10 minutes direct medium heat, grill 20–30 minutes indirect medium heat
Veal loin chop	1 inch thick	**6–8 minutes** direct high heat

All cooking times are for medium-rare doneness, except ground beef (medium).

TYPES OF RED MEAT FOR THE GRILL

TENDER CUTS FOR GRILLING

Beef New York strip steak

Beef porterhouse steak

Beef rib steak/rib eye steak

Beef T-bone steak

Beef tenderloin (filet mignon) steak

Lamb loin chop

Lamb sirloin chop

Veal loin chop

MODERATELY TENDER CUTS FOR GRILLING

Beef flank steak

Beef flat iron steak

Beef hanger steak

Beef skirt steak

Beef top sirloin steak

Lamb shoulder blade chop

Lamb sirloin chop

Veal shoulder blade chop

BIGGER CUTS FOR SEARING AND GRILL-ROASTING

Beef standing rib roast (prime rib)

Beef strip loin roast

Beef tri-tip roast

Beef whole tenderloin

Leg of lamb

Rack of lamb

Rack of veal

TOUGHER CUTS FOR BARBECUING

Beef ribs

Brisket

RED MEAT DONENESS

DONENESS	CHEF STANDARDS	USDA
Rare	120° to 125°F	n/a
Medium rare	125° to 135°F	145°F
Medium	135° to 145°F	160°F
Medium well	145° to 155°F	n/a
Well done	155°F +	170°F

GRILLING LAMB

CUT	THICKNESS/ WEIGHT	APPROXIMATE GRILLING TIME
Chop: loin or rib	¾ inch thick	4–6 minutes direct high heat
	1 inch thick	6–8 minutes direct high heat
	1½ inches thick	8–10 minutes direct high heat
Lamb, ground	¾ inch thick	8–10 minutes direct medium-high heat
Leg of lamb, boneless, rolled	2½–3 pounds	30–45 minutes: sear 10–15 minutes direct medium heat, grill 20–30 minutes indirect medium heat
Leg of lamb, butterflied	3–3½ pounds	30–45 minutes: sear 10–15 minutes direct medium heat, grill 20–30 minutes indirect medium heat
Rack of lamb	1–1½ pounds	15–20 minutes: sear 5 minutes direct medium heat, grill 10–15 minutes indirect medium heat
Rib crown roast	3–4 pounds	1–1¼ hours indirect medium heat

All cooking times are for medium-rare doneness, except ground lamb (medium).

The cuts, thicknesses, weights, and grilling times are meant to be guidelines rather than hard and fast rules. Cooking times are affected by such factors as altitude, wind, outside temperature, and desired doneness. Two rules of thumb: Grill steaks, chops, and kabobs using the direct method for the time given on the chart or to your desired doneness, turning once. Grill roasts and thicker cuts using the indirect method for the time given on the chart or until an instant-read thermometer reaches the desired internal temperature. Let roasts, larger cuts of meat, and thick steaks rest for 5 to 10 minutes before carving. The internal temperature of the meat will rise 5 to 10 degrees during this time.

gr ll SKILLS:
PERFECT BURGERS

Choose Wisely

Hamburgers need some fat to be delicious—about twenty percent, actually. Hamburgers with less fat are destined to be dry and crumbly; however, when the meat has enough milky white fat speckled throughout it, the fat dissolves into mouthwatering moisture that not only feels good on your tongue, but it also tastes good. Fat has its own beefy flavors, and it carries other flavors, too, including the seasonings in the patties and the smokiness of the grill.

Most people get their ground meat from a supermarket, where it has been packed into a foam tray. You can make some very good burgers with this meat, but if you are in search of perfection, ask a butcher to grind the meat for you so that the meat is loosely packed. This type of texture, where you can see long strands of beef just as they came out of the grinder (see photo above), leads to the plumpest, juiciest burgers, assuming the meat has enough fat. This also allows you to choose the best cut. An excellent choice is chuck, a well-exercised, flavorful shoulder cut. Sirloin, a cut from close to the hardworking hip, is another good choice.

Building a Better Burger

1 Put the meat in a bowl and season with salt and pepper before you make the patties.

2 Divide the meat into equal portions before you shape the patties. This step avoids the problem of having too much or too little meat left over for that last patty.

3 With wet hands, gently shape each portion into a loose, round ball. Then flatten each ball into a patty with a thickness between ¾ and 1 inch.

4 Use a spoon or your thumb to create a shallow well in the middle of each patty. This will prevent "the meatball effect," where the patty develops a domed top.

Butter Up

A trick for making really juicy burgers is to nestle a small pat of cold butter in the center of each patty. Just be sure to seal the butter well inside so that it doesn't cause flare-ups.

Grilling Perfect Burgers

A perfect burger is a study in contrasts. The top and bottom of each patty is lightly charred with crispy brown bits all over. Inside each patty the meat is soft, tender, and dripping with juices. The key to this kind of contrast is the magic combination of the patty's thickness (¾ to 1 inch) and the grill's temperature (400° to 500°F). Over the course of 8 to 10 minutes, the surface has just enough time to turn dark brown and delicious while the inside cooks fully without losing much of its juices, assuming the lid is closed.

Cooking with the lid closed reflects heat onto the top of each patty, meaning the patties are cooking on both sides. This speeds up the overall cooking time. Also, closing the lid restricts the amount of air getting to the fire and eliminates a lot of potential flare-ups. And finally, the lid also keeps the cooking grate hot enough to sear the surface of each patty properly.

NO FLIPPING OUT. You should only turn patties once or twice. If you try to turn a patty during the first few minutes, you are bound to leave some meat sticking to the grate. If you can manage to wait 4 minutes or so, the meat will develop a lightly charred crust that releases naturally from the grate.

NO SMASHING. One of the worst things you can do to a patty is to press or smash it with a spatula. The juices run out quickly, causing flare-ups and drying out your burger.

PATTIES

1½ pounds ground chuck (80% lean)
½ teaspoon garlic powder
½ teaspoon kosher salt
½ teaspoon freshly ground black pepper

SALSA

1 large mango, cut into ½-inch dice (about 1 cup)
2 tablespoons roughly chopped fresh cilantro leaves
1 tablespoon fresh lime juice
1 medium serrano chile pepper, seeded and minced
¼ teaspoon kosher salt

4 thin slices pepper jack cheese
4 hamburger buns, split
Dijon mustard

1. Combine the patty ingredients, keeping the mixture crumbly rather than compressed. With wet hands, gently form four loosely packed patties of equal size, each about ¾ inch thick. Don't compact the meat too much or the patties will be tough. Using your thumb or the back of a spoon, make a shallow indentation about 1 inch wide in the center of each patty. This will help the patties cook evenly and prevent them from puffing on the grill.

2. In a nonreactive bowl combine the salsa ingredients. Toss gently and then refrigerate for at least 30 minutes or up to 1 hour. (After an hour, the fruit starts to become mushy.)

3. Prepare the grill for direct cooking over medium-high heat (400° to 500°F).

4. Grill the patties over *direct medium-high heat*, with the lid closed, until cooked to medium doneness, 8 to 10 minutes, turning once when the patties release easily from the grate without sticking. During the last minute of grilling time, place a slice of cheese on each patty to melt and toast the buns, cut side down, over direct heat.

5. Spread the bottom half of each bun with mustard, and serve the patties warm on the buns topped with salsa.

A TOURIST FROM THE TROPICS THAT IS HERE TO STAY

Once upon a time, a couple of decades ago, the exotic mango was little known here in the States, except in stories about shipwrecks on tropical islands.

Nowadays, you can't swing a palm frond without knocking one off a supermarket shelf.

A mainstay of the South Asian diet for centuries, this nutrient-packed stone fruit is becoming ever more common on US grocery lists, thanks to expanding American tastes in food and travel—as well as improvements in cultivation and distribution that make mangoes hardier and easier to ship. Most common in stores is the greenish orange, oblong variety, which is grown for its disease-resistance, portability, and heft. Elsewhere in the frost-free world, the abundant mango crop is much more varied.

Sweet mango is a great match with spicy foods as a cool, juicy side dish, a dessert, or right in the thick of things, mixed into a salsa with fiery chiles, as in the accompanying cheeseburger recipe.

Pick blemish-free, heavy mangoes that give slightly when pressed. And leave the high seas travel to the pros.

SERVES: 4 | PREP TIME: 20 minutes | GRILLING TIME: 10–12 minutes

SAUCE

¼ cup plus 2 tablespoons mayonnaise
1½ tablespoons Dijon mustard
1 teaspoon fresh lemon juice

1½ pounds ground chuck (80% lean)
1 teaspoon dried tarragon
   Kosher salt
½ teaspoon freshly ground black pepper
4 ounces Brie cheese, cut into 8 wedges
4 hamburger buns, split
1 beefsteak tomato, about 8 ounces, cut crosswise
   into 4 slices, each about ½ inch thick
1 tablespoon extra-virgin olive oil
4 leaves Boston lettuce

1. Whisk the sauce ingredients.

2. Prepare the grill for direct cooking over medium-high heat (400° to 500°F).

3. Gently combine the ground chuck, tarragon, 1 teaspoon salt, and the pepper. With wet hands, form four loosely packed patties of equal size, each about ¾ inch thick. Don't compact the meat too much or the patties will be tough. Using your thumb or the back of a spoon, make a shallow indentation about 1 inch wide in the center of each patty. This will help the patties cook evenly and prevent them from puffing on the grill.

4. Grill the patties over *direct medium-high heat*, with the lid closed, until cooked to medium doneness, 8 to 10 minutes, turning once when the patties release easily from the grate without sticking. During the last minute of grilling time, place two pieces of the Brie on each patty to melt and toast the buns, cut side down, over direct heat. Remove from the grill.

5. Brush the tomato slices on both sides with the oil and season with ½ teaspoon salt. Grill over *direct medium-high heat*, with the lid closed, until they are tender and nicely marked, about 2 minutes, turning once. Spread the sauce on the cut sides of each bun. Build each burger with a patty, lettuce, and tomato. Serve warm.

PATTIES

1½ pounds ground chuck (80% lean)
⅔ cup thinly sliced scallions (white and light green parts only)
1½ tablespoons toasted sesame seeds
1½ tablespoons low-sodium soy sauce
 1 tablespoon freshly ground black pepper

 2 tablespoons toasted sesame oil
 2 tablespoons packed dark brown sugar
 4 onion rolls, split
 1 cup loosely packed fresh baby spinach

1. Prepare the grill for direct cooking over medium-high heat (400° to 500°F).

2. Gently combine the patty ingredients. With wet hands, form four loosely packed patties of equal size, each about ¾ inch thick. Don't compact the meat too much or the patties will be tough. Using your thumb or the back of a spoon, make a shallow indentation about 1 inch wide in the center of each patty. This will help the patties cook evenly and prevent them from puffing on the grill.

3. Mix the oil and the brown sugar to form a paste.

4. Grill the patties over *direct medium-high heat*, with the lid closed, for 4 to 5 minutes. Brush half of the paste over the patties, turn them, and brush with the remaining paste. Continue grilling until cooked to medium doneness, 4 to 5 minutes more. During the last minute of grilling time, toast the rolls, cut side down, over direct heat. Serve the patties on the toasted rolls with a handful of the spinach on top.

SERVES: 6 | PREP TIME: 30 minutes, plus 35 minutes for the sauce | CHILLING TIME: 1–5 hours | GRILLING TIME: 11–15 minutes

MEATBALLS

- 1 pound ground chuck (80% lean)
- 1 pound lean ground pork
- ¾ cup dried bread crumbs
- 2 large eggs, lightly beaten
- ½ cup grated pecorino Romano cheese
- ½ cup grated Parmigiano-Reggiano® cheese
- ¼ cup finely chopped yellow onion
- ¼ cup finely chopped fresh Italian parsley leaves
- 2 large garlic cloves, minced or pushed through a press

    Kosher salt
    Freshly ground black pepper

SAUCE

- 1 tablespoon extra-virgin olive oil
- ½ cup minced yellow onion
- 2 garlic cloves, minced or pushed through a press
- 1 can (28 ounces) crushed Italian plum tomatoes
- 1 bay leaf
- 1 teaspoon dried oregano, crumbled
- ⅛ teaspoon crushed red pepper flakes

    Extra-virgin olive oil
- 6 slices French bread, each about ½ inch thick (optional)

1. Thoroughly combine the meatball ingredients, including 1 teaspoon salt and ½ teaspoon pepper, keeping the mixture crumbly rather than compressed. With wet hands, form into equal-sized balls, each about 1½ inches in diameter (yield: about 30 meatballs). Cover with plastic wrap and refrigerate for at least 1 hour or up to 5 hours.

2. In a medium saucepan over medium heat, warm the oil. Add the onion and sauté until tender, 3 to 4 minutes. Add the garlic and sauté for 1 minute more. Add the remaining sauce ingredients, including ½ teaspoon salt and ¼ teaspoon pepper, and simmer, uncovered, until thickened, about 30 minutes. Discard the bay leaf. Keep warm.

3. Prepare the grill for direct cooking over medium heat (350° to 450°F).

4. Brush the meatballs all over with oil. Grill over *direct medium heat*, with the lid closed, until the meatballs are thoroughly cooked but not dry, 11 to 15 minutes, turning occasionally. Serve warm on grilled French bread, if desired, with the sauce spooned on top.

SERVES: 6 | PREP TIME: 20 minutes | DRAINING/COOLING/PICKLING TIME: 5 hours–3 days | GRILLING TIME: 5–7 minutes

4 cups roughly chopped, tightly packed (½-inch pieces) green cabbage
2 Kirby or Persian cucumbers, seeded and cut into ½-inch dice
1 medium yellow onion, chopped
½ red bell pepper, cut into ½-inch dice
2 jalapeño chile peppers, seeded and finely chopped
1 tablespoon kosher salt
1 cup cider vinegar
⅔ cup packed golden brown sugar
1 teaspoon mustard powder
½ teaspoon celery seed
¼ teaspoon ground turmeric
12 all-beef hot dogs
12 hot dog buns, split

1. In a large colander toss the cabbage, cucumbers, onion, bell pepper, jalapeños, and salt. Place a dinner plate on top of the vegetables to weigh them down. Let stand in the sink to drain for 1 hour.

2. In a large saucepan over medium heat, combine the vinegar, brown sugar, mustard powder, celery seed, and turmeric. Bring to a simmer, stirring to dissolve the sugar. Add the cabbage mixture (do not rinse) to the saucepan and cook until the cabbage is crisp-tender, 4 to 6 minutes, stirring occasionally. Transfer to a bowl and let cool for 2 hours at room temperature. Cover and refrigerate for at least 2 hours or up to 3 days.

3. Prepare the grill for direct cooking over medium heat (350° to 450°F).

4. Cut a few shallow slashes in each hot dog. Grill the hot dogs over *direct medium heat*, with the lid closed, until lightly marked on the outside and hot all the way through, 5 to 7 minutes, turning occasionally. During the last minute of grilling time, toast the buns, cut side down, over direct heat.

5. Place the hot dogs in the buns. Using a slotted spoon to drain the excess liquid, spoon about ¼ cup of the vegetables on top of each hot dog. Serve immediately.

grill SKILLS:
PERFECT STEAKS

Choose Wisely

The main thing to look for in steaks is marbling, those visible lines of fat running throughout the meat. This fat is essential to great steaks because, as it melts on the grill, it fills the meat with juice and flavor. On the other hand, wide streaks or hunks of fat, particularly around the outer edges of steaks, can melt and drip so much flammable fat into the fire that you get unwanted flare-ups and risk burning the meat. So choose your steaks well and trim any excess perimeter fat.

Prepping Steaks

1 Pull your steaks out of the refrigerator 15 to 30 minutes before you plan to grill them, and trim the fat around the edges to ¼ inch or less to prevent flare-ups.

2 Lightly coat trimmed steaks with extra-virgin olive oil. This adds flavor and prevents sticking.

3 Rub the oil evenly all over the steaks to prevent them from sticking to the cooking grate. The oil also helps the seasonings adhere to the meat.

4 Season with kosher salt. Within 15 to 30 minutes, the salt seasons the meat deeply, amplifying the steak flavor below the surface. Don't be timid with the salt.

5 Generously season with freshly ground black pepper for a kick of flavor.

Grilling Perfect Steaks

1 Brush the cooking grates clean and place your steaks over direct high heat. A good hot grill won't "seal in the juices," as you may have heard, but it will add tremendous flavor and texture.

2 Leave the steaks alone for at least 2 minutes, preferably 3 minutes. Resist the urge to fiddle with them, unless:

A. You want crosshatch marks. In this case, rotate each steak 90 degrees after about 1½ minutes.
B. You're fighting a flare-up. Move the steaks over indirect heat temporarily, until the flames subside, and then move them back over direct heat.

3 Once you have a deep, delicious sear on the first side, turn the steaks over and sear them on the second side for 2 to 3 minutes.

4 If your steaks are thinner than 1½ inches, finish them over direct heat. If they are 1½ inches or thicker, finish them over indirect heat so that the inside has a chance to cook before the outside burns. Use the handy doneness tests below to help determine when the steaks are ready to come off the grill.

5 Let steaks rest at room temperature for just a few minutes before anyone cuts into them. This does so much to help each steak hold onto its juices.

When Is It Done?

TOUCH TEST. Press the meat surface with your fingertip. When it has the same firmness as the base of your thumb, take the steak off.

HAND TEST: RARE. If you touch your index finger and thumb together and then press the base of your thumb, that's how most steaks feel when they are rare.

HAND TEST: MEDIUM RARE. If you touch your middle finger and thumb together and then press the base of your thumb, that's how most steaks feel when they are medium rare.

TOPPING

¼ cup plus 2 tablespoons mayonnaise
¼ cup finely grated Parmigiano-Reggiano® cheese
2 tablespoons prepared horseradish

4 New York strip steaks, each 8–10 ounces and 1 inch thick, trimmed of excess fat
   Extra-virgin olive oil
   Kosher salt
   Freshly ground black pepper
1 tablespoon balsamic vinegar
4 slices apple wood smoked bacon, cut crosswise into ⅓-inch strips
4 cups loosely packed watercress sprigs, thick stems trimmed (about 1 large bunch)
12 ounces mixed red and yellow cherry tomatoes or grape tomatoes, each cut in half

ALWAYS A KICK

Pungent, assertive horseradish has jumped out of the Bloody Mary and into our spotlight.

This perennial plant, cousin to wasabi, mustard, and broccoli, was long valued for its medicinal as well as its culinary qualities, thanks to that distinct chemical compound—the one that makes you blink and go "whoa!" The grated root mixed with vinegar (as it's found in "prepared horseradish"), however, adds a smack of spicy, inimitable flavor to sauces, spreads, and dressings.

While parts of Europe have always been fans, America forgot about horseradish for a while and let it languish in our fridges in the event of an occasional brunch cocktail. But you've heard it here first, it's back—and it's everywhere.

Use it in sandwiches and in sauces, in potatoes or dips. We top grilled meat with it and love how horseradish's eye-watering potency mellows a bit under the grill lid. And yes, it's still great in the Bloody Mary.

Long live horseradish, in all its sinus-clearing glory.

1. Whisk the topping ingredients.

2. Lightly brush the steaks on both sides with oil and season evenly with 1 teaspoon salt and 1 teaspoon pepper. Allow the steaks to stand at room temperature for 15 to 30 minutes before grilling.

3. Prepare the grill for direct cooking over high heat (450° to 550°F).

4. In a large salad bowl whisk 3 tablespoons oil, the balsamic vinegar, ¼ teaspoon salt, and ¼ teaspoon pepper.

5. In a medium skillet over medium heat, cook the bacon until crisp, 8 to 10 minutes. Using a slotted spoon, transfer the bacon to paper towels to drain.

6. Add the watercress and the tomatoes to the salad bowl, but do not toss.

7. Sear the steaks over *direct high heat*, with the lid closed, for 2 to 3 minutes. Turn the steaks over and spread the top of each steak with an equal amount of the topping. Close the lid and continue grilling until the topping is golden and slightly browned in spots and the steaks are cooked to your desired doneness, 4 to 5 minutes more for medium rare. Remove from the grill and let rest for 3 to 5 minutes.

8. Toss the salad and top with the bacon. Serve the steak warm with the salad.

SERVES: 4 | PREP TIME: 10 minutes | GRILLING TIME: 6–8 minutes

4 New York strip steaks, each 10–12 ounces and
   about 1 inch thick, trimmed of excess fat
1 tablespoon extra-virgin olive oil
1½ teaspoons kosher salt
1 teaspoon freshly ground black pepper
1 cup freshly grated Parmigiano-Reggiano® cheese
2 tablespoons finely chopped fresh basil leaves
¼ cup (½ stick) unsalted butter
2 medium garlic cloves, minced or pushed through a press

1. Lightly brush the steaks on both sides with the oil and season evenly with the salt and pepper. Allow the steaks to stand at room temperature for 15 to 30 minutes before grilling.

2. Prepare the grill for direct cooking over high heat (450° to 550°F).

3. Combine the cheese and the basil.

4. Sear the steaks over *direct high heat,* with the lid closed, for 3 to 4 minutes. Turn the steaks over and generously coat the top of each steak with the cheese and basil mixture. Close the lid and continue grilling until the cheese is melted and the steaks are cooked to your desired doneness, 3 to 4 minutes more for medium rare. Remove from the grill and let rest for 3 to 5 minutes.

5. Meanwhile, in a saucepan over medium heat, combine the butter and the garlic and heat until the butter is melted and the garlic is sizzling, about 3 minutes. Remove from the heat. Spoon the garlic butter over the steaks and serve right away.

SERVES: 4 | PREP TIME: 20 minutes | GRILLING TIME: 3–4 minutes

SPECIAL EQUIPMENT: grill-proof griddle or cast-iron skillet

- 4 New York strip steaks, each about 5 ounces and ¼ inch thick, trimmed of excess fat
- 4 tablespoons extra-virgin olive oil, divided
  Kosher salt
  Freshly ground black pepper
- 1 large yellow onion, cut into ¼-inch half-moons
- 1 small green bell pepper, cut into ¼-inch strips
- 8 ounces button mushrooms, thinly sliced
- 4 French rolls, split
- 8 slices provolone cheese

1. Brush the steaks on both sides with 2 tablespoons oil. Season evenly with 1½ teaspoons salt and ¾ teaspoon pepper. Allow the steaks to stand at room temperature for 15 to 30 minutes before grilling.

2. Prepare the grill for direct cooking over high heat (450° to 550°F) and preheat a grill-proof griddle for 10 minutes.

3. In a bowl mix the onion and bell pepper with 1 tablespoon oil. In another bowl mix the mushrooms with 1 tablespoon oil. Spread the onion and bell pepper in a single layer on the griddle and cook until softened, about 5 minutes, stirring occasionally. Push the onion and bell pepper to one side of the griddle. Add the mushrooms to the griddle and cook them until the juices evaporate and the mushrooms are beginning to brown, about 8 minutes, stirring occasionally. Remove the vegetables from the griddle and season with salt and pepper. Cover and keep warm.

4. Grill the steaks on the cooking grate over *direct high heat*, with the lid closed, for 1½ to 2 minutes, turning when the first side is nicely marked. The second side will only take about 30 seconds to reach medium-rare doneness. Remove from the grill. Toast the rolls, cut side down, over *direct high heat*, for about 1 minute. Remove from the grill and immediately top each roll with two slices of cheese.

5. To assemble, place a steak in each roll and top with an equal amount of the vegetables. Warm the sandwiches on the griddle until the outsides are crusty. If desired, flatten the sandwiches with a grill press. Serve warm.

 Tip

Your butcher should be able to cut the steaks for you. Or buy a 1¼-pound top loin roast, freeze it for a few hours until it is somewhat firm, and cut it crosswise into ¼-inch-thick steaks.

RED MEAT

SERVES: 4 | PREP TIME: 15 minutes | GRILLING TIME: 6–8 minutes

PASTE

  3 *medjool* dates, each cut into quarters
  2 tablespoons red wine vinegar
  ¼ cup extra-virgin olive oil
 1½ teaspoons kosher salt
  1 teaspoon ground cumin
  ½ teaspoon smoked paprika
  ½ teaspoon ground ginger
  ½ teaspoon freshly ground black pepper

  4 T-bone steaks, each about 12 ounces and 1 inch
     thick, trimmed of excess fat

For Moroccan-spiced burgers, gently mix 2 to 3 tablespoons
of the paste into 1 pound of ground chuck.

1. In a small bowl combine the dates and the vinegar. Add just enough hot water to cover, and let stand until the dates are softened, about 10 minutes. Transfer the mixture to a food processor, add the remaining paste ingredients, and process until smooth.

2. Set aside 3 tablespoons of the paste in a small bowl. Spread the remaining paste evenly on both sides of each steak. Allow the steaks to stand at room temperature for 15 to 30 minutes before grilling.

3. Prepare the grill for direct cooking over high heat (450° to 550°F).

4. Grill the steaks over *direct high heat*, with the lid closed, until cooked to your desired doneness, 6 to 8 minutes for medium rare, turning once or twice. Remove from the grill and brush the top of the steaks with the reserved paste. Let rest for 3 to 5 minutes. Serve warm.

SERVES: 4 | PREP TIME: 10 minutes, plus about 25 minutes for the sauce | GRILLING TIME: 6–8 minutes

SPECIAL EQUIPMENT: spice mill, long match

RUB

2   tablespoons four-peppercorn blend
1½ teaspoons mustard seed

   Kosher salt
4   T-bone steaks, each about 12 ounces and 1 inch
   thick, trimmed of excess fat
   Extra-virgin olive oil

SAUCE

1   tablespoon unsalted butter
2   tablespoons finely chopped shallot
¼   cup cognac or brandy
1   cup low-sodium beef broth
1   cup heavy whipping cream
   Freshly ground black pepper
1   teaspoon Dijon mustard

1. Coarsely crush the peppercorns and the mustard seed in a spice mill. Pour into a bowl and mix in 1½ teaspoons salt. Lightly brush the steaks on both sides with oil and season evenly with the rub, pressing the spices into the meat. Allow the steaks to stand at room temperature for 15 to 30 minutes before grilling. Meanwhile, prepare the grill and make the sauce.

2. Prepare the grill for direct cooking over high heat (450° to 550°F).

3. In a saucepan (with a lid) over medium heat, melt the butter. Add the shallot and cook until softened, about 1 minute, stirring often. Remove from the heat and add the cognac. Using a long match, carefully ignite the cognac (the flames will rise high above the pan, so be careful) and let it burn for 30 seconds. If the cognac does not extinguish itself, cover the pan tightly with the lid. Return the saucepan over high heat and add the broth; bring to a boil. Cook until reduced to about 2 tablespoons, about 12 minutes. Add the cream and boil until reduced to about ¾ cup, 8 to 10 minutes, reducing the heat if the sauce starts to boil over. Remove from the heat, season with salt and pepper, and whisk in the mustard. Cover partially to keep warm.

4. Grill the steaks over *direct high heat*, with the lid closed, until cooked to your desired doneness, 6 to 8 minutes for medium rare, turning once or twice. Remove from the grill and let rest for 3 to 5 minutes. Spoon the sauce over the steaks and serve warm.

GARLIC BUTTER

- ½ cup (1 stick) unsalted butter, softened
- ¼ cup finely chopped fresh Italian parsley leaves
- 1½ teaspoons finely grated lemon zest
- 2 teaspoons fresh lemon juice
- 2 large garlic cloves, minced or pushed through a press
- 1 teaspoon freshly ground four peppercorn blend

  Kosher salt
- 1½ pounds red potatoes, unpeeled, each about 2½ inches in diameter, cut in half
  Freshly ground black pepper
- 2 porterhouse steaks, each 1–1¼ pounds and about 1 inch thick, trimmed of excess fat
- 2 tablespoons extra-virgin olive oil
- 2 teaspoons coarsely crushed mixed peppercorns

Tip

A simple and flavorful version of the classic compound butter known as *maître d'hôtel* butter serves as the topping for both the steaks and the potatoes. If you like, add a few tablespoons of chopped fresh chives to the butter mixture to give it a slightly more assertive flavor. Grill some asparagus or sauté some sugar snap peas to serve alongside for a complete meal. If you make the compound butter the day before and refrigerate it, you'll have a delicious and effortless dinner in less than an hour. If you don't have four peppercorn blend on hand, black peppercorns will do.

1. Combine the garlic butter ingredients, including ¾ teaspoon salt, and mash with a fork until well blended. Transfer to a small sheet of plastic wrap and roll into a log 1¼ to 1½ inches in diameter, enclosing the butter completely in the plastic wrap. Refrigerate until cold, about 1 hour. (The butter can be prepared up to a day in advance and kept, wrapped, in the refrigerator. Let stand at room temperature for 30 minutes to 1 hour before using.)

2. Prepare the grill for direct cooking over medium heat (350° to 450°F).

3. Place a sheet of heavy-duty aluminum foil (large enough to enclose the potatoes in a single layer) on a work surface. Place the potatoes, cut side up, on the foil. Lightly season with salt and pepper. Wrap the foil around the potatoes and crimp the edges to seal the packet completely. Place the packet over *direct medium heat,* close the lid, and cook until the potatoes are tender when pierced with a fork, 30 to 40 minutes. Transfer the potatoes to a heatproof bowl. Add half of the garlic butter and coarsely smash the potatoes with a potato masher or a fork, leaving the potatoes chunky. Cover to keep warm.

4. Brush the steaks on both sides with the oil and season evenly with 2 teaspoons salt and the crushed peppercorns. Allow the steaks to stand at room temperature for 15 to 30 minutes before grilling.

5. Increase the temperature of the grill to high heat (450° to 550°F).

6. Grill the steaks over *direct high heat,* with the lid closed, until cooked to your desired doneness, 6 to 8 minutes for medium rare, turning once or twice. Remove from the grill and let rest for 3 to 5 minutes. Cut the steaks across the grain and divide the slices among four plates. Dot the slices with the remaining garlic butter. Reheat the smashed potatoes, if necessary. Serve the steaks warm with the potatoes.

SERVES: 4 | PREP TIME: 25 minutes | CHILLING TIME: about 1 hour | GRILLING TIME: 8–10 minutes

¼ cup white wine vinegar
2 tablespoons finely chopped shallots
3 tablespoons chopped fresh tarragon leaves, divided
1 tablespoon chopped fresh Italian parsley leaves
6 tablespoons (¾ stick) unsalted butter, softened
½ teaspoon finely grated lemon zest
   Kosher salt
   Freshly ground black pepper
4 filets mignons or beef tenderloin steaks, each 6–8 ounces and about 1¼ inches thick
1 tablespoon extra-virgin olive oil

1. In a small saucepan over medium-high heat, combine the vinegar, shallots, 1 tablespoon of the tarragon, and the parsley and bring to a boil. Reduce the heat to medium and continue to boil until only a scant tablespoon of the vinegar remains in the saucepan, 2 to 4 minutes, stirring occasionally. Transfer the mixture to a fine-mesh strainer set over a bowl and press on the solids to extract as much of the vinegar as possible. Reserve the vinegar and transfer the solids to a bowl and let cool.

2. To the bowl with the solids add the butter, lemon zest, ¼ teaspoon salt, ¼ teaspoon pepper, the remaining 2 tablespoons tarragon, and 1 scant teaspoon of the reserved vinegar. Thoroughly blend with a fork. Transfer to a sheet of plastic wrap and roll the mixture into a log about 5 inches long, enclosing the butter completely in the plastic wrap. Refrigerate until cold, about 1 hour.

3. Brush the steaks on both sides with the oil and season evenly with 1 teaspoon salt and 1 teaspoon pepper. Allow the steaks to stand at room temperature for 15 to 30 minutes before grilling.

4. Prepare the grill for direct cooking over high heat (450° to 550°F).

5. Grill the steaks over *direct high heat*, with the lid closed, until cooked to your desired doneness, 8 to 10 minutes for medium rare, turning once or twice. Remove from the grill and let rest for 3 to 5 minutes. Cut the butter log crosswise into ½-inch slices. (Rewrap and refrigerate or freeze the leftover butter for another use.) Immediately top each steak with a slice of the butter. Serve warm.

SERVES: 4–6 | PREP TIME: 25 minutes | DRY BRINING TIME: 4–8 hours | GRILLING TIME: 30–35 minutes

SPECIAL EQUIPMENT: butcher's twine (optional), instant-read thermometer

1   center-cut beef tenderloin roast, about 2 pounds
2   tablespoons kosher salt

SAUCE
2   cups loosely packed fresh Italian parsley leaves
½   cup extra-virgin olive oil
¼   cup fresh lemon juice
2   large garlic cloves
1   teaspoon kosher salt
½   teaspoon freshly ground black pepper
¼   teaspoon crushed red pepper flakes

RUB
2   tablespoons finely chopped fresh thyme leaves
2   tablespoons finely chopped fresh rosemary leaves
2½ teaspoons freshly ground black pepper
3   garlic cloves, minced or pushed through a press

2   tablespoons extra-virgin olive oil

1. At least 4 hours or up to 8 hours before serving, season the roast all over with the salt. This gives the salt enough time to seep into the meat and season more than just the surface. If desired, for a perfectly round appearance, tie the roast with butcher's twine every couple of inches. Wrap in plastic wrap and refrigerate. Allow the roast to stand at room temperature for 30 minutes before grilling.

2. Prepare the grill for direct cooking over medium heat (350° to 450°F).

3. In a food processor combine the sauce ingredients and process until thoroughly combined. Transfer to a bowl, cover, and refrigerate until ready to serve.

4. Combine the rub ingredients, rubbing the herbs between your fingertips to release their oils. Brush the roast all over with the oil and season evenly with the rub, pressing it into the meat.

5. Grill the roast over **direct medium heat**, with the lid closed, until an instant-read thermometer inserted into the thickest part of the roast registers 125°F for medium rare, 30 to 35 minutes, turning four times. Remove from the grill and let rest for about 10 minutes (the internal temperature will rise 5 to 10 degrees during this time). Cut the roast into ½-inch slices. Serve warm with the sauce.

RECIPE REMIX:
Then and Now

Ready for a time warp? May we present Tournedos Héloïse. Back when this recipe was first published in the late '60s, Americans were still riding the postwar wave of Francophile cooking, inspired largely by the incomparable Julia Child. Recipes, while tasty, were heavy, laborious, and required some hard-to-come-by ingredients. Today, we take the classic French flavors of red wine and mushrooms and pair them with lean, juicy beef tenderloin steaks. American bacon stands in for the pâté, and a drizzle of vinaigrette over the finished steaks is a little "merci" to our great culinary influencers.

The Original

Tournedos Héloïse
Recipe from *Sunset Barbecue Cook Book*, © 1967

1/2 pound small mushrooms, washed
2 tablespoons butter or margarine
Salt and pepper to taste
1-1/2 tablespoons lemon juice
1/4 cup heavy cream
1 teaspoon cornstarch or arrowroot
6 artichoke bottoms, 3 inches in diameter (cooked or canned)
2 cans (each 4 ounces) pâté de foie, chilled
6 beef tenderloins, cut 1/4 inch thick
Truffles or ripe olives for garnish
Madeira sauce (recipe follows)

This is a prize steak entrée of many Western restaurants and one that benefits from barbecue cooking; the smoky flavor that permeates the meat as it grills over charcoal is excellent with the other choice ingredients.

Ask your butcher for tournedos, the small tenderloin steaks cut from the fillet. Visit a delicatessen or the gourmet section of your food store for the canned artichoke bottoms, pâté, and truffles.

Using a large frying pan, sauté mushrooms in melted butter. Season with salt and pepper to taste and sprinkle with lemon juice. Blend cream with cornstarch, and stir in; stirring occasionally, cook until thickened. Set aside.

Heat artichoke bottoms in their own liquid. Open both ends of each can of pâté, and push out 3/4 inch and slice, continue to slice the pâté, making 3 rounds from each can. Place pâté on foil, and heat in a 325° oven for 10 minutes.

Meanwhile, barbecue beef over hot coals (allowing about 2 to 3 minutes on a side for rare). Place artichoke bottoms at either end of a platter, top each with a hot tournedo, and arrange a slice of pâté and truffle on top.

Spoon Madeira sauce over (recipe follows), and arrange sautéed mushrooms in center of plate. Makes 6 servings.

Simple Madeira Sauce

Put 1 teaspoon beef extract in a small pan; add 1/4 cup Madeira and simmer until slightly reduced. Blend 1/2 teaspoon cornstarch with 3 tablespoons water and stir in; cook until thickened.

BEEF TENDERLOIN STEAKS
WITH SEARED MUSHROOMS AND RED WINE VINAIGRETTE

The Remix

SERVES: 4 | PREP TIME: 15 minutes | GRILLING TIME: 14–18 minutes

SPECIAL EQUIPMENT: perforated grill pan

4 beef tenderloin steaks, each about 6 ounces and 1¼ inches thick
  Extra-virgin olive oil
  Kosher salt
  Freshly ground black pepper
3 thick slices bacon, cut into ¼-inch dice (2 ounces)
⅓ cup finely diced red onion

VINAIGRETTE

3 tablespoons red wine vinegar
2 teaspoons Dijon mustard
2 garlic cloves, minced or pushed through a press

8 ounces cremini mushrooms, stems removed, each cut into quarters
2 tablespoons finely chopped fresh chives

1. Brush the steaks on both sides with oil and season generously with salt and pepper. Allow the steaks to stand at room temperature for 15 to 30 minutes before grilling.

2. Prepare the grill for direct cooking over high heat (450° to 550°F) and medium heat (350° to 450°F) and preheat a perforated grill pan over medium heat.

3. In a skillet over medium-low heat, cook the bacon and onion until the bacon is crisp, 6 to 8 minutes, stirring occasionally. Remove from the heat.

4. Combine the vinaigrette ingredients, including ¼ cup oil, ½ teaspoon salt, and ¼ teaspoon pepper; whisk until smooth. Put the mushrooms in a medium bowl and add ¼ cup of the vinaigrette. Mix well. Reserve the remaining vinaigrette.

5. Grill the steaks over *direct high heat*, with the lid closed, until cooked to your desired doneness, 8 to 10 minutes for medium rare, turning once or twice. Remove from the grill and let rest for 3 to 5 minutes.

6. Spread the mushrooms in a single layer on the grill pan and grill over *direct medium heat*, with the lid closed, until golden brown and tender, 6 to 8 minutes, turning once or twice. Don't move the mushrooms until the bottom sides are nicely browned. Transfer the mushrooms to the skillet with the bacon and onions and warm over medium heat for about 1 minute, stirring often. Add the chives and mix well. Serve the steaks warm with the mushroom mixture spooned on top. If desired, whisk the reserved vinaigrette and drizzle some over each steak.

SERVES: 4 | PREP TIME: 15 minutes | GRILLING TIME: 3–4 minutes

RUB
- 2 teaspoons kosher salt
- 1½ teaspoons dried oregano
- 1 teaspoon freshly ground black pepper

- 4 boneless rib eye steaks, each about 6 ounces and ½ inch thick, trimmed of all exterior fat
- 1 tablespoon extra-virgin olive oil
- ½ cup mayonnaise
- 2 large garlic cloves, minced or pushed through a press
- 8 slices Italian bread
- 8 thin slices Swiss cheese
- 4 leaves crisp lettuce
- 8 thin slices smoked ham

1. Combine the rub ingredients. Place each steak between two pieces of plastic wrap and pound to an even ¼-inch thickness. Lightly brush the steaks on both sides with the oil and season evenly with the rub, pressing the spices into the meat. Allow the steaks to stand at room temperature for 15 to 30 minutes before grilling.

2. Whisk the mayonnaise and garlic and set aside at room temperature for 15 to 30 minutes before serving.

3. Prepare the grill for direct and indirect cooking over high heat (450° to 550°F).

4. Grill the steaks over *direct high heat*, with the lid closed, until the first side is nicely marked, 2 to 3 minutes, turning once. The second side will only take about 30 seconds to reach medium-rare doneness. Remove from the grill and let rest for 3 to 5 minutes.

5. Grill the bread over *direct high heat*, with the lid open, until lightly toasted, about 30 seconds. Turn the bread over and move to *indirect high heat*. Top four slices of the bread each with two slices of cheese. Grill, with the lid closed, just until the cheese begins to melt, about 1 minute. Remove from the grill. Spread the plain bread slices with the garlic mayonnaise. Top with lettuce, ham slices, a steak, and a cheese-topped bread slice. Serve warm.

SERVES: 2–4 | PREP TIME: 15 minutes | GRILLING TIME: 12–13 minutes

SPECIAL EQUIPMENT: instant-read thermometer

2 bone-in rib steaks, each about 1¼ pounds and
   1¼ inches thick, trimmed of excess fat
   Extra-virgin olive oil

DRESSING
1½ teaspoons finely grated lemon zest
2 tablespoons fresh lemon juice
1 tablespoon red wine vinegar
1 teaspoon Dijon mustard
2 garlic cloves, minced or pushed through a press

2 medium fennel bulbs, trimmed, quartered, cored,
   and very thinly sliced
1½ cups fresh Italian parsley leaves, roughly chopped
   if the leaves are large
   Kosher salt
   Freshly ground black pepper

1. Brush the steaks on both sides with oil. Allow the steaks to stand at room temperature for 15 to 30 minutes before grilling.

2. Prepare the grill for indirect cooking over low heat (250° to 350°F) and direct cooking over high heat (450° to 550°F).

3. In a large bowl whisk the dressing ingredients. Then slowly drizzle and whisk in ¼ cup plus 2 tablespoons oil until it is emulsified. Add the fennel and parsley and toss to combine. Season with ½ teaspoon salt and ¼ teaspoon pepper.

4. Generously season the steaks on both sides with salt. Grill the steaks over *indirect low heat*, without disturbing them, for 5 minutes. Turn them over and continue cooking until an instant-read thermometer inserted into the center of the thickest steak (not touching the bone), registers 110° to 115°F, about 5 minutes more. Move the steaks over *direct high heat* and continue cooking until the internal temperature reaches 130°F (medium rare) or 135°F (medium), 2 to 3 minutes more, turning once. Keep the lid closed as much as possible during grilling. Remove the steaks from the grill and let them rest for 3 to 5 minutes. Season the steaks generously with pepper, and serve warm with some of the fennel salad mounded on top.

The "reverse sear" used here is a clever technique that involves warming thick steaks first over indirect heat and then finishing them with a strong sear over direct heat. Try it. It works great!

RUB

- 1 tablespoon finely ground dark roast coffee
- 1 tablespoon packed golden brown sugar
- 1 tablespoon paprika
- 2 teaspoons ground cumin
- 2 teaspoons kosher salt
- 1 teaspoon freshly ground black pepper

- 4 boneless or bone-in rib eye steaks, each about 12 ounces and 1 inch thick, trimmed of excess fat
  Extra-virgin olive oil

GLAZE

- 2 tablespoons minced shallot
- 1 garlic clove, minced or pushed through a press
- 1 cup low-sodium beef broth
- ½ cup stout or porter
- 1 tablespoon unsulfured molasses
- 1 tablespoon Dijon mustard
- 1 teaspoon kosher salt
- 1 teaspoon freshly ground black pepper

1. Combine the rub ingredients. Lightly brush the steaks on both sides with oil and season evenly with the rub, gently pressing the rub into the meat. Allow the steaks to stand at room temperature for 15 to 30 minutes before grilling.

2. Prepare the grill for direct cooking over high heat (450° to 550°F). Meanwhile, make the glaze.

3. In a medium saucepan over medium heat, warm 1 tablespoon oil. Add the shallot and garlic and sauté until the shallot is tender but not browned, about 2 minutes. Add the remaining glaze ingredients, bring to a boil, and cook until the glaze is reduced by half and has the consistency of maple syrup, 15 to 20 minutes. Keep warm.

4. Grill the steaks over *direct high heat*, with the lid closed, until cooked to your desired doneness, 6 to 8 minutes for medium rare, turning once or twice. Remove from the grill and let rest for 3 to 5 minutes. Serve warm with the glaze.

WHO PUT COFFEE ON MY STEAK?

A steak in its simplest form is iconic. If the meat is well marbled and the griller has adequate skills, this American classic stands proudly at any barbecue, and yet it is also confident enough that it can run with the times. These days, spiced rubs with strong ground coffee beans are all the rage—and why not? The coffee brings a nice touch of bitterness that balances well with the sweetness that you usually find in these rubs. The glaze in this recipe plays with the same sort of flavor balance. You get a little edge of bitterness from the stout that is mellowed by the sweetness of the molasses, and underlying all of that is the richness of concentrated beef broth. Are all of these elements necessary for enjoying a fine steak? No. But occasionally we like to dress our icons in the latest styles.

SERVES: 6–8 | PREP TIME: 20 minutes | GRILLING TIME: 40–48 minutes

3 ears fresh corn, husked
  Extra-virgin olive oil
3 tablespoons fresh lime juice
1 garlic clove, minced or pushed through a press
1 teaspoon dried oregano
  Kosher salt
  Freshly ground black pepper
1 can (15 ounces) pinto beans, rinsed and drained
2 scallions, ends trimmed and finely chopped
½ medium red bell pepper, cut into ½-inch dice
1 jalapeño chile pepper, seeded and minced

RUB
1 tablespoon coarsely ground espresso
2 teaspoons prepared chili powder
2 teaspoons packed golden brown sugar
1 teaspoon dried oregano
¼ teaspoon granulated garlic
¼ teaspoon granulated onion

1 tri-tip roast, about 2¾ pounds and 2 inches thick, trimmed of silver skin and any excess fat

1. Prepare the grill for direct and indirect cooking over medium heat (350° to 450°F).

2. Brush the corn with oil. Grill over *direct medium heat*, with the lid closed, until browned in spots and tender, 8 to 10 minutes, turning occasionally. Remove from the grill, and let cool. In a large bowl whisk the lime juice, garlic, oregano, ½ teaspoon salt, and ½ teaspoon pepper. Slowly whisk in ⅓ cup oil. Add the pinto beans, scallions, bell pepper, and jalapeño. Cut off the corn kernels and add them to the salad.

3. Combine the rub ingredients, including 1 teaspoon salt and ½ teaspoon pepper. Brush the roast on both sides with oil and season evenly with the rub. Allow the roast to stand at room temperature for 15 to 30 minutes. Grill the roast over *direct medium heat*, with the lid closed, until well marked on both sides, 8 to 10 minutes, turning once or twice. Move the roast over *indirect medium heat* and cook to your desired doneness, 24 to 28 minutes for medium rare, turning every 5 minutes. Remove from the grill and let rest for 5 to 10 minutes. Cut the roast across the grain into thin slices and serve with the salad.

If you can't find tri-tip, buy top sirloin. It's typically not as big a piece of meat, so use a little less of the rub and grill for 10 to 12 minutes over direct medium heat, turning once.

SERVES: 6 | PREP TIME: 25 minutes | GRILLING TIME: about 5 minutes

SPECIAL EQUIPMENT: grill-proof wok or 12-inch cast-iron skillet

SAUCE

½ cup low-sodium beef broth
¼ cup oyster sauce
2 tablespoons low-sodium soy sauce
1 tablespoon granulated sugar
2 teaspoons cornstarch

1 tablespoon vegetable oil
1 tablespoon toasted sesame oil
1 tablespoon peeled, finely grated fresh ginger
2 large garlic cloves, minced or pushed through a press
1 pound top sirloin, cut into strips about 3 inches by ¼ inch by ¼ inch
3 large bell peppers, 1 red, 1 green, 1 orange, each cut into ¼-inch strips
1 medium yellow onion, cut vertically in half and thinly sliced
¼ cup fresh cilantro leaves
3 cups cooked rice

1. Whisk the sauce ingredients.

2. Whisk the vegetable oil, sesame oil, ginger, and garlic. Add the sirloin strips and turn to coat.

3. Prepare the grill for direct cooking over high heat (450° to 550°F).

4. Place a grill-proof wok on the cooking grate, close the lid, and preheat it for about 10 minutes. Bring the sauce, top sirloin mixture, bell peppers, onion, and cilantro to the grill and keep close by.

5. When the wok is smoking hot, add the top sirloin mixture, separating the meat as you add it to the wok. Grill over *direct high heat*, with the lid open, until the meat starts to brown and releases easily from the wok, about 1 minute, stirring once after 30 seconds. Add the bell peppers and the onion all at once. Stir to combine and cook until the vegetables turn a shade brighter, about 2 minutes, stirring frequently. Add the sauce, stir for 10 seconds, close the lid, and cook until the sauce comes to a boil, about 1 minute. Simmer until the sauce is thick enough to coat the vegetables, about 1 minute more. Stir in the cilantro. Remove the wok from the grill and serve the stir-fry immediately over warm rice.

For a successful stir-fry, cut all the vegetables and the meat into similar-sized pieces so that they all finish cooking at the same time.

RED MEAT

99

SERVES: 4 | PREP TIME: 20 minutes | MARINATING TIME: 15–30 minutes | GRILLING TIME: 6–8 minutes

SPECIAL EQUIPMENT: metal or bamboo skewers

1   quart water
¾   cup medium-grind bulgur

RUB
1½ teaspoons kosher salt
1½ teaspoons ground cumin
½   teaspoon Aleppo pepper *or* ¼ teaspoon ground cayenne
    pepper plus ¼ teaspoon freshly ground black pepper

2   pounds top sirloin, about 1¼ inches thick, trimmed
    of excess fat, cut into 1¼-inch cubes
    Extra-virgin olive oil
3   tablespoons fresh lemon juice
3   plum tomatoes, seeded and diced
½   cup minced fresh Italian parsley leaves
2   scallions (white and light green parts only),
    finely chopped
½   teaspoon kosher salt
¼   teaspoon freshly ground black pepper

1. If using bamboo skewers, soak in water for at least 30 minutes.

2. In a medium saucepan over high heat, bring 1 quart of water to a boil. Stir in the bulgur and remove from the heat. Let stand until the bulgur is tender, about 30 minutes.

3. Combine the rub ingredients. Place the meat cubes in a large bowl and add enough oil to coat the meat lightly. Add the rub and turn to coat evenly. Thread the meat onto skewers and allow to stand at room temperature for 15 to 30 minutes before grilling.

4. Prepare the grill for direct cooking over high heat (450° to 550°F).

5. In a large bowl whisk the lemon juice with 3 tablespoons oil. Drain the softened bulgur in a fine-mesh strainer. Using your hands, squeeze the excess water from the bulgur. Add the bulgur, tomatoes, parsley, and scallions to the lemon-oil mixture and stir to combine. Season with the salt and pepper.

6. Grill the kabobs over *direct high heat*, with the lid closed, until the meat is cooked to your desired doneness, 6 to 8 minutes for medium rare, turning occasionally. Remove the kabobs from the grill and serve warm with the tabbouleh.

SERVES: 4 | PREP TIME: 20 minutes | MARINATING TIME: 2–4 hours | GRILLING TIME: 6–8 minutes

MARINADE
- 1 Scotch bonnet or habanero chile pepper
- 3 scallions (white and green parts only), chopped
- ⅓ cup roughly chopped fresh basil leaves
- ¼ cup canola oil
- 2 tablespoons cider vinegar
- 2 tablespoons packed dark brown sugar
- 1 tablespoon minced fresh ginger
- 1 teaspoon minced garlic
- 1 teaspoon ground allspice
- 1 teaspoon kosher salt

- 2 pounds top sirloin, about 1¼ inches thick, trimmed of excess fat, cut into 1¼-inch cubes

SALSA
- ½ medium pineapple, cut into ¼-inch cubes
- 1 medium red bell pepper, finely chopped
- 1 scallion (white and light green parts only), finely chopped
- 2 tablespoons finely chopped fresh basil leaves
- 1 teaspoon cider vinegar
- ¼ teaspoon kosher salt

1. If using bamboo skewers, soak in water for at least 30 minutes.

2. Wearing rubber gloves (to avoid burning your skin), remove and discard the stem and seeds from the chile. Put the chile in a food processor along with the remaining marinade ingredients, and process until smooth.

3. Place the meat cubes in a large, resealable plastic bag and pour in the marinade. Press the air out of the bag and seal tightly. Turn the bag to distribute the marinade, place in a bowl, and refrigerate for 2 to 4 hours.

4. Wearing rubber gloves, thread the meat onto skewers and allow to stand at room temperature for 15 to 30 minutes before grilling. Discard the marinade.

5. Prepare the grill for direct cooking over high heat (450° to 550°F).

6. Combine the salsa ingredients.

7. Grill the kabobs over *direct high heat*, with the lid closed, until the meat is cooked to your desired doneness, 6 to 8 minutes for medium rare, turning occasionally. Remove the kabobs from the grill and serve warm with the salsa.

SPINACH- AND MOZZARELLA-STUFFED FLANK STEAK

SERVES: 4 | PREP TIME: 40 minutes | GRILLING TIME: 38–48 minutes

SPECIAL EQUIPMENT: butcher's twine

STUFFING

1½ cups roughly chopped fresh baby spinach (about 2 ounces)
1 cup kalamata olives, roughly chopped
½ cup dried seasoned bread crumbs
2 tablespoons dried currants
1 tablespoon red wine vinegar
1 tablespoon extra-virgin olive oil
2 garlic cloves, minced or pushed through a press

1 flank steak, 1½–1¾ pounds and about ¾ inch thick
4 ounces low-moisture mozzarella or smoked mozzarella cheese, cut into long, thin rectangles
1 tablespoon extra-virgin olive oil
  Kosher salt
  Freshly ground black pepper

1. Combine the stuffing ingredients.

2. Prepare the grill for direct and indirect cooking over medium heat (350° to 450°F).

3. Using a long, flexible knife and keeping the knife parallel to your work surface, split the steak horizontally as shown in photos 1 and 2 below left, opening the two halves as you cut and making sure that they are fairly even in thickness.

4. Pound the butterflied (and unfolded) steak to an even thickness. Ideally you want the steak to be roughly square and 12 to 15 inches long on each side.

5. Arrange the steak so that the grain runs parallel to the edge of your work surface. Place the cheese slices in a single layer on top of the steak, beginning at the bottom and working toward the top. The cheese will not cover the entire surface. Spread the stuffing evenly over the cheese layer and onto the steak, leaving the top 3 inches of the steak uncovered.

6. Starting at the lower edge, roll the steak and stuffing to make a compact roll. Tuck in any stuffing that falls out. Using butcher's twine, snugly tie the roll crosswise every 1½ inches. The roll should be about 4 inches in diameter.

7. Rub the surface of the roll with the oil and season evenly with salt and pepper. Sear over **direct medium heat**, with the lid open, until well marked, about 8 minutes, turning every 2 minutes. Move over **indirect medium heat** and continue grilling, with the lid closed, until cooked to your desired doneness, 30 to 40 minutes more for medium rare. Transfer to a cutting board, cover loosely with foil, and let rest for about 10 minutes. Cut crosswise into thick slices and serve immediately.

1 Using a long, flexible knife that is very sharp, slowly cut the steak open from the top to the bottom.

2 Continue cutting with shallow strokes until you come to within about ½ inch from the opposite edge. Then open the steak like a book.

3 Position the butterflied steak so that the grain of the meat runs parallel to the front and back edges of your work surface.

4 Arrange the cheese and stuffing over the meat, leaving a 3-inch space at the top, and roll the steak snugly.

SERVES: 4 | PREP TIME: 15 minutes | GRILLING TIME: 8–10 minutes

¾   cup water
½   cup balsamic vinegar
2   tablespoons honey
1½ teaspoons tomato paste
1   large bay leaf
1   package (14 ounces) frozen pearl onions, thawed
3½ teaspoons finely chopped fresh thyme leaves, divided
2   teaspoons kosher salt, divided
1   teaspoon freshly ground black pepper, divided
1   flank steak, about 1½ pounds and ¾ inch thick
1   tablespoon extra-virgin olive oil
    Fresh thyme sprigs (optional)

1. In a large skillet combine the water, vinegar, honey, tomato paste, and bay leaf. Add the onions and bring to a simmer over medium-low heat. Cover and simmer for 10 minutes, stirring occasionally. Uncover the skillet and increase the heat to high. Boil until the liquid starts to thicken and is reduced to 4 to 5 tablespoons, about 5 minutes. Remove from the heat and stir in 1½ teaspoons of the thyme, 1 teaspoon of the salt, and ½ teaspoon of the pepper. The sauce will continue to thicken as it cools. If necessary, add water, 1 tablespoon at a time, to thin the mixture to your desired consistency.

2. Combine the remaining 2 teaspoons thyme, 1 teaspoon salt, and ½ teaspoon pepper. Brush the steak on both sides with the oil and season evenly with the spice mixture, pressing the spices into the meat. Allow the steak to stand at room temperature for 15 to 30 minutes before grilling.

3. Prepare the grill for direct cooking over medium heat (350° to 450°F).

4. Grill the steak over *direct medium heat*, with the lid closed, until cooked to your desired doneness, 8 to 10 minutes for medium rare, turning once or twice. Remove from the grill and let rest for 3 to 5 minutes. Cut the steak across the grain into thin slices. Serve immediately with the onions and their sauce. Garnish with thyme, if using.

SERVES: 4 | PREP TIME: 20 minutes | GRILLING TIME: 18–22 minutes

RUB

- 1 teaspoon paprika
- 1 teaspoon ground cumin
- 1 teaspoon granulated garlic
- 1 teaspoon kosher salt
- ¾ teaspoon freshly ground black pepper

- 1 flank steak, about 1½ pounds and ¾ inch thick
- 2 tablespoons extra-virgin olive oil, divided
- 2 poblano or pasilla chile peppers
- 8 ounces button mushrooms, cut into ¼-inch slices
- ¼ cup finely chopped white onion
- 2 medium garlic cloves, minced or pushed through a press
- ½ cup heavy whipping cream
- ¼ teaspoon kosher salt

1. Combine the rub ingredients. Brush the steak on both sides with 1 tablespoon of the oil and season evenly with the rub. Allow the steak to stand at room temperature for 15 to 30 minutes before grilling.

2. Prepare the grill for direct cooking over medium heat (350° to 450°F).

3. Grill the chiles over *direct medium heat,* with the lid closed, until blackened and blistered all over, 10 to 12 minutes, turning occasionally. Put the chiles in a bowl and cover with plastic wrap to trap the steam. Let stand for about 10 minutes. Remove the chiles from the bowl and peel away and discard the charred skin. Cut off and discard the stems and seeds and then cut each chile lengthwise into ½-inch strips.

4. In a large skillet over medium-high heat, warm the remaining 1 tablespoon oil. Add the mushrooms and onion and cook until the mushrooms are lightly browned, about 5 minutes, stirring occasionally. Stir in the garlic and cook until fragrant, about 1 minute. Add the chiles and cream and increase the heat to high. Cook until the cream is thickened and coats the mushrooms, 2 to 3 minutes, stirring occasionally. Season with the salt. Remove from the heat and cover to keep warm.

5. Grill the steak over *direct medium heat,* with the lid closed, until cooked to your desired doneness, 8 to 10 minutes for medium rare, turning once or twice. Remove from the grill and let rest for 3 to 5 minutes. Cut the steak across the grain into thin slices. Serve immediately topped with the creamy poblano and mushroom mixture.

SERVES: 4–6 | PREP TIME: 15 minutes | MARINATING TIME: 2–3 hours | GRILLING TIME: 4–6 minutes

MARINADE

½ cup extra-virgin olive oil
¼ cup finely chopped fresh cilantro leaves
1 teaspoon finely grated lemon zest
3 tablespoons fresh lemon juice
2 tablespoons fresh lime juice
2 teaspoons minced garlic
1¼ teaspoons kosher salt
1 teaspoon ground coriander
½ teaspoon freshly ground black pepper

2 pounds skirt steak, each about ½ inch thick, trimmed of excess surface fat, cut crosswise into 6-inch pieces

1. Combine the marinade ingredients. Pour ¼ cup plus 2 tablespoons of the marinade into a bowl to serve with the steak.

2. Place the steak pieces in a large, resealable plastic bag and pour in the remaining marinade. Press the air out of the bag and seal tightly. Turn the bag to distribute the marinade, place in a bowl, and refrigerate for 2 to 3 hours, turning occasionally. Allow the steaks to stand at room temperature for 15 to 30 minutes.

3. Prepare the grill for direct cooking over high heat (450° to 550°F).

4. Remove the steaks from the bag and discard the marinade. Grill over *direct high heat*, with the lid closed, until cooked to your desired doneness, 4 to 6 minutes for medium rare, turning once or twice. Remove from the grill and let rest for 3 to 5 minutes. Cut the meat across the grain into thin slices and serve warm with the reserved marinade.

SERVES: 4 | PREP TIME: 25 minutes | GRILLING TIME: 4–6 minutes

SALSA

1½	pounds tangerines
½	cup finely chopped red onion
2	tablespoons roughly chopped fresh cilantro leaves
1	tablespoon vegetable oil
1	tablespoon fresh lime juice
1	red jalapeño or serrano chile pepper, seeded and finely chopped
½	teaspoon kosher salt

RUB

2	teaspoons ancho chile powder
1½	teaspoons ground cumin
1	teaspoon kosher salt
¾	teaspoon freshly ground black pepper

1¾ pounds skirt steak, about ½ inch thick, trimmed of excess surface fat, cut crosswise into 6-inch pieces
Vegetable oil
Naan (optional)

1. Cut the peel and white pith from each tangerine. Cut the tangerines crosswise into ½-inch slices, and then cut the slices into ½-inch pieces (you should have about 1½ cups). Transfer to a medium bowl and add the remaining salsa ingredients. Stir gently. Cover and refrigerate.

2. Combine the rub ingredients. Lightly brush the steak pieces on both sides with oil and season evenly with the rub. Allow the steaks to stand at room temperature for 15 to 30 minutes.

3. Prepare the grill for direct cooking over high heat (450° to 550°F).

4. Grill the steaks over *direct high heat*, with the lid closed, until cooked to your desired doneness, 4 to 6 minutes for medium rare, turning once or twice. Remove from the grill and let rest for 3 to 5 minutes. Cut the meat across the grain into thin slices and serve warm with the salsa and the naan, if desired.

SERVES: 4 | PREP TIME: 40 minutes | MARINATING TIME: 4–6 hours | GRILLING TIME: 14–18 minutes

SPECIAL EQUIPMENT: 8 metal or bamboo skewers

MARINADE
½ cup dark beer
2 tablespoons fresh lime juice
2 tablespoons packed dark brown sugar
1 tablespoon hot chili-garlic sauce, such as Sriracha
1 tablespoon Dijon mustard
1 tablespoon vegetable oil
2 teaspoons ground cumin
2 garlic cloves, minced or pushed through a press
1 teaspoon paprika
1 teaspoon kosher salt

1½ pounds skirt steak, about ½ inch thick, trimmed of excess surface fat

SAUCE
1 large green bell pepper
2 garlic cloves
1 cup loosely packed fresh cilantro leaves and tender stems
1 jalapeño chile pepper, seeded and roughly chopped
½ medium poblano or pasilla chile pepper, seeded and roughly chopped
2 tablespoons extra-virgin olive oil
1 tablespoon fresh lime juice
1 teaspoon kosher salt
½ teaspoon ground cumin
½ teaspoon freshly ground black pepper

1. Whisk the marinade ingredients.

2. Cut the steak crosswise into four equal pieces. Then cut each piece lengthwise in half (against the grain). Place the steak pieces in a large, resealable plastic bag and pour in the marinade. Press the air out of the bag and seal tightly. Turn the bag to distribute the marinade, place in a bowl, and refrigerate for 4 to 6 hours, turning occasionally.

3. If using bamboo skewers, soak in water for at least 30 minutes.

4. Prepare the grill for direct cooking over medium heat (350° to 450°F).

5. Grill the bell pepper over *direct medium heat*, with the lid closed, until blackened and blistered all over, 10 to 12 minutes, turning occasionally. Put the pepper in a bowl and cover with plastic wrap to trap the steam. Let stand for about 10 minutes. Remove the pepper from the bowl and peel away and discard the charred skin. Cut off and discard the stem and seeds, and then roughly chop the pepper. Place the pepper and the garlic in a food processor and pulse until finely chopped. Add the remaining sauce ingredients and process to a chunky paste. Transfer to a bowl. Stir the sauce just before serving.

6. Increase the temperature of the grill to high heat (450° to 550°F).

7. Remove the steak from the bag and discard the marinade. Thread the steak pieces onto skewers.

8. Grill the skewers over *direct high heat*, with the lid closed, until cooked to your desired doneness, 4 to 6 minutes for medium rare, turning once. Remove from the grill and serve warm with the sauce.

Tip

When cutting the skirt steak, remember to cut against the grain to ensure tender results. When making the sauce, be sure to taste a small piece of the jalapeño and the poblano to check their heat. If they are too hot, adjust the quantities to taste and remove the ribs for less heat.

SERVES: 4 | PREP TIME: 20 minutes | GRILLING TIME: 8–10 minutes

SALSA

- 1 cup loosely packed fresh mint leaves
- 1 cup loosely packed fresh Italian parsley leaves and tender stems
- 1 teaspoon finely grated lemon zest
- 2 tablespoons fresh lemon juice
- 1 tablespoon roughly chopped shallot
- 1 tablespoon capers, rinsed and drained
- 1 garlic clove, roughly chopped
- ½ teaspoon kosher salt
- ¼ teaspoon crushed red pepper flakes
- ¼ cup extra-virgin olive oil

- 8 lamb loin chops, each about 1¼ inches thick, trimmed of excess fat
  Extra-virgin olive oil
  Kosher salt
  Freshly ground black pepper

1. In a food processor or a blender combine all of the salsa ingredients except the oil. Pulse to roughly chop. With the motor running, add the oil to form a chunky salsa. Transfer to a bowl. Cover the surface with plastic wrap to prevent discoloration and set aside at room temperature. (The salsa can be made up to 4 hours in advance. Cover and refrigerate. Bring to room temperature before serving and stir to combine.)

2. Lightly brush the lamb chops on both sides with oil and season evenly with salt and pepper. Allow the chops to stand at room temperature for 15 to 30 minutes before grilling.

3. Prepare the grill for direct cooking over high heat (450° to 550°F).

4. Grill the chops over *direct high heat*, with the lid closed, until cooked to your desired doneness, 8 to 10 minutes for medium rare, turning once. Remove from the grill and let rest for 3 to 5 minutes. Serve the chops warm with the salsa spooned on top.

SERVES: 4 | PREP TIME: 20 minutes | MARINATING TIME: 20–30 minutes | GRILLING TIME: 19–26 minutes

MARINADE
¼ cup Dijon mustard
¼ cup extra-virgin olive oil
1 tablespoon chopped fresh rosemary leaves
3 garlic cloves, minced or pushed through a press
1½ teaspoons freshly ground black pepper

12 lamb rib chops, each about ¾ inch thick, trimmed of excess fat
2 medium red onions, each about 6 ounces, quartered through the stem and peeled
1 tablespoon extra-virgin olive oil
Kosher salt
¼ teaspoon freshly ground black pepper
½ cup balsamic vinegar
1 tablespoon granulated sugar

1. In a large bowl whisk the marinade ingredients. Put the lamb chops in the bowl and spread the marinade all over them. Marinate at room temperature for 20 to 30 minutes.

2. Prepare the grill for direct cooking over medium heat (350° to 450°F).

3. Brush the onion wedges all over with the oil and season with ½ teaspoon salt and the pepper. Grill the onions over *direct medium heat*, with the lid closed, until tender and slightly charred in spots, 15 to 20 minutes, turning occasionally.

4. In a small saucepan combine the vinegar and sugar and bring to a boil over medium-high heat. Reduce the heat to medium-low and simmer until syrupy, 5 to 7 minutes. Remove from the heat. Increase the grill's temperature to high heat (450° to 550°F).

5. Remove the chops from the bowl and discard the marinade. Lightly season the chops with salt, and grill over *direct high heat*, with the lid closed, until cooked to your desired doneness, 4 to 6 minutes for medium rare, turning once or twice. Remove from the grill and let rest for 3 to 5 minutes. Divide the chops and onions among four serving plates. Drizzle the balsamic syrup over the onions and serve warm.

SERVES: 4 | PREP TIME: 20 minutes | GRILLING TIME: 4–6 minutes

5 ounces baby arugula
1 pint grape tomatoes, each cut in half
1 medium English cucumber, cut lengthwise in half
  and thinly sliced
1 chunk Parmigiano-Reggiano® cheese, about 1½ ounces,
  shaved into strips with a vegetable peeler (about ¾ cup)
¼ cup thinly sliced sweet onion
2 tablespoons fresh lemon juice
  Extra-virgin olive oil
  Kosher salt
  Freshly ground black pepper
4 veal rib chops, each about 8 ounces and ¾ inch thick

1. In a large bowl combine the arugula, tomatoes, cucumber, cheese, and onion. In a small bowl whisk the lemon juice, 2 tablespoons oil, ½ teaspoon salt, and ¼ teaspoon pepper. Set aside.

2. Brush the veal chops on both sides with oil and season evenly with salt and pepper. Allow the chops to stand at room temperature for 15 to 30 minutes before grilling.

3. Prepare the grill for direct cooking over high heat (450° to 550°F).

4. Grill the chops over *direct high heat*, with the lid closed, until cooked to your desired doneness, 4 to 6 minutes for medium rare, turning once. Remove from the grill and let rest for 3 to 5 minutes.

5. Give the dressing another whisk and toss with the salad. Serve the chops warm with the salad.

SERVES: 4 | PREP TIME: 20 minutes | GRILLING TIME: 6–8 minutes

2 tablespoons extra-virgin olive oil
2 teaspoons finely chopped fresh rosemary leaves
1 teaspoon minced garlic
¾ teaspoon kosher salt
¼ teaspoon freshly ground black pepper
4 veal rib chops, each about 12 ounces and 1 inch thick

SAUCE
¼ cup (½ stick) unsalted butter
¾ teaspoon finely chopped fresh rosemary leaves
2 small red bell peppers, thinly sliced
2 tablespoons capers, drained
1½ tablespoons fresh lemon juice
¼ teaspoon kosher salt

1. Combine the oil, rosemary, garlic, salt, and pepper. Brush the veal chops on both sides with the oil mixture. Allow the chops to stand at room temperature for 15 to 30 minutes before grilling.

2. Prepare the grill for direct cooking over high heat (450° to 550°F).

3. Grill the chops over *direct high heat*, with the lid closed, until cooked to your desired doneness, 6 to 8 minutes for medium rare, turning once. Remove from the grill and let rest while you make the sauce.

4. In a small skillet over medium-high heat, melt the butter and then add the rosemary. Cook until the milk solids are toasted and the butter has a nutty smell, 2 to 4 minutes, stirring occasionally. Add the bell peppers and cook until slightly softened, about 2 minutes, stirring once or twice. Add the capers and lemon juice and cook for 1 minute. Remove the skillet from the heat and stir in the salt.

5. Serve the chops warm with the sauce.

SPECIAL EQUIPMENT: large disposable foil pan, instant-read thermometer

1	boneless rib roast, about 5½ pounds, trimmed of excess fat
	Kosher salt
	Freshly ground black pepper
½	cup Dijon mustard
½	cup finely chopped shallots
6	garlic cloves, minced or pushed through a press
2	teaspoons finely chopped fresh thyme leaves
2	pounds meaty beef bones
1½	cups low-sodium beef broth

Tip

The appeal of a roast like this, for entertaining or otherwise, is that it is a showstopper that demands relatively little sweat. Just make sure your grill temperature is nice and even throughout the cooking time and use a reliable meat thermometer. The hardest part of making prime rib may be paying for this pricey cut of meat, which, by the way, has a misleading name. The meat is not necessarily "prime," as in the USDA grade of beef. It just happens to be called prime rib, because when butchers break down an animal into eight large cuts, they refer to those as the primal cuts, and the rib section is called the primal rib or just prime rib. If you want to throw a fancy dinner party and part with a lot of cash, you could make this recipe with USDA prime beef. Then you could call your dinner a prime prime rib.

1. Season the roast evenly with 2 teaspoons salt and 1 teaspoon pepper. Combine the mustard, shallots, garlic, and thyme. Set aside ¼ cup of the mustard mixture for the au jus. Spread the remaining mustard mixture all over the top and sides of the roast. Allow the roast to stand at room temperature for 1 hour before grilling.

2. Prepare the grill for indirect and direct cooking over medium heat (350° to 375°F).

3. Put the bones in a large disposable foil pan and set the roast on top of the bones, fat side facing up. Position the pan on the cooking grate with the thicker end of the roast facing the hottest area of the grill. Grill over *indirect medium heat*, with the lid closed, until an instant-read thermometer inserted into the thickest part of the roast registers 120° to 125°F for medium rare, about 2 hours, rotating the roast once after 1 hour. Start checking the temperature of the roast after 1¼ hours. Keep the grill's temperature between 350° and 375°F.

4. Remove the pan and the roast from the grill, loosely cover the roast with aluminum foil, and let rest for 20 to 30 minutes (the internal temperature will rise 5 to 10 degrees during this time).

5. Transfer the roast to a cutting board. Remove the bones from the pan and discard. Pour off and discard the clear fat, leaving the browned bits in the pan. Return the pan to the grill over *direct medium heat*. Cook until the contents sizzle. Add the broth and the reserved mustard mixture. Holding the pan with an insulated barbecue mitt and using a wooden spoon, scrape up any browned bits from the bottom of the pan. Continue cooking until the mixture is hot. Remove from the grill and season with salt and pepper.

6. Cut the roast into ½-inch slices. Serve warm with the sauce.

SERVES: 2–4 | PREP TIME: 15 minutes, plus about 20 minutes for the sauce | GRILLING TIME: about 2¼ hours

SPECIAL EQUIPMENT: large disposable foil pan fitted with a flat baking rack

RUB

2	tablespoons packed golden brown sugar
1½	tablespoons smoked paprika
1½	teaspoons granulated garlic
1½	teaspoons mustard powder
⅜	teaspoon ground cayenne pepper

Freshly ground black pepper
Kosher salt

1	rack meaty beef ribs (7 ribs), about 5 pounds, membrane removed, rack cut into individual ribs
½	cup low-sodium beef broth *or* water

SAUCE

1	cup ketchup
2	tablespoons unsalted butter
2	tablespoons cider vinegar
1	tablespoon packed golden brown sugar
2	teaspoons prepared chili powder
1	teaspoon Worcestershire sauce
1	large garlic clove, minced or pushed through a press
¼	teaspoon ground cayenne pepper

1. Prepare the grill for direct and indirect cooking over low heat (250° to 350°F).

2. Combine the rub ingredients, including 1 tablespoon black pepper and 2½ teaspoons salt. Season the ribs evenly with the rub. Grill the ribs over *direct low heat*, with the lid closed, until nicely marked, 10 to 12 minutes, turning once. Remove the ribs from the grill and arrange them side by side in a large disposable foil pan fitted with a flat baking rack. Add the broth and cover the pan tightly with aluminum foil. Place the pan over *indirect low heat*, close the lid, and cook for 1 hour. Carefully remove the foil and turn the ribs over. Replace the foil and continue cooking until the ribs are very tender and the meat has shrunk back from the bones, about 1 hour more.

3. In a medium saucepan over medium-low heat, combine the sauce ingredients, including ¼ teaspoon salt and ¼ teaspoon pepper. Stir until the butter melts, cover, and adjust the heat to maintain a gentle simmer. Cook until the sauce is slightly thickened, 15 to 20 minutes, stirring occasionally.

4. Carefully remove the pan from the grill and lift the ribs from the rack. Serve the ribs immediately or, if you want the ribs a little more charred, place them on the cooking grate over *direct low heat*, leave the lid open, and cook for an additional 5 to 10 minutes, turning once or twice. Serve warm with the sauce.

SERVES: 6 | **PREP TIME:** 25 minutes | **GRILLING TIME:** 2–2¾ hours

SPECIAL EQUIPMENT: large disposable foil pan

BRAISING LIQUID

- 1   tablespoon extra-virgin olive oil
- 1   large yellow onion, chopped
- 4   garlic cloves, chopped
- 1   can (14½ ounces) diced fire-roasted tomatoes in juice
- 1   cup merlot
- 1   cup low-sodium beef broth
- 1   tablespoon Italian herb seasoning
- 1   teaspoon kosher salt
- ½   teaspoon freshly ground black pepper

- 12   meaty bone-in beef short ribs, about 7½ pounds total, each 3–4 inches long

GLAZE

- ⅓   cup balsamic vinegar
- ¼   cup packed golden brown sugar
- 3   tablespoons tomato paste

1. Prepare the grill for direct and indirect cooking over medium-low heat (about 350°F).

2. In a medium saucepan over medium-high heat, warm the oil. Add the onion and cook until softened, about 3 minutes, stirring occasionally. Stir in the garlic and cook until fragrant, about 1 minute. Add the remaining braising liquid ingredients and bring to a boil. Arrange the ribs, bone side down, in a single layer in a large disposable foil pan. Pour the braising liquid over the ribs and cover the pan tightly with aluminum foil. Place the pan over *indirect medium-low heat*, close the lid, and cook until the ribs are very tender when pierced with the tip of a knife, 1½ to 2 hours. Transfer the ribs to a platter and tent loosely with foil.

3. Allow the braising liquid in the pan to stand for 5 minutes, then skim the fat from the surface. Pour half of the liquid into a blender, add the glaze ingredients, and puree until smooth. Transfer to a bowl. Pour the remaining liquid in the blender, puree, and add to the bowl. Pour the glaze back into the foil pan and cook over *direct medium-low heat*, with the lid closed, until thickened and reduced, about 25 minutes, stirring frequently.

4. Return the ribs over *direct medium-low heat*, close the lid, brush with some of the glaze, and cook until warmed through and nicely marked, 10 to 15 minutes, turning often and brushing with more glaze at each turn. Serve the ribs warm with any remaining glaze.

RED MEAT

117

SERVES: 8–10 | **PREP TIME: 15 minutes** | **MARINATING TIME: 4 hours** | **GRILLING TIME: 35–45 minutes**

SPECIAL EQUIPMENT: large disposable foil pan

6   small fresh thyme sprigs
1   boneless leg of lamb, 4–5 pounds, butterflied and
    well trimmed
¾   cup zinfandel
    Extra-virgin olive oil
    Kosher salt
    Freshly ground black pepper

COUSCOUS

2   cups low-sodium chicken broth
1   box (10 ounces) couscous
1   can (15½ ounces) chickpeas, rinsed and drained
1   cup ¼-inch diced dried apricots
2   scallions (white and light green parts only), minced
¼   cup sliced almonds, toasted
3   tablespoons sherry vinegar
⅓   cup roughly chopped fresh Italian parsley
    leaves, divided

1. Tuck the thyme sprigs securely in the lamb. In a large baking dish whisk the zinfandel and ¾ cup oil. Place the lamb in the baking dish. Cover and refrigerate for 4 hours, turning once. Allow the lamb to stand at room temperature for 30 to 40 minutes before grilling.

2. Place a large disposable foil pan underneath the cooking grates (over an unlit burner) to catch the drippings. Prepare the grill for direct and indirect cooking over medium heat (350° to 450°F).

3. Remove the lamb from the dish and pat dry with paper towels. Season with salt and pepper. Grill the lamb, fat side up, over *direct medium heat*, with the lid closed, until nicely marked, about 15 minutes, turning once after 10 minutes. Move the lamb, fat side up, over *indirect medium heat* centered over the foil pan, and continue cooking to your desired doneness, 20 to 30 minutes more for medium rare. Remove from the grill and let rest for 5 to 10 minutes.

4. In a saucepan over high heat, bring the broth to a boil and add ½ teaspoon salt. In a heatproof bowl combine the couscous, chickpeas, apricots, and scallions. Stir in the broth. Cover and let stand for 5 minutes. To the bowl add the almonds, ⅓ cup oil, the vinegar, half of the parsley, and ½ teaspoon pepper. Fluff with a fork. Cut the lamb across the grain into thin slices and serve with the couscous. Top with the remaining parsley.

SERVES: 4 | PREP TIME: 15 minutes | MARINATING TIME: 20–30 minutes | GRILLING TIME: about 20 minutes

GLAZE

⅔ cup apricot preserves
½ cup whole-grain mustard
¼ cup extra-virgin olive oil
3 tablespoons finely chopped fresh thyme leaves
6 garlic cloves, minced and pushed through a press

2 racks of lamb, each about 2 pounds, frenched
2 teaspoons kosher salt
1½ teaspoons freshly ground black pepper

1. Whisk the glaze ingredients. Transfer ⅓ cup of the glaze to another bowl and set aside to brush on the racks of lamb when they come off the grill. Rub the remaining glaze all over the lamb, spreading more on the meaty side than the bone side. Marinate the lamb at room temperature for 20 to 30 minutes. Season evenly with the salt and the pepper.

2. Prepare the grill for direct cooking over medium heat (350° to 450°F).

3. Grill the lamb, bone side down first, over *direct medium heat*, with the lid closed, until cooked to your desired doneness, about 20 minutes for medium rare, turning occasionally and watching closely to avoid flare-ups. Remove from the grill and brush with the reserved glaze. Let rest for about 5 minutes.

4. Cut the lamb between the bones into individual chops. Serve warm.

SPECIAL EQUIPMENT: 6 large handfuls mesquite wood chips, instant-read thermometer, extra-large disposable foil pan, large gravy separator

1 whole, untrimmed beef brisket, including both flat and point sections, 10–12 pounds, preferably the *Certified Angus Beef®* brand

PASTE

¼ cup yellow or spicy brown mustard
2 tablespoons unsulfured molasses
2 tablespoons paprika
2 tablespoons packed golden brown sugar
4 teaspoons kosher salt
1 tablespoon Worcestershire sauce
2 teaspoons ground cumin
2 teaspoons prepared chili powder
2 teaspoons granulated garlic
1 teaspoon granulated onion
1 teaspoon freshly ground black pepper
¾ teaspoon celery salt
¾ teaspoon ground allspice

¼ cup (½ stick) unsalted butter
1½ cups low-sodium beef broth
2 teaspoons Worcestershire sauce
  Store-bought barbecue sauce (optional)

1. Using a very sharp knife, trim the fat on the fatty side of the brisket so that it is about ⅓ inch thick, but no less. On the meatier side, remove the web-like membrane so that the coarsely grained meat underneath is visible. Remove any hard clumps of fat on either side of the brisket.

2. Combine the paste ingredients. Massage the paste all over the brisket and allow the brisket to stand at room temperature for 1 hour before cooking.

3. Soak the wood chips in water for at least 30 minutes.

4. Prepare the grill for indirect cooking over very low heat (225° to 250°F).

5. Drain and add two handfuls of the wood chips to the smoker box of a gas grill, following manufacturer's instructions, and close the lid. When the wood begins to smoke, cook the brisket, fat side up, over *indirect very low heat,* with the lid closed, until the internal temperature of the meat reaches 150°F, 4 to 5 hours. Drain and add one handful of the wood chips every 15 to 20 minutes (before the old chips burn out), until all of the wood chips are gone.

6. When the internal temperature of the brisket reaches 150°F, melt the butter in a saucepan over medium heat and then add the beef broth and the Worcestershire sauce. Cook until warmed through, 1 to 2 minutes, stirring often. Pour the liquid into an extra-large disposable foil pan. Carefully transfer the brisket, fat side up, from the grill to the pan. Close the grill lid to maintain the heat. Cover the pan with a double layer of aluminum foil and crimp the edges around the pan to seal it tightly.

7. Place the foil pan with the brisket on the cooking grates over *indirect very low heat,* close the lid, and continue cooking until the meat is so tender that an instant-read thermometer easily tears the meat when it is pushed back and forth, 2 to 4 hours more. The internal temperature should be 195° to 200°F, although tenderness is a more important indicator of doneness than temperature. Remove from the grill and let the brisket rest, still covered with foil in the pan, for 45 minutes.

8. Remove the brisket from the pan and place on a cutting board. Strain the pan juices into a large gravy separator. Allow the juices to stand for 3 minutes to let the fat rise to the top. Pour the pan juices into a medium saucepan and discard the fat. Bring to a boil over high heat and cook until the liquid is reduced by about one-quarter and is starting to look slightly glossy, 8 to 10 minutes, stirring frequently. Remove from the heat. Cut the "flat" section of the brisket across the grain into thin slices. Dip each slice into the reduced pan juices. Roughly chop the fattier "point" section. Serve the brisket warm, with any additional reduced pan juices and your favorite barbecue sauce on the side, if desired.

For the sake of tenderness, brisket should be cut across the grain of the meat, but it is nearly impossible to see the grain when the meat is cooked. So, when the meat is raw, put a bamboo skewer through it (across the grain) to indicate where your knife should make parallel cuts later.

Tip

Plan ahead. First you will need to find and purchase a very large piece of meat, at least 10 to 12 pounds, which you might need to buy from a specialty meat market or special order from a supermarket. The quality of the meat is the most important part of the recipe. Do not try to barbecue a low-quality brisket; it will be tough and dry. Buy a top-quality brisket from a reputable brand, such as the *Certified Angus Beef*® brand. You need a full, untrimmed brisket that includes a flat, relatively lean section (called "the flat") and a thicker, fattier section (called "the point"). When you lift the brisket up from the point end, the flat should flop over easily, indicating there is not too much connective tissue making the meat tight and tough.

PORK

5

GRILLING PORK

CUT	THICKNESS / WEIGHT	APPROXIMATE GRILLING TIME
Bratwurst, fresh	3-ounce link	**20–25 minutes** direct medium heat
Bratwurst, precooked	3-ounce link	**10–12 minutes** direct medium heat
Chop, boneless or bone-in	¾ inch thick	**6–8 minutes** direct medium heat
	1 inch thick	**8–10 minutes** direct medium heat
	1¼–1½ inches thick	**10–12 minutes:** sear 6 minutes direct medium heat, grill 4–6 minutes indirect medium heat
Loin roast, boneless	3½ pounds	**28–40 minutes:** sear 8–10 minutes direct high heat, grill 20–30 minutes indirect high heat
Loin roast, bone-in	3–5 pounds	**1¼–1¾ hours** indirect medium heat
Pork shoulder (Boston butt), boneless	5–6 pounds	**5–7 hours** indirect low heat
Pork, ground	½ inch thick	**8–10 minutes** direct medium heat
Ribs, baby back	1½–2 pounds	**3–4 hours** indirect low heat
Ribs, spareribs	2½–3½ pounds	**3–4 hours** indirect low heat
Ribs, country-style, boneless	1 inch thick	**12–15 minutes** direct medium heat
Ribs, country-style, bone-in	1 inch thick	**45–50 minutes** indirect medium heat
Tenderloin	1 pound	**15–20 minutes** direct medium heat

The USDA recommends that pork is cooked to 160°F, but most chefs today cook it to 145°F or 150°F, when it still has some pink in the center and all the juices haven't been driven out. Of course, the doneness you choose is entirely up to you. Let roasts, larger cuts of meat, and thick chops rest for 5 to 10 minutes before carving. The internal temperature of the meat will rise 5 to 10 degrees during this time.

TYPES OF PORK FOR THE GRILL

TENDER CUTS FOR GRILLING
- Center-cut chop
- Loin or rib chop
- Tenderloin

MODERATELY TENDER CUTS FOR GRILLING
- Ham steak
- Shoulder blade steak
- Sirloin chop

BIGGER CUTS FOR GRILL-ROASTING
- Center loin roast
- Center rib roast
- Country-style ribs
- Cured ham
- Rack of pork

TOUGHER CUTS FOR BARBECUING
- Baby back ribs
- Shoulder (Boston butt)
- Spareribs

gr i ll SKILLS:
PERFECT PORK CHOPS

Choose Wisely

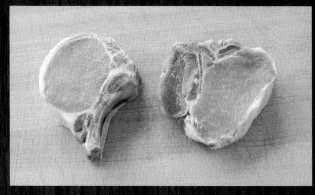

A lot of chops fall under the category of pork chops, but they are not all the same. They are all cut from a pig's loin, which extends from the shoulder blade to the hip, but along that loin you will find significant differences. The chops from the shoulder area (blade chops and country-style ribs) have quite a bit of fat and chewy sinew, which makes them less than ideal for grilling. The chops cut from the hip area (sirloin chops) are often too lean and dry for this kind of cooking. The chops you should be grilling are from middle of the loin, aka, the "center-cut rib chops" and "center-cut loin chops." They are very similar to one another in taste and texture. Each loin chop features a T-shaped bone that separates the loin meat from some tenderloin meat on the other side. Each rib chop has a large bone (from a rack of baby back ribs) running down one side of some sumptuous loin meat. With either of these chops, try to find a thickness of at least ¾ inch. Thinner chops tend to dry out too quickly.

Making Mock Chops

Pork tenderloins are not chops, but if you cut them crosswise into thick disks and flatten them with your hand, you've got little medallions that cook and taste very much like chops.

Brining Pork Chops

1 For brag-worthy results, brine your chops in a salt-and-sugar solution before grilling. This is how master grillers achieve especially juicy results. It only takes 30 minutes or so for pork chops to absorb some of that flavorful brine.

2 Once you have removed the chops from the brine, pat them dry with paper towels, and then coat them with oil and a spice rub. Because of the salt in the brine, you will not need as much salt in the spice rub.

3 As with any piece of meat destined for the grill, it's smart to let it sit at room temperature for 15 to 30 minutes before grilling. After that, the chops will cook faster and stay juicier.

Grilling Perfect Pork Chops

1 High heat tends to char the outside of pork chops too quickly and leave the centers rare or medium rare, like a steak, so go with medium heat instead for an even doneness. For chops that are less than 1½ inches thick, direct medium heat is all you really need.

2 For chops that are thicker than 1½ inches, grill them over direct medium heat until you have the color of grill marks you like, and then move the chops to indirect heat for the final few minutes of cooking.

3 If any of your chops have a layer of undercooked fat around the perimeter, you might want to stand it on its edge over direct heat for up to 1 minute. Be mindful here because the fat can burn quickly, but if you work carefully, you will give your pork chop a crispy, sizzling edge.

When Is It Done?

Chances are good that you learned somewhere that 165°F is the safe internal temperature for pork. The USDA was touting that temperature for years. It's still true that ground pork must be cooked to 165°F, but chops are safe to eat when they reach 145°F. This is hot enough to eliminate the risk of trichinosis, a parasitic disease contracted from undercooked pork, but not so hot that you run every last drop of moisture out of the meat.

Remove the chops from the grill and give them a few minutes to rest at room temperature so that the juices settle throughout the meat. When you cut a perfect pork chop open, you should see a very light pink color and a glistening sheen of moisture. The pork chop on the left, with raw meat in the center, is clearly undercooked. The chop on the right, with a dry, gray appearance, is overcooked. The chop in the middle, with a little bit of pink in the center, is cooked to 150°F (just right). See how the meat gives a little under pressure.

PORK CHOPS
WITH ROASTED PLUMS IN RED WINE REDUCTION

SERVES: 4 | PREP TIME: 30 minutes | MARINATING TIME: 2–4 hours | GRILLING TIME: 12–18 minutes

MARINADE
- ¼ cup low-sodium soy sauce
- 2 tablespoons red wine vinegar
- 1 tablespoon packed dark brown sugar
- 1 tablespoon grated fresh ginger
- 1 garlic clove, minced or pushed through a press

Vegetable oil

- 4 bone-in pork loin chops, each about 8 ounces and 1 inch thick, trimmed of excess fat
- 4 firm but ripe plums, about 1 pound total, each cut in half
- 2 garlic cloves, minced or pushed through a press
- 1 cup fruity, full-bodied red wine, such as Syrah
- ¾ cup low-sodium beef broth
- ⅓ cup plum jam or preserves
- 2 teaspoons red wine vinegar
- 1 sprig fresh rosemary, about 6 inches long
- 1½ teaspoons cold unsalted butter

Kosher salt

Freshly ground black pepper

REDUCTION SAUCES: WHEN LESS REALLY IS MORE

One way to add flavor to a dish is to keep adding ingredients, but of course that approach comes with limits and dangers, as the flavors can get muddled and confused. When you are making a sauce, there is an entirely different approach that does more with less. Borrowed from classical European cuisine, reduction sauces get more and more flavorful by concentrating whatever liquids you already have.

Take, for example, this red wine reduction sauce. You begin the process by sautéing some garlic. Then you add a full cup of rich red wine and boil it until only one-quarter of its original volume is left. All of the wine's richness, fruitiness, and acidity have been packed into a much smaller volume now. Then you add beef broth to the wine and boil it, too. As the water evaporates, the remaining meaty flavors get stronger. Now you just need to thicken this liquid reduction with some syrupy jam, which is actually its own kind of reduction, but that's another story. The sweetness of the jam is a bit much, so add a little vinegar for balance. To smooth out the whole thing, swirl a little butter into the reduction sauce before combining it with roasted plums.

1. Whisk the marinade ingredients, including 3 tablespoons oil. Place the pork chops in a large, resealable plastic bag and pour in the marinade. Press the air out of the bag and seal tightly. Turn the bag to distribute the marinade, place in a bowl, and refrigerate for 2 to 4 hours, turning occasionally.

2. Prepare the grill for direct cooking over medium heat (350° to 450°F).

3. Lightly brush the plums on both sides with oil. Grill them over *direct medium heat*, with the lid closed, until they begin to soften, 4 to 8 minutes, turning once (the cooking time will vary depending on the ripeness of the plums). Remove from the grill and cut them into ¼-inch slices.

4. Remove the chops from the bag and allow them to stand at room temperature for 15 to 30 minutes before grilling. Discard the marinade.

5. In a saucepan over medium-high heat, warm 2 teaspoons oil. Add the garlic and sauté until fragrant, about 1 minute. Add the wine and bring to a boil. Boil rapidly until it is reduced to ¼ cup, 7 to 8 minutes. Add the broth, return to a boil, and cook until the mixture is again reduced to ¼ cup, 8 to 9 minutes. Stir in the jam, vinegar, and rosemary sprig, reduce the heat to medium-low, and simmer until slightly thickened, about 3 minutes, stirring occasionally. Remove from the heat and discard the rosemary. Add the butter and swirl until melted. Season with ¼ teaspoon salt and ⅛ teaspoon pepper, add the plums, and set aside.

6. Lightly season the chops on both sides with salt and pepper. Grill them over *direct medium heat*, with the lid closed, until they are still slightly pink in the center, 8 to 10 minutes, turning once or twice. Remove from the grill and let rest for 3 to 5 minutes. Serve warm with the roasted plums.

BISTRO-STYLE PORK CHOPS
WITH CREAMY SHALLOT SAUCE

SERVES: 4 | PREP TIME: 35 minutes | GRILLING TIME: 8–10 minutes

4   bone-in pork loin chops, each about 8 ounces and
1 inch thick, trimmed of excess fat
2   tablespoons extra-virgin olive oil
2   tablespoons finely chopped fresh tarragon
leaves, divided
     Kosher salt
     Freshly ground black pepper
3   tablespoons unsalted butter, divided
1½   cups thinly sliced shallots
½   cup thinly sliced dill gherkins
1½   tablespoons whole-grain mustard
¾   cup low-sodium chicken broth
3   tablespoons frozen apple juice concentrate, thawed
⅓   cup heavy whipping cream

1. Lightly brush the pork chops on both sides with the oil and season evenly with 1½ tablespoons of the tarragon, 1 teaspoon salt, and ¾ teaspoon pepper. Allow the chops to stand at room temperature for 15 to 30 minutes before grilling.

2. Prepare the grill for direct cooking over medium heat (350° to 450°F).

3. Grill the chops over *direct medium heat*, with the lid closed, until they are still slightly pink in the center, 8 to 10 minutes, turning once or twice.

4. Meanwhile, in a large skillet over medium heat, melt 2 tablespoons of the butter. Add the shallots and sauté until they are tender and deep golden brown, 6 to 7 minutes. Stir in the gherkins, mustard, broth, and apple juice concentrate. Bring to a boil and cook until the mixture is slightly thickened and the liquid is reduced, 1 to 2 minutes. Add the cream, return to a gentle boil, and cook until the mixture is thickened to a cream sauce consistency, 2 to 3 minutes. Season with the remaining 1½ teaspoons tarragon, ¼ teaspoon salt, and ¼ teaspoon pepper. Whisk in the remaining 1 tablespoon butter. Remove from the heat and cover to keep warm.

5. Remove the chops from the grill and let rest for 3 to 5 minutes to allow the juices to accumulate. Pour the juices into the sauce and stir to blend. Serve the chops warm with the sauce.

SERVES: 4 | PREP TIME: 20 minutes | GRILLING TIME: 8–10 minutes

SAUCE
- 1 tablespoon unsalted butter
- ½ cup finely chopped yellow onion
- 1 garlic clove, minced or pushed through a press
- ⅓ cup ketchup
- ⅓ cup unsulfured molasses
- ¼ cup bourbon
- 1 tablespoon Worcestershire sauce
- 1 tablespoon balsamic vinegar
- ½ teaspoon hot pepper sauce

RUB
- 1 teaspoon prepared chili powder
- ½ teaspoon kosher salt
- ½ teaspoon freshly ground black pepper

- 4 boneless center-cut pork loin chops, each about 8 ounces and 1 inch thick, trimmed of excess fat
  Vegetable oil
- 4 slices bacon

1. In a saucepan over medium heat, melt the butter. Add the onion and cook until golden brown, about 5 minutes, stirring often. Stir in the garlic and cook until fragrant, about 1 minute.

Add the remaining sauce ingredients and bring to a simmer. Reduce the heat to low and simmer until the sauce is lightly thickened, 10 to 15 minutes, stirring often. Reserve ¼ cup of the sauce for brushing on the pork chops while on the grill and the remaining sauce to serve with the chops.

2. Combine the rub ingredients. Brush the chops on both sides with oil and season with the rub. Allow the chops to stand at room temperature for 15 to 30 minutes before grilling.

3. Prepare the grill for direct cooking over medium heat (350° to 450°F).

4. In a skillet over medium heat or in a microwave oven on high, cook the bacon until the fat is slightly rendered, about 2 minutes. Wrap a slice of bacon around the perimeter of each chop and secure with a toothpick.

5. Grill the chops over *direct medium heat*, with the lid closed, until they are still slightly pink in the center and the bacon is crisp, 8 to 10 minutes, turning once or twice and brushing with some of the sauce during the last 4 to 5 minutes of grilling time. Remove from the grill and let rest for 3 to 5 minutes. Serve warm with the remaining sauce.

HERB-CRUSTED PORK CHOPS
STUFFED WITH PROVOLONE AND PROSCIUTTO

SERVES: 4 | PREP TIME: 20 minutes | MARINATING TIME: 20–30 minutes | GRILLING TIME: 16–18 minutes

PASTE

¼ cup extra-virgin olive oil
2 tablespoons roughly chopped fresh rosemary leaves
2 tablespoons fresh oregano leaves
1 tablespoon fresh thyme leaves
1 tablespoon finely grated lemon zest
2 large garlic cloves, peeled
1 teaspoon kosher salt
½ teaspoon crushed red pepper flakes

4 double bone-in pork loin chops, each 12–14 ounces and about 2 inches thick, trimmed of excess fat
4 thin slices provolone cheese
4 thin slices prosciutto

1. In a food processor or a blender combine the paste ingredients and puree until the mixture forms a thick paste.

2. Place the pork chops on a work surface. Using a small, sharp knife, make a slit in the side of the meat opposite the bone. Enlarge this slit into a pocket by cutting to the left and right, slowly creating an opening that extends throughout the chop to within ½ inch of the bone. Stuff each chop with one slice of the cheese and one slice of the prosciutto, folding them in half, if necessary, so that they will fit. Spread the paste all over the chops and marinate at room temperature for 20 to 30 minutes.

3. Prepare the grill for direct cooking over medium heat (350° to 450°F).

4. Grill the chops over *direct medium heat*, with the lid closed, until they are still slightly pink in the center, 16 to 18 minutes, turning occasionally. Remove from the grill and let rest for 3 to 5 minutes. Serve warm.

SERVES: 6 | **PREP TIME: 15 minutes** | **MARINATING TIME: 30 minutes–1 hour** | **GRILLING TIME: 19–21 minutes**

MARINADE

½   pineapple, coarsely chopped
1   medium white onion, coarsely chopped
¼   cup tequila
2   tablespoons distilled white or cider vinegar
1   canned chipotle chile pepper in adobo sauce
2   large garlic cloves
1   teaspoon dried oregano, preferably Mexican
1   teaspoon ground cumin
1   teaspoon kosher salt
¼   teaspoon ground cinnamon

2¼   pounds boneless country-style ribs or boneless blade pork chops, about 1 inch thick, trimmed of excess fat

SALSA

½   pineapple, cut crosswise into ½-inch slices, cored
½   medium white onion, cut crosswise into ¼-inch slices
⅓   cup roughly chopped fresh cilantro leaves
1   jalapeño chile pepper, seeded and minced

    Kosher salt
12   corn or flour tortillas (6 inches)
2   limes, cut into wedges

1. In a food processor puree the marinade ingredients until smooth. Place the pork chops in a large resealable plastic bag and pour in the marinade. Press the air out of the bag and seal tightly. Turn the bag to distribute the marinade, place in a bowl, and refrigerate for 30 minutes to 1 hour.

2. Prepare the grill for direct cooking over medium heat (350° to 450°F).

3. Grill the pineapple and onion slices over *direct medium heat*, with the lid closed, until grill marks appear, about 8 minutes, turning once or twice. Remove from the grill and cut into small dice. Combine all the salsa ingredients. Set aside.

4. Remove the chops from the bag, allowing some of the marinade to cling to the meat. Discard the remaining marinade. Season the chops with salt. Grill the chops over *direct medium heat*, with the lid closed, until the meat is still slightly pink in the center, 10 to 12 minutes, turning once. (The grill marks might be dark because of the natural sugar in the marinade, but that's okay.) Remove from the grill and let rest for 3 to 5 minutes. Warm the tortillas over *direct medium heat* for about 1 minute, turning once. Cut the meat across the grain into ½-inch slices. Fill each tortilla with pork and salsa, and serve with the lime wedges.

RECIPE REMIX:
Then and Now

What was it with the '70s and stuffings? Anything that could be filled with one was, and even things that couldn't somehow were. Maybe it was the "more bang for your buck" trend of the oil crisis era, or perhaps it was just the novelty of surprise, but these days we like our flavors, more or less, where we can see them. The original pork loin roast recipe does have potential, especially with the traditional pairings of apples and nuts, both of which we've borrowed for our Remix. This time around we're using brined pork chops coated with a sophisticated, tangy Dijon glaze, upon which sautéed apples are piled high. The only surprise here is extraordinary flavor.

The Original

Stuffed Pork Loin Roast
Recipe from *Elegant Fare from the Weber Kettle*, ©1977

1 boned, rolled pork loin (4 pounds), trimmed

Pork Stuffing
3 tablespoons butter
2 medium onions, chopped
2 apples, cored, peeled and chopped
1/2 cup chopped boiled ham
3/4 cup chopped ripe olives
1/2 cup chopped walnuts
1 cup soft bread crumbs
1/2 teaspoon salt
1/4 teaspoon thyme
3 tablespoons melted butter

This is the stout, hearty fare that has brought fame to the tables of Germany. The presentation is impressive, with the roast fanning out beautifully.

Using a sharp knife, slice the roast halfway down at 1-inch intervals. Continue each slice to form deep pockets, leaving a 1-inch wall on the sides and bottom.

Heat the butter in a skillet and sauté the onions, stirring occasionally, until they are limp and transparent. Add the apples and cook 1 minute more. Combine with the remaining ingredients and mix well.

Generously stuff the roast, and then tie at 1-inch intervals around the outside to hold the roast together.

Cook by Indirect Heat Method for charcoal or by Indirect Heat Method (Low Heat) for gas, for 1-1/2 to 2 hours or until a meat thermometer buried halfway in the center pork slice registers 170°.

Remove roast from kettle and allow to stand 10 minutes before carving. Remove the strings and slice through the meat between pockets to yield individually stuffed chop portions. Roast Potatoes and a fresh green vegetable would be nice additions.

Serves 8.

DIJON-GLAZED PORK CHOPS
WITH APPLE-TARRAGON RELISH

The Remix

SERVES: 6 | PREP TIME: 30 minutes | BRINING TIME: 30 minutes–2 hours | GRILLING TIME: 5–7 minutes

BRINE

- 4 cups cold water
- ⅓ cup kosher salt
- ⅓ cup packed golden brown sugar
- 3 bay leaves
- 2 teaspoons freshly ground black pepper
- 4 cups ice cubes

- 6 bone-in pork loin chops, each about 6 ounces and ¾ inch thick, trimmed of excess fat

RELISH

- Extra-virgin olive oil
- 1 large yellow or red onion, finely chopped (about 2 cups)
- 2 medium Fuji apples, cored and cut into ¼-inch dice (about 2 cups)
- 1 teaspoon finely grated lemon zest
- 1 tablespoon fresh lemon juice
- 1 tablespoon finely chopped fresh tarragon leaves
- ½ teaspoon kosher salt
- Freshly ground black pepper

- 2 tablespoons Dijon mustard
- 30 pistachio nuts, shelled and roughly chopped (about 3 tablespoons)

1. In a large saucepan mix the cold water with the salt and the sugar, and whisk over medium heat until the salt and sugar are dissolved. Remove from the heat and stir in the bay leaves and the pepper. Add the ice cubes. Put the pork chops in the brine and allow them to stand at room temperature for about 30 minutes, or refrigerate for 2 hours. Meanwhile, make the relish.

2. In a 12-inch skillet over medium heat, warm 2 tablespoons oil and add the onion. Sauté until tender and slightly golden, about 10 minutes, stirring often. Stir in the apples and cook for 2 minutes more. Remove from the heat and stir in the lemon zest, lemon juice, tarragon, salt, and ¼ teaspoon pepper.

3. Prepare the grill for direct cooking over medium heat (350° to 450°F).

4. Whisk the mustard with 3 tablespoons oil and ¼ teaspoon pepper. Lift the pork chops from the brine and pat them dry with paper towels. Discard the brine. Brush the chops on both sides with the mustard mixture.

5. Grill the chops over *direct medium heat*, with the lid closed, until the meat is still slightly pink in the center, 5 to 7 minutes, turning once after 3 minutes. Remove from the grill and let rest for 3 to 5 minutes. Reheat the relish. Serve the chops warm with the relish, and top with the nuts.

ROASTED PORK LOIN
WITH MAPLE-MUSTARD CREAM SAUCE

SERVES: 8–10 | PREP TIME: 20 minutes, plus about 40 minutes to make the sauce | GRILLING TIME: 28–40 minutes

SPECIAL EQUIPMENT: instant-read thermometer

SAUCE

1½	tablespoons unsalted butter
¾	cup finely chopped shallots
3	tablespoons cider vinegar
2¼	cups low-sodium beef broth
1	cup heavy whipping cream
¼	cup maple syrup
3	tablespoons country-style Dijon mustard
½	teaspoon kosher salt

RUB

2	teaspoons smoked paprika
1½	teaspoons kosher salt
1	teaspoon garlic powder
¾	teaspoon freshly ground black pepper

1	boneless center-cut pork loin roast, about 3½ pounds
1	tablespoon extra-virgin olive oil
2	tablespoons finely chopped fresh Italian parsley leaves

SEAR AND SLIDE

We roast pork for at least a couple reasons: the outside and the inside. We like the outside of the loin to have a glistening golden sheen with lightly charred edges of lip-smacking fat. We like the inside of the loin to have a succulent, delicate texture that gives easily to even a dull dinner knife. The trouble is, one heat alone will not get us to both outcomes.

That's why we sear the meat first over direct heat and then slide it over indirect heat to finish. While searing the meat right over the hot flames for eight to ten minutes, we dry the surface and develop the foundation of a sizzling, flavorful crust. If we continued to sear the meat over direct heat like that, the surface would get darker and darker and eventually burn; yet, the inside would still be undercooked. So we slide the meat instead over indirect heat. With almost all the heat now circulating more gently around the roast, the inside of the meat cooks gradually, with only a little more browning of the crust. In a sense, the inside now has an opportunity to catch up with the outside.

1. In a medium saucepan over medium heat, melt the butter. Add the shallots and cook until slightly softened, 5 to 6 minutes, stirring often. Add the vinegar and cook until evaporated, 1 to 2 minutes. Pour in the broth and the cream, increase the heat to high, and bring to a boil. Reduce the heat to medium and gently simmer until the mixture is reduced to 1¾ cups and is thick enough to coat the back of a spoon, 20 to 30 minutes, stirring occasionally. Stir in the syrup and simmer for 3 minutes. Remove from the heat and stir in the mustard and the salt. Set aside while you prepare the roast; or, let cool, cover, and refrigerate for up to 3 hours.

2. Combine the rub ingredients. Brush the roast all over with the oil and season evenly with the rub. Allow the roast to stand at room temperature for 30 minutes before grilling.

3. Prepare the grill for direct and indirect cooking over high heat (450° to 550°F).

4. Sear the roast over *direct high heat*, with the lid closed, until the surface is well marked, 8 to 10 minutes, turning occasionally (watch for flare-ups, especially when searing the fatty side). Move the roast over *indirect high heat* and grill, fat side up, with the lid closed, until an instant-read thermometer inserted into the center of the roast registers 140° to 145°F, 20 to 30 minutes more. Transfer to a cutting board, tent loosely with foil, and let rest for about 15 minutes (the internal temperature will rise 5 to 10 degrees during this time).

5. Reheat the sauce gently over medium-low heat and add the parsley. Cut the roast crosswise into slices and serve warm with the sauce.

SERVES: 4 | **PREP TIME:** 20 minutes | **MARINATING TIME:** 4 hours | **GRILLING TIME:** 15–20 minutes

MARINADE

- ¾ cup cola (not diet)
- ¼ cup fresh orange juice
- 2 tablespoons fresh lime juice
- 1½ tablespoons peeled, grated fresh ginger
- 1 tablespoon packed dark brown sugar
- 2 teaspoons mustard powder
- 2 teaspoons kosher salt
- 3 garlic cloves, minced or pushed through a press
- 1 teaspoon freshly ground black pepper
- 1 teaspoon ground cumin
- ½ teaspoon ground cardamom

- 2 pork tenderloins, each about 1 pound, trimmed of silver skin and any excess fat
- 1 tablespoon extra-virgin olive oil

1. Whisk the marinade ingredients. Place the pork in a large, resealable plastic bag and pour in the marinade. Press the air out of the bag and seal tightly. Turn the bag to distribute the marinade, place in a bowl, and refrigerate for 4 hours. Remove the pork from the bag and reserve the marinade. Allow the pork to stand at room temperature for 15 to 30 minutes before grilling.

2. Prepare the grill for direct cooking over medium heat (350° to 450°F).

3. Pour the marinade into a small saucepan. Bring to a boil over medium-high heat and simmer until slightly reduced and thickened, about 4 minutes. Set aside.

4. Brush the pork all over with the oil. Grill over *direct medium heat*, with the lid closed, until well marked on two sides, about 5 minutes, turning once. Lightly baste with the reduced marinade and continue to grill until the outsides are evenly browned and the centers are barely pink, 10 to 15 minutes more, turning and basting every 5 minutes (if the tenderloins stick, move them to a clean part of the cooking grate when you turn them). Remove from the grill and let rest for 3 to 5 minutes. Cut into slices and serve warm. Serving suggestion: Summer Corn, Tomato, and Avocado Salad (for the recipe, see page 267).

SERVES: 4 | PREP TIME: 30 minutes | GRILLING TIME: 15–20 minutes

GLAZE

- 1 jar (12 ounces) apple jelly
- 3 tablespoons cider vinegar
- 2 tablespoons unsalted butter
- 4 teaspoons Dijon mustard

  Kosher salt
  Freshly ground black pepper
- 4 teaspoons minced fresh thyme leaves
- 2 pork tenderloins, each about 1 pound, trimmed of silver skin and any excess fat
  Extra-virgin olive oil
- 4 large garlic cloves, thinly sliced
- ⅛ teaspoon crushed red pepper flakes
- 1 pound mustard greens, stems trimmed and leaves roughly chopped
- ⅓ cup golden raisins
- ½ cup low-sodium chicken broth
- 2 teaspoons cider vinegar
- 4 slices cooked bacon, finely chopped

1. In a saucepan over medium heat, cook the jelly until it melts, 1 to 2 minutes, stirring constantly. Add the remaining glaze ingredients, including ½ teaspoon salt and ¼ teaspoon pepper, and whisk until the mixture is smooth. Remove from the heat and reserve ½ cup of the glaze for brushing on the pork during grilling. Leave the remaining glaze in the saucepan.

2. Prepare the grill for direct cooking over medium heat (350° to 450°F).

3. Combine the thyme, 1½ teaspoons salt, and 1 teaspoon pepper. Lightly brush the pork all over with oil and season with the spices. Grill over *direct medium heat*, with the lid closed, until the outsides are evenly seared and the centers are barely pink, 15 to 20 minutes, turning three times. During the last 3 minutes of grilling time, brush the pork with the reserved glaze. Remove from the grill and let rest for 3 to 5 minutes.

4. In a large, deep skillet over medium-high heat, warm 2 tablespoons oil. Add the garlic and the red pepper flakes and cook until the garlic is fragrant, about 1 minute, stirring constantly. Add the greens and toss until lightly wilted, about 2 minutes. Stir in the raisins and broth and bring to a boil. Cook until the broth is absorbed and the greens are just tender, 2 to 4 minutes more. Stir in the vinegar and season with salt and pepper. Reheat the glaze in the saucepan. Cut the pork into slices. Divide the greens, pork, and bacon among four plates. Spoon the glaze over the top, and serve right away.

VIETNAMESE PORK SANDWICHES
WITH LEMON MAYONNAISE AND PICKLED VEGETABLES

SERVES: 6 | PREP TIME: 30 minutes | GRILLING TIME: 5–6 minutes

½ English cucumber, about 6 ounces, thinly sliced
1 red onion, about 4 ounces, cut in half vertically, thinly sliced
1 medium carrot, peeled and grated using the large holes of a box grater
1 tablespoon granulated sugar
3 teaspoons kosher salt, divided
¾ teaspoon crushed red pepper flakes
¼ cup white wine vinegar
¼ cup extra-virgin olive oil
2 pork tenderloins, each about 1 pound, trimmed of silver skin and any excess fat
   Vegetable oil
1 teaspoon freshly ground black pepper, divided
¾ cup mayonnaise
1 tablespoon finely grated lemon zest
1 loaf ciabatta, about 1 pound, cut into 6 equal pieces, each piece halved horizontally
½ cup coarsely chopped fresh cilantro leaves
½ cup coarsely chopped fresh mint leaves

1. Combine the vegetables with the sugar, 1 teaspoon of the salt, the red pepper flakes, vinegar, and olive oil. Set aside.

2. Cut off the thin, tapered ends from each tenderloin and reserve for another use. Cut each tenderloin crosswise into three equal pieces. Place the pieces of pork, cut side up, on a work surface and, using your hand, pound each piece until it is an even ½ inch thick. Lightly brush the pork pieces on both sides with vegetable oil and season them evenly with the remaining 2 teaspoons salt and ½ teaspoon of the pepper.

3. Combine the mayonnaise and the lemon zest.

4. Prepare the grill for direct cooking over high heat (450° to 550°F).

5. Grill the pork over *direct high heat*, with the lid closed, until barely pink in the center, 5 to 6 minutes, turning once or twice. During the last minute of grilling time, toast the ciabatta, cut side down, over direct heat. Remove the pork and the ciabatta from the grill. Let the pork rest for 3 to 5 minutes.

6. Thoroughly drain the vegetables and discard the liquid. Build the sandwiches with lemon mayo, pork, pickled vegetables, cilantro, and mint. Serve immediately.

SERVES: 6–8 | PREP TIME: 15 minutes | MARINATING TIME: 4–8 hours | GRILLING TIME: 8–10 minutes

SPECIAL EQUIPMENT: metal or bamboo skewers

MARINADE
⅓ cup finely chopped fresh Italian parsley leaves and tender stems
¼ cup extra-virgin olive oil
2 tablespoons minced red onion
1 tablespoon sherry vinegar
1 tablespoon smoked paprika
2 teaspoons ground cumin
2 teaspoons minced garlic
¼ teaspoon ground cayenne pepper

Kosher salt
2 pork tenderloins, each about 1 pound, trimmed of silver skin and any excess fat, cut into 1¼-inch cubes
2 large bell peppers, 1 red and 1 green, cut into 1¼-inch squares

1. Whisk the marinade ingredients, including ½ teaspoon salt. Put the pork cubes in a large, resealable plastic bag and pour in the marinade. Press the air out of the bag and seal tightly. Turn the bag to distribute the marinade, place in a bowl, and refrigerate for 4 to 8 hours, turning occasionally.

2. If using bamboo skewers, soak in water for at least 30 minutes.

3. Prepare the grill for direct cooking over high heat (450° to 550°F).

4. Remove the pork from the bag and discard the marinade. Thread the pork and bell pepper squares alternately onto skewers.

5. Grill the kabobs over *direct high heat*, with the lid closed, until the pork is barely pink in the center, 8 to 10 minutes, turning once or twice. Remove from the grill and season with salt. Serve warm.

PORK AND CHORIZO BURGERS
WITH LIME-JALAPEÑO SLAW

SERVES: 4 | PREP TIME: 30 minutes | CHILLING TIME: 30 minutes–6 hours | GRILLING TIME: 12–13 minutes

SPECIAL EQUIPMENT: instant-read thermometer

PATTIES

14	ounces lean ground pork
10	ounces fresh chorizo
½	cup *panko* bread crumbs
3	tablespoons minced shallot
2	tablespoons finely chopped fresh Italian parsley leaves
4	garlic cloves, minced or pushed through a press
1	teaspoon ground cumin
½	teaspoon smoked paprika
½	teaspoon dried thyme
½	teaspoon kosher salt
¼	teaspoon freshly ground black pepper

SLAW

¾	cup loosely packed fresh cilantro leaves, finely chopped
½	jalapeño chile pepper, seeded and minced
2	tablespoons fresh lime juice
2	tablespoons sour cream
2	tablespoons mayonnaise
½	teaspoon kosher salt
¼	teaspoon prepared chili powder
12	ounces green cabbage, cored and thinly sliced
1	medium carrot, peeled and coarsely grated

4	hamburger buns, split
	Extra-virgin olive oil
	Mayonnaise
8	thin slices tomato
4	leaves lettuce

1. In a large bowl gently combine the patty ingredients until thoroughly blended. With wet hands, form four loosely packed patties, each about 4 inches in diameter and 1 inch thick. Don't compact the meat too much or the patties will be tough. Using your thumb or the back of a spoon, make a shallow indentation about 1 inch wide in the center of each patty. This will help the patties cook evenly and prevent them from puffing on the grill. Refrigerate in a single layer for at least 30 minutes or up to 6 hours (cover with plastic wrap if chilling for more than 1 hour).

2. In a large bowl whisk the cilantro, jalapeño, lime juice, sour cream, mayonnaise, salt, and chili powder. Add the cabbage and the carrot and toss to mix. If time allows, cover and refrigerate for 1 hour to allow the flavors to develop. Remove from the refrigerator about 20 minutes before serving (the slaw tastes better when it is not too cold).

3. Prepare the grill for direct cooking over medium heat (350° to 450°F).

4. Lightly brush the cut side of each bun with oil. Grill the patties over *direct medium heat*, with the lid closed, until an instant-read thermometer inserted into the center of the patties registers 145°F, 12 to 13 minutes, turning once when the patties release easily from the grate without sticking (if flare-ups occur, move temporarily over indirect heat). Looking at the patties will not be an accurate measure of whether they are done since chorizo stays slightly pink when cooked. During the last minute of grilling time, toast the buns, cut side down, over direct heat. Remove the patties and the buns from the grill.

5. Spread the cut sides of each bun with mayonnaise. Build each burger with lettuce, a patty, and two tomato slices. Toss the slaw to redistribute the dressing and serve alongside the burgers.

TEXAS PORK SLIDERS
WITH BLACK BEAN SALSA

SERVES: 6 | PREP TIME: 20 minutes | GRILLING TIME: 6–8 minutes

SALSA

1	can (15 ounces) black beans, rinsed and drained
¾	cup finely chopped green bell pepper
¼	cup coarsely grated red onion
2	tablespoons extra-virgin olive oil
2	tablespoons minced fresh cilantro leaves
1	tablespoon red wine vinegar
½	teaspoon dried oregano
¼	teaspoon hot pepper sauce, or to taste
¼	teaspoon smoked paprika
¼	teaspoon kosher salt

PATTIES

1½	pounds lean ground pork
¼	cup coarsely grated red onion
1	teaspoon mustard powder
1	teaspoon dried oregano
1	teaspoon kosher salt
½	teaspoon smoked paprika
½	teaspoon freshly ground black pepper
12	small dinner rolls, split

1. Combine the salsa ingredients. Set aside.

2. Prepare the grill for direct cooking over medium heat (350° to 450°F).

3. Gently combine the patty ingredients. With wet hands form 12 loosely packed patties of equal size, each about 3 inches in diameter. Don't compact the meat too much or the patties will be tough. Using your thumb or the back of a spoon, make a shallow indentation about ½ inch wide in the center of each patty. This will help the patties cook evenly and prevent them from puffing on the grill.

4. Grill the patties over *direct medium heat*, with the lid closed, until fully cooked, 6 to 8 minutes, turning once or twice. During the last minute of grilling time, toast the rolls, cut side down, over direct heat. Remove from the grill and assemble the patties in the rolls with the salsa on top (you may have leftover salsa). Serve immediately.

SERVES: 4 | **PREP TIME: 30 minutes** | **GRILLING TIME: 37–48 minutes**

SPECIAL EQUIPMENT: 10-inch cast-iron skillet

    3   poblano chile peppers, about 14 ounces total
    1½ teaspoons canola oil
    12 ounces fresh chorizo sausages, casings removed
    3   large garlic cloves, minced or pushed through a press
    1   cup sliced scallions (white and light green parts only)
    2   teaspoons ground cumin
    1   can (28 ounces) diced plum tomatoes in juice
    1   can (15 ounces) black beans, rinsed and drained
        Kosher salt
        Freshly ground black pepper
    3½ ounces pepper jack cheese, coarsely grated
    4   large eggs
    8   corn tortillas (6 inches)

1. Prepare the grill for direct cooking over high heat (450° to 550°F).

2. Grill the poblanos over *direct high heat*, with the lid closed, until blackened and blistered all over, 10 to 12 minutes, turning occasionally. Put the poblanos in a bowl and cover with plastic wrap to trap the steam. Let stand for about 10 minutes. Peel away and discard the charred skin. Cut off and discard the stems and seeds, and then roughly chop the poblanos.

3. Place a 10-inch cast-iron skillet over *direct high heat*, add the oil, and warm for 1 minute. Add the chorizo and break into small pieces using a wooden spoon. Cook until the chorizo is lightly browned, 5 to 6 minutes, stirring occasionally. Stir in the garlic, scallions, and poblanos and cook for 2 to 3 minutes. Stir in the cumin, the tomatoes in juice, the beans, ½ teaspoon salt, and ½ teaspoon pepper. Bring to a boil and cook until the flavors are blended, the liquid is reduced by two-thirds, and only a small amount of liquid remains in the bottom of the skillet, 12 to 16 minutes, stirring occasionally. Top evenly with the cheese and cook until most of the cheese is melted, 3 to 4 minutes. Keep the lid closed as much as possible during grilling.

4. Make four shallow indentations in the chile-bean mixture. Crack one egg into each indentation. Continue cooking over *direct high heat*, with the lid closed, until the egg whites are set but the yolks are still soft and runny, 3 to 5 minutes. Season the eggs with salt and pepper. Carefully remove the skillet from the grill.

5. Put four tortillas in each of two foil packets. Warm the packets over *direct high heat* for about 1 minute, turning once. Serve the huevos rancheros with warm tortillas.

GRILLED PIZZAS
WITH SAUSAGE, PEPPERS, AND HERBS

SERVES: 6–8 | PREP TIME: 30 minutes | GRILLING TIME: 18–22 minutes

SPECIAL EQUIPMENT: pizza stone at least 14 inches in diameter, pizza peel (optional)

- 2 balls (each about 1 pound) premade pizza dough
  Extra-virgin olive oil
- 1 medium red or green bell pepper, cut into ¼-inch strips
- ½ small yellow onion, thinly sliced
- 8 ounces mild or spicy Italian sausage
  All-purpose flour
- 1 can (8 ounces) tomato sauce
- ¼ cup thinly sliced black olives
- 2 tablespoons finely chopped fresh Italian parsley leaves
- 1 tablespoon finely chopped fresh thyme leaves
- 2 teaspoons finely chopped fresh rosemary leaves
- 1½ cups shredded mozzarella cheese

1 Cold pizza dough is difficult to stretch, so take it out of the refrigerator about an hour before grilling, and then roll it to a thickness of about ⅓ inch.

2 Move the dough onto a pizza peel or a rimless baking sheet lightly coated with flour so that it slides easily.

3 Use whatever toppings you like, but be sure all of them will be fully cooked after just 10 minutes on the grill.

4 Slide your pizza onto a preheated pizza stone so that the front edge of the dough grips the stone. Then slowly pull the peel or pan back toward you.

1. Remove the balls of dough from the refrigerator, if necessary, about 1 hour before grilling so that the dough is easier to roll.

2. In a large skillet over medium-high heat, warm 1 tablespoon oil. Add the bell pepper and the onion and cook until softened but not browned, about 3 minutes, stirring occasionally. Remove the vegetables from the skillet and set aside.

3. Add the sausage to the skillet, breaking it into medium-sized pieces. Cook over medium-high heat until lightly browned and fully cooked, about 3 minutes, stirring occasionally and breaking the sausage into smaller pieces. Remove the skillet from the heat, and let the sausage cool in the skillet.

4. Prepare the grill for direct cooking over medium heat (350° to 450°F) and preheat a pizza stone for at least 15 minutes, following manufacturer's instructions. Meanwhile, prepare your first pizza.

5. Using a rolling pin on a lightly floured work surface, roll out the dough, one ball at a time, into rounds about 12 inches wide and ⅓ inch thick. (If the dough retracts, cover it with a kitchen towel, let it rest for 5 minutes, and then continue.) Set the first round aside while you roll out the second.

6. Carefully transfer your first round of pizza dough onto a pizza peel (or a rimless baking sheet) lightly coated with flour. Spread ½ cup of the sauce over the dough. Scatter half of the sausage, half of the pepper-and-onion mixture, half of the olives, and half of the parsley, thyme, and rosemary on top. Finish by scattering half of the cheese on top of everything.

7. Slide your first pizza onto the preheated pizza stone and cook over *direct medium heat*, with the lid closed, until the crust is golden brown and the cheese is melted, 9 to 11 minutes. Using a pizza peel or a large spatula, remove the pizza from the pizza stone and let rest for a few minutes. Cut into wedges and serve warm.

8. Repeat steps 6 and 7 with the remaining dough, sauce, and toppings.

STUFFED PIZZA WITH THE WORKS

SERVES: 6–8 | PREP TIME: 30 minutes | GRILLING TIME: 40–50 minutes

SPECIAL EQUIPMENT: 10-inch cast-iron skillet

FILLING
1 tablespoon extra-virgin olive oil
3 cups finely chopped yellow onions
1½ cups diced green bell pepper
1 pound button mushrooms, sliced
4 large garlic cloves, minced or pushed through a press
1 teaspoon kosher salt
½ teaspoon freshly ground black pepper

SAUCE
1 can (8 ounces) tomato sauce
¼ cup freshly grated Parmigiano-Reggiano® cheese
2 tablespoons tomato paste
1 tablespoon extra-virgin olive oil
½ teaspoon dried oregano
½ teaspoon dried basil
1 garlic clove, minced or pushed through a press
¼ teaspoon dried thyme

Extra-virgin olive oil
1½ pounds premade pizza dough (if you'd rather make your own dough, see page 286)
All-purpose flour
7 ounces grated mozzarella cheese (about 2 cups)
5 ounces sliced pepperoni

1. Prepare the grill for direct and indirect cooking over medium heat (350° to 450°F).

2. In a large skillet over medium heat, warm the oil. Add the onions and bell pepper and cook until slightly softened, about 3 minutes, stirring occasionally. Add the mushrooms and cook until tender and lightly browned and any liquid they have released is evaporated, about 12 minutes. During the last minute, stir in the garlic, salt, and pepper. Remove the filling from the heat and set aside to cool.

3. Combine the sauce ingredients. Remove the dough from the refrigerator, if necessary, about 1 hour before grilling so that the dough is easier to roll.

4. Lightly coat a 10-inch cast-iron skillet with oil. Divide the dough into two balls, one with two-thirds of the dough and the other with the remaining one-third. On a lightly floured work surface, roll, pat, and stretch the larger ball into a 14-inch round. (If the dough retracts, cover it with a kitchen towel, let it rest for 5 minutes, and then continue rolling.) Transfer the dough to the skillet, letting the excess hang over the sides to keep the dough from sliding into the skillet. Gently stretch the dough to fit the skillet, pressing it into the corners but being careful not to tear the dough. Spread 1 cup of the mozzarella on top of the dough. Spread one-half of the filling on top of the cheese and then place one-half of the pepperoni in a single layer on top of the filling. Repeat with another layer using the remaining filling and the remaining pepperoni. Top evenly with ½ cup of the mozzarella. Roll, pat, and stretch the remaining piece of dough into a 10-inch round. Place the round on top of the filling and press down to remove any visible air pockets. Brush some water on the edges of the top and bottom pieces of dough where they come together, and then roll and pinch the edges to seal them. Prick the dough in several places to release any new air pockets that may have formed. Spread the sauce over the top crust, leaving the edges where the dough is sealed uncovered. Top the sauce with the remaining ½ cup mozzarella.

5. Place the skillet over *direct medium heat*, close the lid, and cook until the edges of the dough look set and somewhat dry, about 5 minutes. Move the skillet over *indirect medium heat* and continue cooking, with the lid closed, until the crust is golden brown, 35 to 45 minutes. Remove the skillet from the grill and let the pizza rest for 10 minutes. Using a wide spatula, slide the pizza onto a serving platter. Cut into wedges and serve warm.

1 Line the skillet with two-thirds of the dough, gently pressing it into the corners.

2 Layer the mozzarella, the vegetable filling, and the pepperoni inside the dough.

3 Place a round of the remaining dough on top, and press out any air pockets.

4 Moisten the top and bottom crusts, seal them snugly, and prick the top crust in spots.

KIELBASA SUBMARINE SANDWICHES
WITH BEER-BRAISED ONIONS

SERVES: 4 | PREP TIME: 15 minutes | GRILLING TIME: 31–36 minutes

SPECIAL EQUIPMENT: 10-inch cast-iron skillet

6   ounces sauerkraut, rinsed and drained
2   red onions, 10–12 ounces total, halved and
     very thinly sliced
2   bottles (each 12 ounces) beer
1   teaspoon granulated sugar
½   teaspoon caraway seed
⅛   teaspoon celery seed
1   pound kielbasa, halved lengthwise, each half cut
     crosswise into 2 pieces
4   submarine sandwich rolls, each about 6 inches
     long, split
     Yellow or brown deli mustard

1. Prepare the grill for direct cooking over medium heat (350° to 450°F).

2. In a 10-inch cast-iron skillet combine the sauerkraut, onions, beer, and sugar. Place the skillet over *direct medium heat*, close the lid, and bring the mixture to a simmer. Simmer for 25 to 30 minutes, stirring occasionally. After 20 minutes, add the caraway seed and the celery seed. At the same time, grill the kielbasa, cut side down first, over *direct medium heat*, until nicely browned, 7 to 8 minutes, turning once. Remove the kielbasa from the grill and cut into 1-inch pieces. After the sauerkraut mixture has simmered for 25 to 30 minutes, add the kielbasa to the skillet and continue to cook for 5 minutes more, stirring occasionally.

3. Toast the rolls, cut side down, over *direct medium heat* until warmed through and lightly browned, about 1 minute.

4. Fill the rolls with the onion and kielbasa mixture. Serve with mustard.

Everyone in the pool! After these kielbasa sausages get a good sear on the grill, they join onions, sauerkraut, and beer in a simmering pool of savory flavors.

SERVES: 6–8 | **PREP TIME:** 25 minutes | **GRILLING TIME:** 2½–3 hours

SPECIAL EQUIPMENT: 2 large handfuls mesquite wood chips, large disposable foil pan, instant-read thermometer

1 tablespoon prepared chili powder
¾ teaspoon granulated garlic
   Kosher salt
1 bone-in pork shoulder roast (Boston butt), about 3½ pounds, trimmed of excess fat
   Extra-virgin olive oil
8 crusty rolls, each about 6 inches long, split

GUACAMOLE
2 Hass avocados, cut into ½-inch dice
2 plum tomatoes, seeded and cut into ½-inch dice
3 tablespoons minced red onion
1 tablespoon finely chopped fresh cilantro leaves
1 tablespoon fresh lime juice
1 garlic clove, minced or pushed through a press
½ teaspoon prepared chili powder

8 leaves red lettuce
8 slices tomato
1 red onion, thinly sliced and separated into rings
   Pickled jalapeño chile pepper slices, drained

1. Soak the wood chips in water for at least 30 minutes.

2. Prepare the grill for indirect cooking over medium-low heat (about 325°F).

3. Combine the chili powder, granulated garlic, and 2 teaspoons salt. Lightly brush the roast all over with oil and season evenly with the spices. Place the roast in a large disposable foil pan. Drain and add half of the wood chips to the charcoal or to the smoker box of a gas grill, following manufacturer's directions, and close the lid. When smoke appears, place the pan over *indirect medium-low heat*, close the lid, and cook for 1½ hours, draining and adding the remaining wood chips after 45 minutes. If you're using a charcoal grill, replenish the charcoal as needed to maintain a steady temperature. After 1½ hours, cover the pan tightly with aluminum foil and continue cooking until an instant-read thermometer inserted into the thickest part of the roast (not touching the bone) registers 190°F, 1 to 1½ hours more. Remove from the grill, cover, and let rest for 15 to 30 minutes. Save the pan juices. Toast the rolls, cut side down, over direct heat for about 1 minute.

4. Combine the guacamole ingredients and roughly mash with a fork. Season with salt. Cut the meat across the grain into thin slices. Skim the fat from the pan juices. Build the tortas on rolls with lettuce, tomato, onion, jalapeño slices, pork, pan juices, and guacamole. Serve warm.

PORK

151

APPLE-SMOKED PULLED PORK SANDWICHES

SERVES: 10–12 | PREP TIME: 30 minutes | GRILLING TIME: 6–7 hours

SPECIAL EQUIPMENT: 6 large handfuls apple wood chips, 1 large disposable foil pan (2 if you're using a charcoal grill), instant-read thermometer

RUB

- 1 tablespoon packed dark brown sugar
- 1 tablespoon kosher salt
- 2 teaspoons paprika
- 1 teaspoon granulated garlic
- 1 teaspoon prepared chili powder
- 1 teaspoon chipotle chile powder

- 1 bone-in pork shoulder roast (Boston butt), 5½–6 pounds, trimmed of excess fat

SAUCE

- 1 tablespoon unsalted butter
- ½ cup minced yellow onion
- 1 cup ketchup
- 1 cup unsweetened apple juice
- ½ cup cider vinegar
- 2 tablespoons packed dark brown sugar
- 1 tablespoon unsulfured molasses
- 1 tablespoon soy sauce
- ½ teaspoon hot pepper sauce, or to taste

SLAW

- ⅓ cup mayonnaise
- 3 tablespoons sour cream
- 2 tablespoons cider vinegar
- 1 tablespoon granulated sugar
- ¾ teaspoon kosher salt
- ¼ teaspoon freshly ground black pepper
- ½ medium head green cabbage, thinly sliced (about 4 cups)
- 2 medium carrots, peeled, coarsely grated (about 1 cup)

- 12 hamburger buns, split

1. Soak the wood chips in water for at least 30 minutes.

2. Combine the rub ingredients. Coat the surface of the roast evenly with the rub. Allow the roast to stand at room temperature for 30 minutes before grilling.

3. Prepare the grill for indirect cooking over very low heat (250° to 300°F). If you're using a charcoal grill, make sure the charcoal covers no more than one-third of the charcoal grate. Place a large disposable foil pan on the empty side of the charcoal grate. Fill the pan about halfway with warm water.

4. Drain and add two handfuls of the wood chips to the charcoal or to the smoker box of a gas grill, following manufacturer's instructions, and close the lid. When the wood begins to smoke, cook the roast, fat side up, over *indirect very low heat*, with the lid closed, for 4 hours. Drain and add one handful of the wood chips to the charcoal or to the smoker box every 45 minutes to 1 hour until they are gone. If you're using a charcoal grill, replenish the charcoal as needed to maintain a steady temperature, adding about 8 unlit briquettes every 45 minutes to 1 hour. Leave the lid off the grill for about 5 minutes to help the new briquettes light.

5. After 4 hours, use an instant-read thermometer to check the internal temperature of the roast. If it has not reached 160°F, continue cooking until it does. If it has reached 160°F, place the roast in a large disposable foil pan and cover tightly with aluminum foil. Return the pan to the grill and cook over *indirect very low heat*, with the lid closed, until the internal temperature in the thickest part of the roast (not touching the bone) registers 190°F, 2 to 3 hours more. Remove from the grill and let rest, in the covered foil pan, for 1 hour. While the roast rests, make the sauce.

6. In a large saucepan over medium heat, melt the butter. Add the onion and cook until softened, 5 to 6 minutes, stirring occasionally. Whisk in the remaining sauce ingredients, bring to a simmer, reduce the heat to medium-low, and cook until slightly thickened, 10 to 15 minutes, stirring occasionally. Remove from the heat.

7. In a large bowl whisk the mayonnaise, sour cream, vinegar, sugar, salt, and pepper until smooth. Add the cabbage and the carrots. Mix until the vegetables are evenly coated.

8. When the roast is cool enough to handle, pull the meat apart into shreds. Discard any large pieces of fat and sinew. In a large saucepan over low heat, moisten the pork with as much of the sauce as you like, and cook until warmed through, stirring occasionally. Pile the pork on buns and top with coleslaw. Serve with any additional sauce.

SERVES: 8 | PREP TIME: 20 minutes | MARINATING TIME: 12–24 hours | GRILLING TIME: 4–5 hours

SPECIAL EQUIPMENT: large disposable foil pan, instant-read thermometer

MARINADE

- 2 cans (each 12 ounces) cola (not diet)
- 1 medium yellow onion, thinly sliced
- 2 lemons, peel and pith removed, cut crosswise into ¼-inch slices
- ½ cup low-sodium soy sauce
- ⅓ cup packed golden brown sugar
- 3 garlic cloves, coarsely chopped
- 3 cinnamon sticks, each about 2 inches long
- 1 canned chipotle chile pepper in adobo sauce, coarsely chopped
- 1 tablespoon dried oregano

- 1 bone-in pork shoulder roast (Boston butt), 5–6 pounds, trimmed of excess fat

1. In a large bowl combine the marinade ingredients and stir until the sugar is dissolved. Score the fat on the roast in a crosshatch pattern, cutting slashes through the fat just to the flesh about 2 inches apart. Place the roast in the bowl with the marinade and turn to coat. Cover and refrigerate for 12 to 24 hours, turning occasionally. Allow the roast to stand at room temperature for 1 hour before grilling.

2. Prepare the grill for indirect cooking over low heat (250° to 350°F).

3. Place the roast, fat side down, in a large disposable foil pan. Pour the marinade and the solids over the roast. Grill over *indirect low heat*, with the lid closed, until an instant-read thermometer inserted into the thickest part of the roast (not touching the bone) registers 190°F, 4 to 5 hours, turning once after 1½ hours. Remove the roast and the pan from the grill.

4. Transfer the roast to a platter, cover loosely with aluminum foil, and let rest for 20 minutes. Discard the marinade. Cut the roast into ½-inch slices. Serve warm.

SERVES: 6–8 | PREP TIME: 25 minutes | GRILLING TIME: 5–6 hours

SPECIAL EQUIPMENT: 4 large handfuls hickory wood chips, instant-read thermometer

1   bone-in pork shoulder roast (Boston butt), 4–5 pounds
1   tablespoon kosher salt
1   teaspoon freshly ground black pepper

SAUCE
1   tablespoon vegetable oil
1   teaspoon toasted sesame oil
1   tablespoon peeled, grated fresh ginger
3   garlic cloves, minced or pushed through a press
½   cup hoisin sauce
1   tablespoon low-sodium soy sauce
2   tablespoons dry sherry
2   teaspoons hot chili-garlic sauce, such as Sriracha
3   scallions, ends trimmed, thinly sliced, divided
½   teaspoon finely grated orange zest

4   cups cooked white rice
3   tablespoons roughly chopped fresh cilantro leaves

1. Soak the wood chips in water for at least 30 minutes. Trim the roast of excess fat and season with the salt and pepper. Cover and allow the roast to stand at room temperature for 30 minutes.

2. Prepare the grill for indirect cooking over low heat (250° to 350°F). Keep the grill's temperature as close to 300°F as possible.

3. Drain and add half of the wood chips to the charcoal or to the smoker box of a gas grill, and close the lid. When the wood begins to smoke, cook the roast, fat side up, over *indirect low heat*, with the lid closed, for 1 hour. Drain and add the remaining wood chips after 30 minutes of cooking time. Continue cooking until an instant-read thermometer inserted into the thickest part of the roast (not touching the bone) registers 190°F, 4 to 5 hours more. If you're using a charcoal grill, replenish the charcoal as needed to maintain a steady temperature. Transfer the roast to a cutting board, cover loosely with foil, and let rest for about 20 minutes.

4. In a saucepan over medium heat, warm the oils. Add the ginger and the garlic and cook until fragrant and just starting to brown, about 1 minute. Stir in the hoisin, soy sauce, sherry, and chili-garlic sauce, reduce the heat to medium, and cook until warm, 2 to 3 minutes, stirring occasionally. Remove from the heat and stir in half the scallions and the orange zest. Pull the pork apart into shreds, discarding any large pieces of fat. Combine the pork and the sauce and toss to moisten. Serve warm, spooned over the rice and topped with the remaining scallions and the cilantro.

SERVES: 4 | PREP TIME: 10 minutes | GRILLING TIME: 3–5 minutes

SPECIAL EQUIPMENT: grill-proof griddle, cast-iron grill press (optional)

- 4 soft French rolls, each about 6 inches long, split
- ¼ cup Dijon mustard
- 8 slices Black Forest ham, each about ⅛ inch thick
- 4 ounces Brie cheese, cut into 8 pieces, each about ¼ inch thick
- 1 large ripe pear or apple, cored and cut lengthwise into 8 slices
- 4 crisp leaves romaine lettuce
- ¼ cup (½ stick) unsalted butter, melted

Tip

You will need something to flatten these sandwiches as they grill. A cast-iron skillet is too big and might slide off. You are better off using a small, cast-iron grill press or a sturdy spatula to press straight down on each sandwich one at a time.

1. Prepare the grill for direct cooking over medium heat (350° to 450°F) and preheat a grill-proof griddle for about 10 minutes.

2. Spread the cut side of the rolls with the mustard. Top the bottom half of each roll with two ham slices, two cheese slices, two pear slices, a lettuce leaf, and the top half of the roll. Press down on each sandwich so it is compacted. Brush the sandwiches on both sides with the melted butter.

3. Place the sandwiches on the griddle over *direct medium heat* and press them down, one at a time, with a grill press or a wide, sturdy spatula. Grill until the rolls are toasted and golden and the cheese is melted, 3 to 5 minutes, turning once and pressing them flat after turning. Remove from the grill and serve right away.

SMOKY MARMALADE-GLAZED HAM
WITH ORANGE-DILL SAUCE

SERVES: 8–10 | PREP TIME: 20 minutes | GRILLING TIME: 1¾–2½ hours

SPECIAL EQUIPMENT: large disposable foil pan, instant-read thermometer

1   bone-in smoked ham, butt end, 6–7 pounds

GLAZE
⅓   cup whole-grain mustard
⅓   cup orange marmalade
2   tablespoons fresh lime juice
½   teaspoon freshly ground black pepper

SAUCE
⅔   cup mayonnaise
⅔   cup sour cream
¼   cup prepared horseradish
    Finely grated zest and ¼ cup juice of 2 oranges
2   tablespoons minced fresh dill
1   teaspoon white wine vinegar
½   teaspoon kosher salt
¼   teaspoon freshly ground black pepper

1. Allow the ham to stand at room temperature for 30 to 40 minutes before grilling.

2. Prepare the grill for indirect cooking over medium heat (350° to 450°F).

3. Combine the glaze ingredients. Score the ham in a large crisscross pattern about ½ inch deep on all sides, except the cut side, and place it cut side down in a large disposable foil pan. Brush half of the glaze on the top and sides of the ham. Grill over *indirect medium heat*, with the lid closed, for 1 hour. Baste with the remaining glaze and continue grilling until an instant-read thermometer inserted into the thickest part of the ham (not touching the bone) registers 160°F, 45 minutes to 1½ hours more. If the glaze gets too dark, cover the ham loosely with aluminum foil for the remainder of the grilling time. Remove from the grill, tent loosely with foil, and let rest for 15 to 45 minutes.

4. In a nonreactive bowl whisk the sauce ingredients. Carve the ham and serve warm with the sauce.

By scoring a ham, you expose more of the rind to the heat and develop gloriously sweet, crispy edges where the glaze has seeped into the creases.

PORK

157

grill SKILLS:
PERFECT RIBS

Cracking the Code

If you ask ten barbecue fanatics about the features that add up to perfect ribs, you will get about ten different (and probably legitimate) answers. Ribs are that personal. Having said that, most of us agree on some basic elements. The meat itself should be so tender and moist that when you take a bite, it pulls clean off the bone. The seasonings should be a complementary mélange of hot, sweet, savory, and salty, and no flavor should stick out from the crowd. The smoke from whatever kind of wood you like should blend into the meat as an ethereal background flavor. The sauce can vary from the sweet, smoky, tomato-based style of Missouri to the tangy, mustardy style of South Carolina to the spicy, chile-laced style of New Mexico—but no sauce should ever smother the nuances of the meat underneath it. In the end, if you can get the meat, spices, smoke, and sauce to play together nicely, you are well on your way to perfecting ribs.

Removing the Membrane

For the meat to be tender, you need to remove the tough membrane first. Slide a dull knife under the membrane and along a bone far enough that you can pry an edge of the membrane loose.

Then grab the loose edge and peel off the membrane in one big sheet or a few smaller pieces. You can use a paper towel if the membrane is hard to grip.

Season, Smoke, Mop, and Sauce

1 Season the racks generously, especially on the meaty side. Then let the racks stand at room temperature for 45 minutes so that they are not too cold going onto the grill.

2 If you stand them upright in a rib rack, you can cook twice as many racks in the same amount of space.

3 Create a small pile of charcoal to one side of the grill and feed it with more charcoal about once an hour (more often during cold or windy weather). A foil pan filled with water will help to maintain a steady temperature.

4 Once an hour, add a couple dry wood chunks or a couple handfuls of soaked and drained wood chips to the coals to maintain a steady stream of smoke during the first half of the cooking time.

5 Occasionally baste the ribs with a seasoned liquid called a "mop." Something as simple as apple juice with a little cider vinegar will moisten any areas that are drying out.

6 Barbecue sauce should not go on until the final 20 to 30 minutes of cooking; otherwise, the sugar in the sauce is likely to burn. Brush it on lightly—it should glaze the meat, not drown it.

7 For really tender ribs, glaze each rack with some sauce or mop, and wrap it in heavy-duty aluminum foil. Return each rack over indirect heat for the final 30 minutes to 1 hour of cooking time.

When Is It Done?

You will know you have reached perfect tenderness when each rack passes the bend test.

When you lift a rack at one end, bone side up, and the rack bends so easily in the middle that the meat tears open, the ribs are done.

KANSAS CITY PIT MASTER BABY BACK RIBS

SERVES: 6-8 | PREP TIME: 30 minutes | GRILLING TIME: 2¾-3 hours

SPECIAL EQUIPMENT: rib rack, 4 large handfuls hickory wood chips, large disposable foil pan (if you're using a charcoal grill), basting mop or brush

RUB
2	tablespoons paprika
1½	tablespoons packed dark brown sugar
1	tablespoon prepared chili powder
1	tablespoon granulated garlic
1	tablespoon kosher salt
1½	teaspoons onion powder
1½	teaspoons freshly ground black pepper
½	teaspoon ground thyme
½	teaspoon ground cayenne pepper

4 racks baby back ribs, each 2½-3 pounds

SAUCE
1	cup ketchup
⅔	cup unsweetened apple juice
⅓	cup cider vinegar
2	tablespoons packed dark brown sugar
2	tablespoons unsulfured molasses
1	tablespoon Worcestershire sauce
1	teaspoon prepared chili powder
1	teaspoon smoked paprika
½	teaspoon ground cumin
¼	teaspoon freshly ground black pepper

MOP
1	cup unsweetened apple juice
6	tablespoons sauce (from above)
¼	cup cider vinegar

1. Mix the rub ingredients. Using a dull knife, slide the tip under the membrane covering the back of each rack of ribs. Lift and loosen the membrane until you can pry it up, then grab a corner of it with a paper towel and pull it off. Season the racks evenly with the rub. Arrange the racks in a rib rack, standing each rack to face in the same direction. Allow the racks to stand at room temperature for 45 minutes before grilling.

2. Soak the wood chips in water for at least 30 minutes.

3. Prepare the grill for indirect cooking over low heat (300° to 350°F). If you're using a charcoal grill, make sure the charcoal covers no more than one-third of the charcoal grate. Place a large disposable foil pan on the empty side of the charcoal grate. Fill the pan about halfway with warm water.

4. Drain and add half of the wood chips to the charcoal or to the smoker box of a gas grill, following manufacturer's instructions, and close the lid. When smoke appears, place the racks over *indirect low heat*, close the lid, and cook for 1 hour. Maintain the temperature of the grill between 300° and 350°F. If you're using a charcoal grill, place the racks in the rib rack over the foil pan as far from the charcoal as possible, with the bone side facing toward the charcoal. Close the vent in the top lid about halfway.

5. In a saucepan combine the sauce ingredients. Bring to a simmer over medium heat and cook until slightly thickened, about 15 minutes, stirring occasionally. Remove from the heat.

6. Whisk the mop ingredients. After the first hour of cooking, drain and add the remaining wood chips to the charcoal or to the smoker box. If you're using a charcoal grill, replenish the charcoal as needed to maintain a steady temperature, adding about 8 unlit briquettes every 45 minutes to 1 hour. Leave the lid off the grill for about 5 minutes to help the new briquettes light. Lightly brush the racks with the mop, particularly the areas looking a little dry. Close the lid and cook for a second hour. Maintain the temperature of the grill between 300° and 350°F.

7. After the second hour of cooking, remove the racks from the rib rack, close the grill lid, and brush the racks thoroughly with the remaining mop. Put the racks back in the rib rack, again all facing the same direction, but this time turned over so that the ends that were facing down earlier now face up. Also position any racks that appear to be cooking faster than the others toward the back of the rib rack, farthest from the heat. Cook for another 30 minutes.

8. After 2½ hours, the meat will shrink back from most of the bones by ¼ inch or more. If it has not, continue to cook until it does. Then remove the rib rack from the grill. Close the lid to maintain the heat. Remove the racks from the rib rack and lightly brush each rack on both sides with some of the sauce.

9. Return the racks to the grill over *indirect low heat*. At this point you can pile the racks on top of one another. Continue to cook over *indirect low heat*, with the lid closed, until tender and succulent, 15 to 30 minutes. They are done when you lift a rack at one end with tongs, bone side up, and the rack bends so much in the middle that the meat tears easily. If the meat does not tear easily, continue to cook until it does. Remove from the grill and let rest for 5 to 10 minutes. Just before serving, lightly brush the racks with sauce again. Cut the racks into individual ribs and serve warm with any extra sauce on the side.

1 The first step toward tender ribs is peeling off the tough membrane on the back of each rack.

2 Another step toward serious flavor is a spice rub that strikes a balance with salt, sugar, chili powder, and herbs.

3 Your next priority should be a steady, low temperature between 300° and 350°F, the lower the better.

4 Brushing the ribs with a tangy mop is a brilliant way of keeping them moist and adding another layer of flavor.

HONEY- AND LIME-GLAZED BABY BACK RIBS

SERVES: 4 | PREP TIME: 15 minutes | MARINATING TIME: 4–6 hours | GRILLING TIME: 2¼–2½ hours

SPECIAL EQUIPMENT: 18-inch-wide heavy-duty aluminum foil

MARINADE

- ⅔ cup peanut or vegetable oil
- ¼ cup plus 2 tablespoons low-sodium soy sauce
- ¼ cup fresh lime juice
- 2 tablespoons grated lemon zest
- 2 tablespoons minced garlic
- 2 tablespoons Vietnamese or Thai fish sauce
- 2 tablespoons honey
- 2 teaspoons freshly ground black pepper

- 2 racks baby back ribs, each 1½–2 pounds, membrane removed (see page 158)
- 2 limes, cut into wedges
- 2 tablespoons chopped fresh basil leaves

1. Whisk the marinade ingredients. Place the racks on a rimmed sheet pan and pour the marinade over the racks. Turn to coat both sides. Cover and refrigerate for 4 to 6 hours, turning occasionally. Allow the racks to stand at room temperature for 45 minutes before grilling.

2. Prepare the grill for indirect cooking over low heat (250° to 350°F).

3. Remove the racks from the sheet pan and pour the marinade into a small saucepan. Bring to a boil and then reduce the heat to maintain a simmer. Cook for 2 minutes, stirring occasionally. Remove from the heat.

4. Wrap each rack in a sheet of heavy-duty aluminum foil, crimping the seams well. Grill the foil-wrapped racks, bone side down, over *indirect low heat*, with the lid closed, for 1¼ hours. Remove from the grill and let rest for about 10 minutes. When the packets are cool enough to handle, open them and pour any accumulated juices into the reduced marinade. Skim off the excess fat from the marinade. Return the ribs to the grill, meaty side down, and baste with the marinade. Cook over *indirect low heat*, with the lid closed, for 15 minutes. Turn the ribs over and cook until the meat has shrunk back from the ends of most of the bones by ¼ inch or more, 45 minutes to 1 hour, basting occasionally. The ribs are done when you lift a rack at one end with tongs, bone side up, and the rack bends so much in the middle that the meat tears easily. Remove from the grill and let rest for 5 to 10 minutes. Serve with lime wedges and top with the basil.

JERK-SPICED BABY BACK RIBS
WITH DARK RUM–PINEAPPLE SALSA

SERVES: 4 | PREP TIME: 20 minutes | MARINATING TIME: 3–4 hours | GRILLING TIME: 2½–3 hours

PASTE

½	cup roughly chopped white onion
1–2	serrano chile peppers, seeded
3	scallions, ends trimmed, roughly chopped
2	tablespoons extra-virgin olive oil
2	tablespoons fresh lime juice
2	tablespoons granulated sugar
6	garlic cloves, chopped
1	tablespoon ground allspice
1	teaspoon dried thyme
¾	teaspoon freshly ground black pepper

Kosher salt

2 racks baby back ribs, each 1¾–2¼ pounds, membrane removed (see page 158)

SALSA

2	cups finely diced fresh pineapple (about 12 ounces)
¼	cup finely diced red bell pepper
¼	cup finely diced white onion
2	tablespoons roughly chopped fresh cilantro leaves
½	teaspoon hot pepper sauce, or to taste
1	tablespoon fresh lime juice
1	tablespoon dark or spiced rum

1. In a food processor combine the paste ingredients, including 1½ teaspoons salt, and process until fairly smooth. Spread the paste all over the racks. Cover and refrigerate for 3 to 4 hours, turning occasionally. Allow the ribs to stand at room temperature for 45 minutes before grilling.

2. Prepare the grill for indirect cooking over low heat (250° to 350°F).

3. In a nonreactive bowl combine the salsa ingredients, including 1 teaspoon salt. Cover and refrigerate until just before serving.

4. Season the racks evenly with salt. Grill, bone side down first, over *indirect low heat*, with the lid closed, for 2½ to 3 hours, turning the racks over, rotating them, and switching their positions about every 40 minutes so that both sides of each rack spend the same amount of time closest to the heat. Also, baste them occasionally with water to keep the surface moist. The ribs are done when the meat has shrunk back from the ends of most of the bones by ¼ inch or more. Lift a rack by picking up one end with tongs. It should bend in the middle and the meat should tear easily. If the meat does not tear easily, continue to cook until it does, up to 1 hour more. Transfer to a platter and let rest for 5 to 10 minutes. Stir the lime juice and rum into the salsa. Cut each rack into individual ribs and serve with the salsa.

BABY BACK RIBS
WITH SPICY RUB AND MOLASSES BARBECUE SAUCE

SERVES: 4 | PREP TIME: 20 minutes | GRILLING TIME: 3¼–4¼ hours

RUB

- 2 tablespoons packed golden brown sugar
- 1 tablespoon kosher salt
- 2 teaspoons chipotle chile powder
- 2 teaspoons garlic powder
- 1 teaspoon prepared chili powder
- 1 teaspoon ground cayenne pepper
- 1 teaspoon freshly ground black pepper

- 2 racks baby back ribs, each 2–2½ pounds

SAUCE

- 2 tablespoons unsalted butter
- 1 yellow onion, 7–8 ounces, finely chopped
- 1 cup ketchup
- ¾ cup light molasses (not blackstrap)
- ½ cup beer, preferably lager
- ¼ cup cider vinegar
- 3 tablespoons tomato paste
- 1½ teaspoons mustard powder
- 1 teaspoon garlic powder

- 1 cup beer, preferably lager

1. Combine the rub ingredients. Using a dull knife, slide the tip under the membrane covering the back of each rack of ribs. Lift and loosen the membrane until you can pry it up, then grab a corner of it with a paper towel and pull it off. Season the racks all over with the rub, and allow them to stand at room temperature for 45 minutes before grilling.

2. Prepare the grill for indirect cooking over low heat (250° to 350°F).

3. Meanwhile, in a saucepan over medium-high heat, melt the butter. Add the onion and cook until slightly softened, 3 to 4 minutes, stirring occasionally. Stir in the remaining sauce ingredients and bring to a boil. Reduce the heat to medium-low and simmer, uncovered, until thickened, for 18 to 20 minutes. Remove from the heat.

4. Place the racks, bone side down, over *indirect low heat*, as far from the heat as possible, close the lid, and cook for 3 hours. After the first hour, baste the racks with beer, particularly any areas that are looking a little dry. Continue to baste with beer every hour or so. After 3 hours, check to see if one or both racks are ready to come off the grill. They are done when the meat has shrunk back from the ends of most of the bones by ¼ inch or more. Lift a rack by picking up one end with tongs. It should bend in the middle and the meat should tear easily. If the meat does not tear easily, return the racks to the grill, close the lid, and continue cooking for up to 1 hour more.

5. Remove the racks from the grill and lightly brush them on both sides with some of the sauce. Return the racks to the grill and cook over *indirect low heat*, with the lid closed, until the surface is slightly crispy, 10 to 20 minutes, turning occasionally. Remove from the grill and let rest for 5 to 10 minutes. Cut the racks between the bones into individual ribs and serve warm with the remaining sauce.

SPARERIBS
WITH HONEY-ORANGE GLAZE

SERVES: 4 | PREP TIME: 15 minutes | GRILLING TIME: about 1½ hours

SPECIAL EQUIPMENT: 1 large handful hickory wood chips, 18-inch-wide heavy-duty aluminum foil

GLAZE
½ cup honey
2 tablespoons frozen orange juice concentrate, thawed
1 tablespoon balsamic vinegar

RUB
1 tablespoon kosher salt
2 teaspoons ancho chile powder
2 teaspoons ground cumin
2 teaspoons dried oregano
1 teaspoon freshly ground black pepper

2 racks St. Louis–style spareribs, each 3–3½ pounds, membrane removed (see page 158)

1. Soak the wood chips in water for at least 30 minutes.

2. Prepare the grill for direct cooking over medium heat (350° to 450°F).

3. Whisk the glaze ingredients.

4. Combine the rub ingredients. Cut each rack in half to create two smaller racks. Season the racks evenly with the rub. Using eight 18-by-24-inch sheets of heavy-duty aluminum foil, double wrap each half rack in its own packet and seal tightly. Place the foil-wrapped racks on the grill over *direct medium heat*, close the lid, and cook for 1¼ hours, turning the packets over once or twice for even cooking, making sure not to pierce the foil. If you're using a charcoal grill, replenish the charcoal as needed to maintain a steady temperature. Remove the packets from the grill and let rest for about 10 minutes. Carefully open the packets, remove the racks, and discard the rendered fat and foil.

5. Drain and add the wood chips to the charcoal or to the smoker box of a gas grill, following manufacturer's instructions, and close the lid. When the wood begins to smoke, return the racks to the grill. Cook over *direct medium heat*, with the lid closed, until the racks are sizzling, about 5 minutes, turning once or twice. Brush both sides with the glaze and cook until the racks are shiny and slightly crispy, about 5 minutes more, turning once or twice and applying more glaze after each turn. Remove from the grill and let rest for 5 to 10 minutes. Serve warm.

SERVES: 4 | PREP TIME: 20 minutes | GRILLING TIME: about 3½ hours

SPECIAL EQUIPMENT: 18-inch-wide heavy-duty aluminum foil

RUB

- 3 tablespoons packed golden brown sugar
- 2 teaspoons freshly ground black pepper
- 1 teaspoon ground ginger
- ½ teaspoon mustard powder
- ½ teaspoon Chinese five spice

    Kosher salt
- 2 racks St. Louis–style spareribs, each 3–3½ pounds, membrane removed (see page 158)
- 2 teaspoons toasted sesame oil
- 1 tablespoon peeled, grated fresh ginger
- 3 garlic cloves, minced or pushed through a press
- ½ cup apricot preserves
- 3 tablespoons low-sodium soy sauce

1. Prepare the grill for indirect and direct cooking over low heat (250° to 300°F).

2. Combine the rub ingredients, including ¾ teaspoon salt. Season the racks all over with the rub, putting more of the rub on the meaty side. Allow the racks to stand at room temperature for 45 minutes before grilling.

3. Grill the racks, bone side down, over *indirect low heat*, with the lid closed, for 2 hours. Meanwhile, in a saucepan over medium-high heat, warm the oil. Add the ginger and the garlic and cook until fragrant and just starting to brown, about 1 minute, stirring often. Stir in ¾ teaspoon salt, the preserves, and the soy sauce. Bring to a boil and cook until slightly thickened, 2 to 3 minutes, stirring occasionally. Remove from the heat.

4. Remove the racks from the grill and brush both sides with three-fourths of the apricot-soy glaze. Wrap each rack in heavy-duty aluminum foil. Return the foil-wrapped racks to the grill and continue cooking over *indirect low heat*, with the lid closed, until the meat has shrunk back from the ends of most of the bones at least ¼ inch or more in several places and the meat tears easily when you lift each rack, about 1½ hours more. Remove from the grill and let rest until cool enough to handle. Carefully remove the racks from the foil and discard the rendered fat and foil. Brush the racks with the remaining glaze, return to the grill over *direct low heat*, close the lid, and cook until they are lightly charred, about 5 minutes, turning occasionally. Remove from the grill and let rest for 5 to 10 minutes. Serve warm.

6

POULTRY

GRILLING POULTRY

CUT	THICKNESS / WEIGHT	APPROXIMATE GRILLING TIME
Chicken breast, bone-in	10–12 ounces	**23–35 minutes:** 3–5 minutes direct medium heat, 20–30 minutes indirect medium heat
Chicken breast, boneless, skinless	6–8 ounces	**8–12 minutes** direct medium heat
Chicken drumstick	3–4 ounces	**26–40 minutes:** 6–10 minutes direct medium heat, 20–30 minutes indirect medium heat
Chicken thigh, bone-in	5–6 ounces	**36–40 minutes:** 6–10 minutes direct medium heat, 30 minutes indirect medium heat
Chicken thigh, boneless, skinless	4 ounces	**8–10 minutes** direct medium heat
Chicken thigh, ground	¾ inch thick	**12–14 minutes** direct medium heat
Chicken, whole	4–5 pounds	**1¼–1½ hours** indirect medium heat
Chicken, whole leg	10–12 ounces	**48 minutes–1 hour:** 40–50 minutes indirect medium heat, 8–10 minutes direct medium heat
Chicken wing	2–3 ounces	**35–43 minutes:** 30–35 minutes indirect medium heat, 5–8 minutes direct medium heat
Cornish game hen	1½–2 pounds	**50 minutes–1 hour** indirect high heat
Duck breast, boneless	10–12 ounces	**9–12 minutes:** 3–4 minutes direct low heat, 6–8 minutes indirect high heat
Duck, whole	5½–6 pounds	**40 minutes** indirect high heat
Turkey breast, boneless	2½ pounds	**1–1¼ hours** indirect medium heat
Turkey, whole, not stuffed	10–12 pounds	**2½–3½ hours** indirect medium-low heat

The cuts, thicknesses, weights, and grilling times are meant to be guidelines rather than hard and fast rules. Cooking times are affected by such factors as altitude, wind, and outside temperature. Cooking times are for the USDA's recommendation of 165°F. Let whole poultry rest for 10 to 15 minutes before carving. The internal temperature of the meat will rise 5 to 10 degrees during this time.

grill SKILLS:
PERFECT CHICKEN PARTS

Choose Wisely

Most chicken parts these days are mass-produced for the lowest cost possible. With the help of a lively mix of spices or an interesting marinade, along with some solid grilling technique, these conventional parts can be good. If, however, you are willing to spend more for organic, free-range chicken parts, you will appreciate an obvious difference. When chickens are fed a diet free of artificial ingredients and growth-promoting antibiotics, and when they are able to run and forage in the great outdoors, they have a cleaner, more pronounced chicken flavor and their texture is firm without being tough.

The darker meat on the left comes from an organic, free-range chicken with pure, natural flavors. Whenever you see chicken like the paler breast on the right, with thin white lines, you are looking at a conventional chicken that will be relatively bland and a little chewier.

Every Minute Counts

When you take the bones away from a chicken, especially the breasts, and expose that lean meat to the grill, there is a matter of only a couple of minutes between underdone and overcooked. The precise timing depends on the heat of the grill and the thickness of each breast, so you must pay close attention to those details. With direct medium heat (about 400°F), the thin breast on the left will be fully cooked in about eight minutes, but the thicker breast on the right will require at least ten minutes, and maybe twelve, to cook all the

Cutting Up a Whole Chicken

Using a sharp knife, cut off each wing at the second joint.

Leave the rest of each wing attached to the breast.

Run your knife down the middle of the breast to divide it.

This technique will give you six meaty pieces.

Cut through the skin between each leg and the rest of the body.

Bend each leg to expose the thigh joint, and cut through it.

The Bones Matter

Boneless chicken pieces are thin enough that you can grill them entirely over direct heat, but when bones are involved, the parts take longer to cook, so it is important to use both direct and indirect heat. Otherwise the surface will burn to a crisp before the meat at the bones has lost its pink color.

Cut off the part of the rib cage below the breast on each side.

Finish each cut just below the remaining part of each wing.

You can start grilling bone-in parts over direct heat to brown the outer surfaces and then finish the parts over indirect heat, or you can start the parts slowly over indirect heat and finish them over direct heat for a final crisping of the skin. Either way works, though it is usually safest to begin the cooking over indirect heat. That way you are less likely to experience flare-ups, because some fat will render out of the skin before you set the parts right over the flames.

When Is It Done?

Check the thigh meat by inserting the probe of an instant-read thermometer into the thickest part (but not touching the bone). If you don't have a thermometer, cut into the center of the meat. The juices should run clear and the meat should no longer be pink at the bone.

Make a shallow cut at the top of the rib cage.

Bend the chicken with both hands to crack the rib cage.

CHICKEN BREASTS ON SWISS CHARD
WITH WARM BACON DRESSING

SERVES: 4 | PREP TIME: 45 minutes | GRILLING TIME: 8–12 minutes

1 pound red Swiss chard
4 boneless, skinless chicken breast halves,
  each about 6 ounces
  Extra-virgin olive oil
2½ tablespoons finely chopped fresh thyme
  leaves, divided
  Kosher salt
  Freshly ground black pepper
4 slices apple wood smoked bacon, cut crosswise
  into ⅓-inch strips
3 tablespoons sherry vinegar, divided
½ cup low-sodium chicken broth
1 tablespoon Dijon mustard
3 large shallots, thinly sliced (about 1 cup)
3 large garlic cloves, thinly sliced

1. Cut the thick center ribs from the chard and finely chop them. Roughly chop the leaves and set them aside separately. You should have about 10 cups of packed leaves and about 1 cup of chopped center ribs.

2. Prepare the grill for direct cooking over medium heat (350° to 450°F).

3. Lightly brush the chicken breasts on both sides with 1 tablespoon oil and season evenly with 1½ tablespoons of the thyme, 1 teaspoon salt, and ¾ teaspoon pepper.

4. To make the dressing: In a medium skillet over medium-high heat, cook the bacon until crisp, 8 to 10 minutes, stirring occasionally. Using a slotted spoon, transfer the bacon to paper towels to drain. Add 1 tablespoon oil to the skillet with the bacon drippings and warm over medium heat. Carefully add 2 tablespoons of the vinegar, the remaining 1 tablespoon thyme, ¼ teaspoon salt, and ¼ teaspoon pepper (it will bubble vigorously) and cook for 30 seconds, stirring constantly. Remove the skillet from the heat.

5. Grill the chicken, smooth (skin) side down first, over *direct medium heat*, with the lid closed, until the meat is firm to the touch and opaque all the way to the center, 8 to 12 minutes, turning once or twice.

6. Meanwhile, in a small bowl whisk the chicken broth, the remaining 1 tablespoon vinegar, and the mustard. In a large, deep skillet over medium-high heat, warm 2 tablespoons oil. Add the shallots and sauté until tender and golden, 3 to 4 minutes. Add the garlic and the chard center ribs and cook for 2 minutes, stirring occasionally. Increase the heat to high, add the chard leaves, and toss with tongs until just wilted, about 2 minutes. Stir in the broth-mustard mixture and toss until the liquid is almost evaporated but the chard is still bright green, 2 to 4 minutes longer. Season with salt and pepper.

7. Remove the chicken from the grill and let rest for 3 to 5 minutes. Divide the chard among four plates and top each with a chicken breast. Return the skillet with the dressing over medium heat. Add the bacon and warm through, about 1 minute. Spoon the dressing over the chicken and serve warm.

MARINATED CHICKEN
WITH GREEN OLIVE AND CAPER VINAIGRETTE

SERVES: 4 | PREP TIME: 15 minutes | MARINATING TIME: 1–2 hours | GRILLING TIME: 8–12 minutes

VINAIGRETTE

- 3 tablespoons red wine vinegar
- 1 tablespoon finely chopped shallot
- 2 teaspoons finely chopped fresh rosemary leaves
- 1 teaspoon kosher salt
- 1 medium garlic clove, finely chopped
- ¼ teaspoon crushed red pepper flakes
- ⅔ cup extra-virgin olive oil

- 4 boneless, skinless chicken breast halves, each about 6 ounces
- ⅓ cup chopped green olives
- 2 tablespoons capers, rinsed and drained

1. Whisk all the vinaigrette ingredients except the oil. Add the oil in a steady stream, whisking constantly to emulsify. Pour half of the vinaigrette into a 13-by-9-inch glass or ceramic baking dish and reserve the remaining vinaigrette at room temperature for serving. Add the chicken breasts to the baking dish and turn to coat. Cover and refrigerate for at least 1 hour or up to 2 hours.

2. Prepare the grill for direct cooking over medium heat (350° to 450°F).

3. Remove the chicken from the dish, letting any excess vinaigrette drip back into the dish, and discard the vinaigrette. Grill the chicken, smooth (skin) side down first, over *direct medium heat*, with the lid closed, until the meat is firm to the touch and opaque all the way to the center, 8 to 12 minutes, turning once or twice. Remove from the grill and let rest for 3 to 5 minutes.

4. Stir the olives and the capers into the reserved vinaigrette. Serve each chicken breast with a spoonful of the vinaigrette on top.

SERVES: 4 | **PREP TIME:** 30 minutes | **GRILLING TIME:** 9–10 minutes

SPECIAL EQUIPMENT: 8 metal or bamboo skewers

½ teaspoon grated lime zest
½ teaspoon ground cumin, divided
　Kosher salt
　Freshly ground black pepper
4 boneless, skinless chicken breast halves, each about 6 ounces, cut into 1-inch cubes
1 slice yellow onion, about 1 inch thick, separated into rings, cut into 1-inch pieces
½ cup mayonnaise
2 teaspoons fresh lime juice
2 teaspoons minced canned chipotle chile pepper in adobo sauce

SALSA
2 large or 3 small Hass avocados, diced
2 medium plum tomatoes, seeded and finely diced
3 scallions (white and light green parts only), minced
2 tablespoons fresh lime juice
1 tablespoon minced fresh cilantro leaves
¼ teaspoon hot pepper sauce

　Extra-virgin olive oil
8 flour tortillas (8 inches)

1. If using bamboo skewers, soak in water for at least 30 minutes.

2. In a large bowl mix the lime zest, ¼ teaspoon of the cumin, ½ teaspoon salt, and ¼ teaspoon pepper. Place the chicken cubes and the onion pieces in the bowl with the seasonings and toss to combine; thread the chicken and the onion alternately onto skewers.

3. Prepare the grill for direct cooking over medium heat (350° to 450°F).

4. Whisk the mayonnaise, lime juice, chipotle chile, and the remaining ¼ teaspoon cumin. Stir in water, 1 teaspoon at a time, until the mixture reaches a thick drizzling consistency.

5. Combine the salsa ingredients, including ½ teaspoon salt.

6. Brush the skewers all over with oil and season with salt and pepper. Grill over *direct medium heat*, with the lid closed, until the meat is firm to the touch and opaque all the way to the center, about 8 minutes, turning once or twice. Remove from the grill and let rest for 2 to 3 minutes. Meanwhile, warm the tortillas over *direct medium heat*, with the lid open, for 1 to 2 minutes, turning once. Push the chicken and onion off the skewers onto tortillas and serve with chipotle mayo and salsa.

MOROCCAN-SPICED CHICKEN KABOBS
WITH LEMON YOGURT SAUCE

SERVES: 4 | PREP TIME: 30 minutes | MARINATING TIME: 4 hours | GRILLING TIME: 8–10 minutes

SPECIAL EQUIPMENT: metal or bamboo skewers

MARINADE

¼	cup extra-virgin olive oil
¼	cup chopped fresh cilantro leaves
¼	cup chopped fresh mint leaves
2	tablespoons fresh lemon juice
2	teaspoons honey
1½	teaspoons kosher salt
1	teaspoon paprika
1	teaspoon ground cumin
2	garlic cloves, minced or pushed through a press
½	teaspoon ground coriander
½	teaspoon ground cinnamon
¼	teaspoon ground cayenne pepper

4 boneless, skinless chicken breast halves, each about 6 ounces, cut into 1½-inch pieces

SAUCE

2	cups whole-milk Greek yogurt
1	teaspoon finely grated lemon zest
½	cup fresh lemon juice
¼	cup finely chopped fresh mint leaves
2	medium garlic cloves, minced or pushed through a press
1	teaspoon kosher salt

2 large bell peppers, 1 green and 1 red, each cut into 1½-inch squares
1 small red onion, cut into 8 wedges and separated into layers

1. Whisk the marinade ingredients. Pour ¼ cup of the marinade into a medium nonreactive bowl and reserve for the vegetables. Place the chicken pieces in a large, resealable plastic bag and pour in the marinade. Press the air out of the bag and seal tightly. Turn the bag to distribute the marinade, place in a bowl, and refrigerate for 4 hours, turning occasionally.

2. If using bamboo skewers, soak in water for at least 30 minutes.

3. Whisk the sauce ingredients. Cover and refrigerate until ready to serve.

4. Prepare the grill for direct cooking over medium heat (350° to 450°F).

5. Put the vegetables in the medium bowl with the reserved marinade, and turn to coat. Remove the chicken from the bag and discard the marinade. Remove the vegetables from the bowl. Thread the chicken, peppers, and onion alternately onto skewers.

6. Grill the kabobs over *direct medium heat*, with the lid closed, until the meat is firm to the touch and opaque all the way to the center, 8 to 10 minutes, turning once or twice. Remove from the grill and let rest for 2 to 3 minutes. Serve warm with the sauce.

To avoid soaking bamboo skewers each time you need them, soak a big batch once for an hour or so, drain them, and then freeze them in a plastic bag. When it's time to grill, pull out as many skewers as you need.

CHICKEN BREAST AND PECAN SALAD
WITH WHEAT BERRIES

SERVES: 4 | PREP TIME: 20 minutes, plus 1 hour for the wheat berries | MARINATING TIME: 2 hours | GRILLING TIME: 8–12 minutes

2   boneless, skinless chicken breast halves, each about 6 ounces
1   cup sweet pickle brine (from the jar of sweet gherkins)
⅔   cup wheat berries
1   cup finely chopped celery
⅔   cup chopped sweet gherkins
½   cup chopped pecans
½   cup mayonnaise
¼   cup cider vinegar
1   tablespoon chopped fresh dill *or* 1 teaspoon dried dill
1   teaspoon freshly ground black pepper
½   teaspoon kosher salt
¼   teaspoon celery seed
2   large tomatoes, cut crosswise into thick slices

Tip

If you don't want to cook the wheat berries yourself, look for cooked wheat berries at the salad bar of many large and gourmet supermarkets. You'll need about 1⅔ cups of cooked wheat berries for this recipe.

1. Place the chicken breasts in a small baking dish and pour the pickle brine on top. Cover and refrigerate for 2 hours, turning once or twice.

2. Meanwhile, place the wheat berries in a small saucepan and fill about two-thirds full of water. Bring to a boil over high heat. Reduce the heat to low, partially cover, and cook until tender, about 1 hour. Drain and then rinse with cool water to bring the wheat berries to room temperature. Drain again.

3. Prepare the grill for direct cooking over medium heat (350° to 450°F).

4. Remove the chicken from the dish and discard the brine. Grill the chicken, smooth (skin) side down first, over *direct medium heat*, with the lid closed, until the meat is firm to the touch and opaque all the way to the center, 8 to 12 minutes, turning once or twice. Remove from the grill and let rest for 3 to 5 minutes. Cut the chicken into ½-inch pieces.

5. Place the chicken and the wheat berries in a large serving bowl and add all of the remaining ingredients except the tomatoes. Stir until well combined. Serve warm or at room temperature over the sliced tomatoes.

SERVES: 4 | PREP TIME: 45 minutes | MARINATING TIME: 1–1½ hours | GRILLING TIME: 8–12 minutes

MARINADE

- 2 tablespoons extra-virgin olive oil
- 2 tablespoons fresh lemon juice
- 2 teaspoons paprika
- 3 medium garlic cloves, minced or pushed through a press
- 1 teaspoon kosher salt
- ½ teaspoon freshly ground black pepper

- 4 boneless, skinless chicken breast halves, each about 6 ounces

SALAD

- 3 tomatoes, about 1 pound total, seeded and diced
- 1 English cucumber, about 12 ounces, diced
- 1 medium green bell pepper, diced
- 4 scallions (white and light green parts only), chopped
- ¼ cup fresh lemon juice
- ¼ cup extra-virgin olive oil
- ¼ cup roughly chopped fresh Italian parsley leaves
- 2 tablespoons roughly chopped fresh mint leaves
- 1 teaspoon kosher salt
- ½ teaspoon freshly ground black pepper

- 4 ounces crumbled feta cheese

1. In a medium nonreactive bowl whisk the marinade ingredients. Add the chicken, turn to coat, cover, and refrigerate for 1 to 1½ hours.

2. Prepare the grill for direct cooking over medium heat (350° to 450°F).

3. In a large serving bowl combine the salad ingredients.

4. Remove the chicken from the bowl and discard the marinade. Grill the chicken, smooth (skin) side down first, over *direct medium heat*, with the lid closed, until the meat is firm to the touch and opaque all the way to the center, 8 to 12 minutes, turning once or twice. Remove from the grill and let rest for 3 to 5 minutes. Cut the chicken into ¼-inch cubes, add to the salad, and toss well to combine. Top with the feta and serve immediately.

SERVES: 4 | PREP TIME: 20 minutes | MARINATING TIME: 4–6 hours | GRILLING TIME: 10–14 minutes

DRESSING

- 1 cup mayonnaise
- ⅔ cup buttermilk
- ¼ cup coarsely grated yellow onion
- 1 tablespoon cider vinegar
- ½ teaspoon celery seed
- ½ teaspoon celery salt
- 1 garlic clove, minced or pushed through a press
- ¼ teaspoon freshly ground black pepper

- 4 boneless, skinless chicken breast halves, each about 6 ounces
- 2 hearts of romaine, about 12 ounces total, each cut lengthwise in half, trimmed
  Extra-virgin olive oil
- 1 pint small cherry tomatoes, each cut in half
- 2 tablespoons finely chopped fresh Italian parsley leaves
  Kosher salt
  Freshly ground black pepper

1. Whisk the dressing ingredients. Place the chicken in a large, resealable plastic bag and pour in 1 cup of the dressing. Press the air out of the bag and seal tightly. Turn the bag to distribute the dressing, place in a bowl, and refrigerate for 4 to 6 hours, turning occasionally. Cover and refrigerate the remaining dressing.

2. Prepare the grill for direct cooking over medium heat (350° to 450°F).

3. Remove the chicken from the bag, shaking off and discarding the excess dressing. Grill the chicken, smooth (skin) side down first, over *direct medium heat*, with the lid closed, until the meat is firm to the touch and opaque all the way to the center, 8 to 12 minutes, turning once or twice. Remove from the grill and let rest for 3 to 5 minutes. Cut the chicken into chunks.

4. Lightly brush the romaine halves on both sides with oil and grill over *direct medium heat*, with the lid closed, until slightly wilted, about 2 minutes, turning once. Remove from the grill.

5. Serve the romaine warm with the chicken, dressing, tomatoes, and parsley. Season with salt and pepper.

SERVES: 4 | PREP TIME: 25 minutes | SOAKING TIME: 30–45 minutes | GRILLING TIME: 8–12 minutes

½ cup thinly sliced red onion
3 large tangerines
3 boneless, skinless chicken breast halves, each about 6 ounces
2 tablespoons extra-virgin olive oil
½ teaspoon kosher salt
¼ teaspoon freshly ground black pepper

VINAIGRETTE
¼ cup plus 2 tablespoons extra-virgin olive oil
2 tablespoons sherry vinegar
1 tablespoon Dijon mustard
1 teaspoon coarsely ground black pepper
¼ teaspoon kosher salt

3 small bunches watercress, thick stems trimmed
3 Hass avocados, cut into thick slices

1. In a medium bowl filled with ice water, soak the onion until it is crisp and the flavor is mellowed, 30 to 45 minutes.

2. Finely grate enough zest from the tangerines to make 1 teaspoon. Remove the peel and white pith from the tangerines. Cut between the flesh and the white membranes separating the individual segments, working over a strainer set over a bowl so you can catch the tangerine juice for the dressing. You'll need 2 tablespoons juice. Set aside the tangerine zest, segments, and juice.

3. Prepare the grill for direct cooking over medium heat (350° to 450°F).

4. Brush the chicken breasts on both sides with the oil and season evenly with the salt and pepper.

5. Whisk the vinaigrette ingredients, including the reserved 1 teaspoon tangerine zest and the reserved 2 tablespoons tangerine juice, until smooth and emulsified.

6. Grill the chicken, smooth (skin) side down first, over *direct medium heat*, with the lid closed, until the meat is firm to the touch and opaque all the way to the center, 8 to 12 minutes, turning once or twice. Remove from the grill and let rest for 3 to 5 minutes.

7. Meanwhile, drain the onions and pat them dry with paper towels. Combine the onions, tangerine segments, and watercress. Drizzle with just enough vinaigrette to coat the ingredients lightly and toss gently. Cut the chicken breasts crosswise into slices. Divide the salad, chicken, and avocado among four plates and serve with the remaining vinaigrette.

PULLED CHICKEN SLIDERS
WITH ROOT BEER BARBECUE SAUCE

SERVES: 4 | PREP TIME: 15 minutes, plus about 20 minutes for the sauce | GRILLING TIME: 8–10 minutes

SAUCE
1 tablespoon extra-virgin olive oil
½ cup finely chopped yellow onion
⅔ cup ketchup
½ cup root beer
2 tablespoons unsulfured molasses
2 tablespoons fresh lemon juice
1 teaspoon prepared chili powder
½ teaspoon garlic powder
⅛ teaspoon ground cayenne pepper

RUB
2 teaspoons smoked paprika
1 teaspoon ground cumin
1 teaspoon garlic powder
1 teaspoon kosher salt

1½ pounds boneless, skinless chicken thighs
Extra-virgin olive oil
8 small, soft hamburger buns or rolls, split
Store-bought coleslaw (optional)

1. In a medium saucepan over medium heat, warm the oil. Add the onion and cook until softened, 3 to 5 minutes, stirring occasionally. Stir in all the remaining sauce ingredients. Increase the heat to medium-high, bring to a boil, reduce the heat to medium, and simmer until slightly thickened, 10 to 15 minutes, stirring occasionally.

2. Prepare the grill for direct cooking over medium heat (350° to 450°F).

3. Combine the rub ingredients. Lightly brush the chicken thighs on both sides with oil and season evenly with the rub.

4. Grill the chicken over *direct medium heat*, with the lid closed, until the meat is firm to the touch and the juices run clear, 8 to 10 minutes, turning once or twice. Remove from the grill and let rest until just cool enough to handle, 3 to 5 minutes. Shred the chicken, add to the sauce, and heat through over medium heat, stirring occasionally.

5. Fill the buns with the chicken mixture. Serve with coleslaw, if desired.

Tip

The sauce can be made several days ahead of time and kept refrigerated until ready to use. Try it brushed on grilled pork, or slather it on top of your favorite burger.

CHICKEN AND BROCCOLI STIR-FRY
WITH PEANUTS AND SCALLIONS

SERVES: 4 | PREP TIME: 15 minutes | GRILLING TIME: 7–9 minutes

SPECIAL EQUIPMENT: grill-proof wok or 12-inch cast-iron skillet

SAUCE
⅓ cup hoisin sauce
¼ cup low-sodium chicken broth
1 tablespoon low-sodium soy sauce
1 teaspoon hot chili-garlic sauce, such as Sriracha
   or ½–1 teaspoon crushed red pepper flakes

2 tablespoons vegetable oil
1 tablespoon peeled, minced fresh ginger
2 teaspoons minced garlic
1 pound boneless, skinless chicken thighs, cut into
   ¾-inch pieces
12 ounces broccoli florets
1 red bell pepper, cut into ¾-inch pieces
⅓ cup lightly salted peanuts
3 scallions (white and light green parts only), thinly
   sliced on the diagonal
2 cups cooked rice

Tip

Cut all the vegetables and meat into similar-sized pieces
so that they all finish cooking at the same time.

1. Whisk the sauce ingredients.

2. In a large bowl whisk the oil, ginger, and garlic. Add the chicken pieces and turn to coat.

3. Prepare the grill for direct cooking over high heat (450° to 550°F).

4. Place a grill-proof wok on the cooking grate over *direct high heat*, close the lid, and preheat it for about 10 minutes. Bring the sauce, chicken mixture, broccoli, bell pepper, peanuts, and scallions out to the grill and keep close by.

5. When the wok is smoking hot, add the chicken mixture and stir-fry over *direct high heat*, with the grill lid open, for 3 minutes, using wok spatulas or wooden spoons to toss the chicken frequently. Add the broccoli and bell pepper and continue to stir-fry until the broccoli is bright green, 2 to 3 minutes, stirring frequently. Add the sauce and stir well. Close the grill lid and cook until the sauce is bubbling, about 1 minute. Add the peanuts and the scallions. Cook until the broccoli is crisp-tender and the chicken is cooked through, 1 to 2 minutes. Remove the wok from the grill and serve the stir-fry immediately over warm rice.

SERVES: 6 | PREP TIME: 15 minutes | GRILLING TIME: 14–18 minutes

SALSA
¼ medium white onion, cut through the root end and peeled
8 tomatillos, about 1 pound total, papery skins removed and tomatillos rinsed
  Extra-virgin olive oil
⅓ cup tightly packed fresh cilantro leaves
2 garlic cloves, roughly chopped
½ jalapeño chile pepper, seeded and roughly chopped
  Kosher salt

RUB
2 teaspoons pure ancho chile powder
1 teaspoon kosher salt
½ teaspoon ground cumin
½ teaspoon garlic powder

1½ pounds boneless, skinless chicken thighs
2 tablespoons extra-virgin olive oil
12 corn or flour tortillas (6 inches)
4 cups loosely packed shredded lettuce

1. Prepare the grill for direct cooking over medium heat (350° to 450°F).

2. Lightly coat the onion and the tomatillos with oil. Grill the onion, cut side down, and the tomatillos over *direct medium heat*, with the lid closed, until the onion is lightly charred and the tomatillos are softened and beginning to collapse, turning as needed. The onion will take 4 to 6 minutes and the tomatillos will take 6 to 8 minutes. Remove from the grill as they are done. Roughly chop the onion and the tomatillos, and place them in a food processor or a blender with the cilantro, garlic, and jalapeño. Puree until smooth. Season with salt.

3. Combine the rub ingredients. Lightly brush the chicken thighs on both sides with the oil and season evenly with the rub. Grill the chicken over *direct medium heat*, with the lid closed, until the meat is firm to the touch and the juices run clear, 8 to 10 minutes, turning once or twice. Remove from the grill and let rest for 3 to 5 minutes. Cut the chicken into slices.

4. Warm the tortillas over *direct medium heat*, with the lid open, about 30 seconds, turning once. Remove from the grill and gently fold in half. Fill each tortilla with some chicken, lettuce, and salsa. Serve immediately.

SMOKED CHICKEN ENCHILADA PIE

SERVES: 6–8 | PREP TIME: 20 minutes | GRILLING TIME: about 50 minutes

SPECIAL EQUIPMENT: 2 large handfuls mesquite wood chips, 12-inch cast-iron skillet

1½   pounds boneless, skinless chicken thighs
     Extra-virgin olive oil
½   teaspoon kosher salt
¼   teaspoon freshly ground black pepper
18   corn tortillas (6 inches)
1   medium yellow onion, chopped
2   large garlic cloves, minced or pushed through a press
1   can (28 ounces) enchilada sauce
1½   cups fresh or frozen and thawed corn kernels
1   can (7 ounces) chopped fire-roasted green chiles, drained
8   ounces Mexican cheese blend, grated (2 cups)
     Sour cream
     Chopped fresh cilantro leaves
     Store-bought guacamole

Tip

Change it up by substituting drained canned black or pinto beans for some or all of the corn. The enchilada sauce will determine the heat level of the overall dish, so choose carefully.

1. Soak the wood chips in water for at least 30 minutes.

2. Prepare the grill for direct and indirect cooking over medium heat (350° to 450°F).

3. Brush the chicken thighs on both sides with 1 tablespoon oil and season evenly with the salt and pepper.

4. Grill the tortillas over *direct medium heat*, with the lid open, until lightly browned, about 1 minute, turning once. Remove from the grill and place the tortillas in a single layer on baking sheets to cool. Once cooled, tear the tortillas into quarters.

5. Drain and add half of the wood chips to the lit charcoal or to the smoker box of a gas grill, following manufacturer's instructions, and close the lid. When smoke appears, cook the chicken over *direct medium heat*, with the lid closed, until the meat is firm to the touch and the juices run clear, 8 to 10 minutes, turning once or twice. Remove from the grill and set aside. When the chicken is cool enough to handle, shred the meat into bite-sized pieces.

6. Meanwhile, in a medium skillet over medium heat, warm 1 tablespoon oil. Add the onion and the garlic and cook until softened, about 3 minutes, stirring occasionally. Remove from the heat.

7. Lightly oil a 12-inch cast-iron skillet. Spread ½ cup of the enchilada sauce in the bottom of the skillet. Top with one-third of the tortilla pieces, and cover with 1 cup of the enchilada sauce. Scatter with half of the chicken, half of the corn, half of the onion-garlic mixture, and half of the chiles. Top with ⅔ cup of the cheese. Repeat these layers (chicken, corn, onion-garlic mixture, and chiles), and then add the remaining tortilla pieces, sauce, and cheese.

8. Drain and add the remaining wood chips to the charcoal or to the smoker box. If using a charcoal grill, replenish the charcoal as needed to maintain a steady temperature, adding 6 to 10 unlit briquettes after 45 minutes to help the new briquettes light. Cover the skillet with aluminum foil and cook the enchilada pie over *indirect medium heat*, with the lid closed, until the sauce starts to bubble and the cheese is melted, about 20 minutes. Remove the foil and continue to cook until the center of the pie is hot, about 20 minutes more. Remove the skillet from the grill, uncover, and let rest for 5 minutes. Serve warm with sour cream, cilantro, and guacamole.

CREOLE CHICKEN BREASTS
WITH BLACK-EYED PEA AND TOMATO SALAD

SERVES: 4 | PREP TIME: 25 minutes | GRILLING TIME: 30–45 minutes

DRESSING

4½ tablespoons extra-virgin olive oil
3 tablespoons cider vinegar
1 tablespoon creole mustard
1 tablespoon honey

SALAD

2 cans (each 15 ounces) black-eyed peas, rinsed and drained
10 ounces grape tomatoes, each cut in half (about 2 cups)
4 ounces smoked ham, cut into ⅓-inch cubes
⅓ cup finely chopped celery

Kosher salt
Freshly ground black pepper
4 chicken breast halves (with bone and skin), each 10–12 ounces
1 tablespoon extra-virgin olive oil
2½ teaspoons Cajun seasoning
¼ cup plus 2 tablespoons creole mustard
1 tablespoon honey
2 teaspoons minced fresh thyme leaves
4 cups loosely packed watercress sprigs, thick stems trimmed (about 1 bunch)

1. In a large bowl whisk the dressing ingredients. Add the salad ingredients and toss to coat with the dressing. Season with salt and pepper. Cover and refrigerate until ready to serve.

2. Prepare the grill for indirect cooking over medium heat (350° to 450°F).

3. Brush the chicken breasts on both sides with the oil and season evenly with the Cajun seasoning, 1½ teaspoons salt, and 1 teaspoon pepper.

4. Whisk the creole mustard and the honey together. Place close by the grill.

5. Grill the chicken, bone side down, over *indirect medium heat*, with the lid closed, until the meat is almost firm to the touch, 25 to 35 minutes. Brush the honey mustard evenly over the chicken. Continue to grill until the juices run clear and the meat is no longer pink at the bone, 5 to 10 minutes more, brushing occasionally with the remaining honey mustard. Remove from the grill and season the skin side of the chicken evenly with the thyme. Let the chicken rest for 3 to 5 minutes.

6. Add the watercress to the salad and toss gently to combine. Serve the chicken warm with the salad.

THE CAJUN-CREOLE CONNECTION

North of New Orleans, there's an assumption that "Cajun" and "Creole" are interchangeable. Don't ever tell a Louisianan that. Yes, the two styles of cooking have technique and ingredient overlap, but Cajun tends to be humbler, more casual, and reflective of its history as the rustic "peasant" cooking of French Canadian immigrants who settled in the bayous. Creole is a little richer and fancier, with the European flair and Caribbean and African flavors of Louisiana's previous settlers. Our chicken owes its Creole connection to the use of its signature mustard, a zippier, concentrated version of the condiment often found in rémoulade sauce. And as a nod to the Cajuns, we use their peppery, robust seasoning to add unmistakable spice (but not heat). The result is a simple, elegant dish that will make all Louisianans proud.

SPICY CRUSTED LEMONGRASS CHICKEN
WITH CILANTRO PESTO

SERVES: 4 | **PREP TIME: 20 minutes** | **MARINATING TIME: 1–6 hours** | **GRILLING TIME: 8–12 minutes**

MARINADE
- 2 stalks lemongrass
- ¼ cup cider vinegar
- ¼ cup peanut oil
- 2 scallions, ends trimmed and roughly chopped
- 2 tablespoons finely chopped fresh cilantro leaves
- 1 tablespoon peeled, minced fresh ginger
- 1 teaspoon minced garlic

  Kosher salt
  Freshly ground black pepper
- 4 boneless chicken breast halves (with or without skin), each about 6 ounces

PESTO
- 2 cups coarsely chopped fresh cilantro leaves
- ¾ cup loosely packed fresh Italian parsley leaves
- ¼ cup plus 1 tablespoon extra-virgin olive oil
- 1 tablespoon peeled, coarsely chopped fresh ginger
- 1 garlic clove, coarsely chopped
- ⅛ teaspoon ground cayenne pepper

- ½ cup *panko* bread crumbs
- 2 tablespoons all-purpose flour
- 1 teaspoon crushed red pepper flakes
  Olive oil cooking spray

1. Peel away the dry outer layers of the lemongrass stalks, trim the ends, and mince the tender parts; you should have about ¼ cup. In a large nonreactive bowl whisk the lemongrass with the remaining marinade ingredients, including ¾ teaspoon salt and ½ teaspoon pepper. Place the chicken in the bowl with the marinade and turn to coat. Cover and refrigerate for 1 to 6 hours, turning occasionally.

2. In a food processor combine the pesto ingredients, including ½ teaspoon salt and ¼ teaspoon pepper. Puree until fairly smooth.

3. Prepare the grill for direct cooking over medium heat (350° to 450°F).

4. Remove the chicken from the bowl and discard the marinade. Using paper towels, blot the chicken mostly dry, leaving some of the solid bits clinging to the chicken. In a shallow dish stir the *panko* with the flour, red pepper flakes, and ¼ teaspoon salt. Coat the chicken with the mixture, pressing lightly so that the mixture adheres. Lightly spray the chicken all over with oil.

5. Grill the chicken, smooth (skin) side down first, over **direct medium heat**, with the lid closed, until the meat is firm to the touch and opaque all the way to the center, 8 to 12 minutes, turning once. Remove from the grill and let rest for 3 to 5 minutes. Serve warm with the pesto.

SERVES: 4 | PREP TIME: 30 minutes, plus 25 minutes for the rice | MARINATING TIME: 4–8 hours | GRILLING TIME: 8–12 minutes

MARINADE

- ¼ cup gold tequila
- ¼ cup fresh lime juice
- 1 tablespoon packed golden brown sugar
- 2 teaspoons Dijon mustard
- 2 teaspoons ancho chile powder
- 2 garlic cloves, smashed
- 1 teaspoon ground cumin
- 1 teaspoon freshly ground black pepper

  Extra-virgin olive oil
  Kosher salt
- 4 boneless chicken breast halves (with skin), each about 6 ounces

RICE

- 1 tablespoon unsalted butter
- ¼ cup finely chopped yellow onion
- 1 garlic clove, minced or pushed through a press
- 1 teaspoon paprika
- 1 teaspoon dried oregano
- ¼ teaspoon ground cayenne pepper
- 1½ cups long-grain white rice
- 2¼ cups low-sodium chicken broth
- ¼ cup thinly sliced scallions, ends trimmed

1. Whisk the marinade ingredients, including 1 tablespoon oil and 1 teaspoon salt. Place the chicken in a large resealable plastic bag and pour in the marinade. Press the air out of the bag and seal tightly. Turn the bag to distribute the marinade, place in a bowl, and refrigerate for 4 to 8 hours.

2. Prepare the grill for direct cooking over medium heat (350° to 450°F).

3. In a medium saucepan over medium heat, warm the butter and 1 tablespoon oil. Add the onion and the garlic and sauté until the onion softens and begins to turn golden brown, about 3 minutes. Add the paprika, oregano, cayenne pepper, and 1 teaspoon salt and sauté until fragrant, about 30 seconds. Add the rice and stir until coated in the oil, about 1 minute. Add the broth and bring to a boil. Cover the pan and reduce the heat to low. Simmer until all of the liquid is absorbed, 20 to 25 minutes. Remove from the heat, fluff the rice with a fork, and stir in the scallions. Cover and keep warm.

4. Remove the chicken from the bag and discard the marinade. Grill the chicken, skin side up first, over *direct medium heat*, with the lid closed, until the meat is firm to the touch and no longer pink in the center, 8 to 12 minutes, turning once after 7 to 9 minutes. Remove from the grill and let rest for 3 to 5 minutes. Serve warm with the rice.

POULTRY

193

HERBED CHICKEN THIGHS
WITH HONEY-LEMON GLAZE

SERVES: 4 | PREP TIME: 20 minutes | GRILLING TIME: 36–40 minutes

GLAZE

- 2 teaspoons extra-virgin olive oil
- 3 medium garlic cloves, minced or pushed through a press
- 1 tablespoon peeled, grated fresh ginger
- ½ cup honey
- 3 tablespoons fresh lemon juice
- 2 teaspoons cornstarch dissolved in 2 teaspoons water
- 1 teaspoon finely grated lemon zest

RUB

- 1 teaspoon dried marjoram
- 1 teaspoon dried basil
- 1 teaspoon garlic powder
- 1 teaspoon kosher salt
- ¾ teaspoon freshly ground black pepper
- ¼ teaspoon ground cinnamon

- 8 chicken thighs (with bone and skin), each 5–6 ounces, trimmed of excess fat and skin

Tip

Coat a measuring cup with oil before adding the honey. The honey will come out easily with no mess.

1. Prepare the grill for direct and indirect cooking over medium heat (350° to 450°F).

2. In a small saucepan over medium-high heat, warm the oil. Stir in the garlic and the ginger and cook until they just start to brown, 1 to 2 minutes, stirring often. Add the honey, bring to a boil, and cook for 2 minutes, watching carefully and reducing the heat if necessary so the mixture doesn't boil over. Add the lemon juice and cook for 1 minute. Stir in the cornstarch mixture, return to a boil, and cook until slightly thickened, about 1 minute. Remove from the heat and stir in the lemon zest. The glaze will continue to thicken as it cools.

3. Combine the rub ingredients. Season the chicken thighs evenly with the rub.

4. Grill the chicken, skin side down first, over *direct medium heat*, with the lid closed, until golden brown, 6 to 10 minutes, turning occasionally. Move the chicken over *indirect medium heat*, brush with some of the glaze, and cook until the juices run clear and the meat is no longer pink at the bone, about 30 minutes more, turning once or twice and occasionally brushing with the remaining glaze. Remove from the grill and let rest for 3 to 5 minutes. Serve warm.

CRISPY CHICKEN THIGHS
WITH BASIL AND PROSCIUTTO BUTTER

SERVES: 4 | PREP TIME: 15 minutes | GRILLING TIME: 20–24 minutes

BUTTER
¼ cup (½ stick) unsalted butter, softened
1 ounce prosciutto, finely chopped
1 medium shallot, minced
1 tablespoon finely chopped fresh basil leaves
1 tablespoon finely grated Parmigiano-Reggiano® cheese
¼ teaspoon kosher salt
¼ teaspoon freshly ground black pepper

8 chicken thighs (with bone and skin), each
  5–6 ounces, trimmed of excess fat and skin
½ teaspoon kosher salt
¼ teaspoon freshly ground black pepper

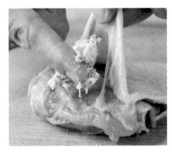

Lift the skin and spread
the butter mixture all
over the exposed meat.

1. Using a fork, combine the butter ingredients. Divide the seasoned butter into eight equal portions.

2. Prepare the grill for indirect and direct cooking over medium-high heat (400° to 500°F).

3. Pat the chicken thighs dry with paper towels. Using your fingertips, gently loosen the skin of the thighs, being careful not to completely separate the skin from the meat. Lift the skin up and place a portion of the butter underneath. Smooth the skin over the butter and massage it gently to spread it evenly over the top of the meat. Season the thighs on both sides with the salt and pepper.

4. Grill the thighs, skin side up first, over *indirect medium-high heat*, with the lid closed, until sizzling, slightly firm, and lightly marked on the bottom, 18 to 20 minutes. Then turn the thighs over and cook over *direct medium-high heat*, with the lid closed, until the juices run clear, the skin is blistered and crisp, and the meat is no longer pink at the bone, 2 to 4 minutes more (if flare-ups occur, move the thighs temporarily over indirect heat). Remove from the grill and let rest for 3 to 5 minutes. Serve warm.

SERVES: 4 | PREP TIME: 20 minutes | GRILLING TIME: 25–30 minutes

GLAZE

1	cup peach preserves
½	cup peach nectar
4	teaspoons prepared chili powder
1	teaspoon finely grated lime zest
2	tablespoons fresh lime juice
½	cup chopped fresh cilantro leaves

	Kosher salt
	Freshly ground black pepper
12	chicken drumsticks, 2¾–3 pounds total
4	firm but ripe peaches, each cut in half
2	teaspoons canola oil

1. In a small saucepan over medium-high heat, combine the preserves, nectar, and chili powder. Bring to a simmer, whisking until the mixture is well blended and almost smooth, about 1 minute. Remove the saucepan from the heat and whisk in the lime zest and juice. Let cool to lukewarm, then whisk in the cilantro, ⅛ teaspoon salt, and ⅛ teaspoon pepper.

2. Divide the glaze equally between two small bowls: one for brushing on the chicken while grilling and the other for serving.

3. Prepare the grill for direct cooking over medium heat (350° to 450°F).

4. Pat the drumsticks dry with paper towels and season evenly with 1¼ teaspoons salt and 1 teaspoon pepper. Brush the cut side of the peach halves lightly with the oil.

5. Grill the drumsticks over *direct medium heat*, with the lid closed, until the skin is golden brown and the meat is almost firm to the touch, about 20 minutes, turning occasionally. Brush the peach glaze from the first bowl evenly over the drumsticks. Continue grilling, with the lid closed, until the juices run clear and the meat is no longer pink at the bone, 5 to 10 minutes more, turning once or twice and brushing occasionally with more of the glaze. During the last 5 minutes of grilling time, grill the peach halves, cut side down, over *direct medium heat* until lightly charred and beginning to soften (check after 3 minutes). Remove the drumsticks and the peaches from the grill and let the drumsticks rest for 3 to 5 minutes. Serve the drumsticks and the peaches warm with the reserved glaze.

POULTRY

197

SPICE-RUBBED CHICKEN
WITH ORANGE-CHIPOTLE BARBECUE SAUCE

SERVES: 4 | PREP TIME: 30 minutes | GRILLING TIME: 40–50 minutes

RUB

1½	teaspoons kosher salt
1	teaspoon freshly ground black pepper
1	teaspoon granulated garlic
1	teaspoon dried thyme
¼	teaspoon ground allspice

4	whole chicken legs, each 10–12 ounces, excess skin and fat removed
	Extra-virgin olive oil

SAUCE

½	cup minced yellow onion
2	garlic cloves, minced or pushed through a press
1	cup fresh orange juice
1	cup ketchup
2	canned chipotle chile peppers in adobo sauce, minced
1	tablespoon packed golden brown sugar
1	tablespoon cider vinegar
1	teaspoon Worcestershire sauce
¼	teaspoon ground allspice

1. Prepare the grill for indirect and direct cooking over medium heat (350° to 450°F).

2. Combine the rub ingredients. Lightly brush the chicken on both sides with oil and season evenly with the rub.

3. In a small saucepan over medium heat, warm 2 tablespoons oil. Add the onion and the garlic and cook until the onion is tender but not browned, 3 to 5 minutes, stirring occasionally. Add the remaining sauce ingredients and whisk until smooth. Simmer over medium heat for 5 to 7 minutes, stirring occasionally. Remove from the heat.

4. Grill the chicken, skin side up, over *indirect medium heat*, with the lid closed, until the juices run clear and the meat is no longer pink at the bone, 35 to 40 minutes, brushing once with the sauce after 30 minutes. Brush with the sauce again and then move the chicken over *direct medium heat*. Continue cooking, with the lid open, until the skin is well browned, 5 to 10 minutes more, turning once or twice. Remove from the grill and let rest for 3 to 5 minutes. Serve the chicken warm with the remaining sauce.

Tip

Trimming the excess skin and fat from the chicken legs helps to minimize flare-ups on the grill. When you move the chicken over direct heat to finish cooking it, watch for excess smoke coming from the grill, which could be an indicator that you need to move the chicken temporarily over indirect heat.

RECIPE REMIX:
Then and Now

It's a classic combination: onion, garlic, and
... MSG? With all due respect to this "oldie,"
some of these ingredients were not "goodies." Once
a showstopper at martini-fueled dinner parties,
Chicken a la Vermouth has a swanky pedigree worth
revisiting. Adapted for the grill—and modern
sensibilities—some elements were swapped out (so
long, MSG and vermouth) for fresher flavors (hello,
fragrant rosemary and dry, crisp white wine) to
bring this retro gem up to date.

The Original

Chicken a la Vermouth
Recipe from *14 Exotic Gourmet Recipes for
Weber Covered Barbecue Kettle*, ca. 1960

Use a well-rounded 2-1/2 to 3 lb. whole broiling chicken.
For juicier chickens it is always better to barbecue,
broil, or roast the chickens whole. When you do cut-up
chicken, it has already been bled of 75% of its natural
juices. Try doing chickens whole and taste the difference.

Pour 5 lbs. of charcoal or approximately 1/2 bag into
your WEBER BARBECUE KETTLE, light, and while it is getting
started prepare your chicken or *chickens as follows:

Saturate and rub with Peanut Oil, and Dry Mustard. Insert
a 1 inch thick square of butter into the cavity of the
chicken. Sprinkle with:

Dehydrated Onion and Garlic
Soya Sauce
1/2 tsp. Oregano
1 tsp. Sweet Basil
Monosodium Glutamate
Parsley
Soya Sauce
Paprika

The chicken is ready for the WEBER COVERED BARBECUE KETTLE.
The dampers underneath and vent on the cover wide open
for the first 30 minutes, then cut the dampers down to
1/2 open, and leave alone for the next 1 hour. Then pour
1 ounce of Dry Vermouth into the chicken cavity with the
melted butter, insert a basting brush, stir and mix the
butter and vermouth and baste every 5 minutes for the
next 20 minutes. Take off and serve. Complete cooking time
1 hour 50 minutes.

*On a WEBER COVERED BARBECUE KETTLE you can barbecue one
chicken or ten 2-1/2 pound broilers in the same cooking
time, by placing them in a rosette on your top grill. This
is an ideal serving for 20 to 30 people with very little
work involved.

ROSEMARY CHICKEN
BASTED WITH GARLIC AND BUTTER

The Remix

SERVES: 4 | PREP TIME: 15 minutes | MARINATING TIME: 4–12 hours | GRILLING TIME: 35–45 minutes

MARINADE
- 1 cup dry white wine
- 3 tablespoons extra-virgin olive oil
- 1 tablespoon finely chopped fresh rosemary leaves
- 1 tablespoon Dijon mustard
- 4 garlic cloves, minced or pushed through a press
- 1 teaspoon dried thyme
- 1 teaspoon kosher salt
- ½ teaspoon freshly ground black pepper

- 1 whole chicken, 4–5 pounds, cut into 6 pieces (see page 173)
- 1 tablespoon unsalted butter
- 12 multicolored mini sweet peppers
- 1 tablespoon extra-virgin olive oil
- ¼ teaspoon kosher salt

1. In a large resealable plastic bag set inside a medium bowl, mix the marinade ingredients. Add the chicken pieces, press the air out of the bag, and seal tightly. Turn the bag several times to distribute the marinade, return to the bowl, and refrigerate for at least 4 hours or up to 12 hours.

2. Prepare the grill for indirect and direct cooking over medium heat (350° to 450°F).

3. Remove the chicken from the bag and reserve the marinade. Grill the chicken, meatier sides down first, over *indirect medium heat*, with the lid closed, for 30 minutes. Meanwhile, make the basting sauce using the reserved marinade.

4. Pour the marinade into a small saucepan and bring to a boil. Simmer briskly until reduced by about half, 4 to 6 minutes. Remove the saucepan from the heat and whisk in the butter.

5. Brush the peppers all over with the oil and season evenly with the salt.

6. After the chicken pieces have been on the grill for 30 minutes, lightly brush them with the basting sauce, and then move them over *direct medium heat*. Continue grilling until the juices run clear and the meat is no longer pink at the bone, 5 to 15 minutes more, turning occasionally (the breasts and wings will be done first). Before removing any piece of chicken from the grill, move it over indirect heat and brush it with the basting sauce once more. During the last 8 to 10 minutes of grilling time, grill the peppers over *direct medium heat* until lightly charred, turning occasionally. Serve the chicken warm with the peppers.

grill SKILLS:
PERFECT WHOLE CHICKEN

Done right, a roast chicken dinner from the grill is spectacular. When its golden skin turns crisp, and warm juices run throughout the tender meat, it is worth every minute and every dollar spent. The first step toward such a dinner happens at the store, because nowadays there is a big difference between a factory-farmed, commodity chicken and an organic, free-range chicken. Commodity birds are often fed hormones and artificial ingredients to grow quickly with large breasts and yellowish skins. They may look good, but organic birds are definitely more flavorful and their texture has a tender, meaty integrity that is also quite moist if you cook it right.

Classic Roast Chicken

1 Prepare the grill for indirect medium heat (350° to 450°F). For a particularly crisp skin, get the temperature somewhere between 400° and 450°F.

2 Remove any excess fat from inside the cavity. Also remove the giblets, if there are any. The wing tips tend to burn and they don't have much meat, so either cut them off or tuck the tips under the back of the chicken.

3 Lightly coat the surface of the chicken with good olive oil and season inside and outside with salt and pepper, especially the outside of the chicken. Salt is crucial for a deliciously crisp skin. If you like, stuff the cavity with some herb sprigs and a quartered lemon for added flavors.

4 Truss the chicken to make it evenly compacted and to protect the top of the breasts with the ends of the drumsticks.

5 Set the chicken over indirect heat and let it roast for an hour or so. Let it rest at room temperature for 10 to 15 minutes, cut it up, and serve warm.

Spatchcocked Chicken

Spatchcocking, or butterflying, a chicken is a clever way of cooking it more evenly and more quickly.

1 Set the chicken, with the breast side facing down, on a work surface. Using sharp kitchen shears, cut from the tail end along both sides of the backbone.

2 Remove the backbone and discard it. Flatten the chicken with both hands to crack the rib cage. Then use a sharp knife to cut a shallow slit at the top of the rib cage. Run your fingertips alongside both sides of the breastbone to expose it.

3 Dig your fingertips down along the breastbone until it comes loose from the meat. Then pull it out and discard it.

4 Cut a small hole in the loose skin on both sides at the leg end of the chicken. Pull the end of each drumstick through the hole on its side. This will hold the legs in place on the grill.

Beer Can Chicken

This wacky looking idea is actually kinda brilliant. With the chicken standing upright on a can, you have a solution to an age-old problem of cooking whole birds, which is that the breast meat cooks faster than the leg meat and tends to turn dry by the time the leg meat is done. In this showstopping situation, the legs are closer to the heat source, so they get a little hotter and cook a little faster than the breasts. Now both areas are done at the same time. Genius! Also, the entire surface of the bird gets full exposure to the dry, caramelizing heat of the grill, so you get a handsome, crisp skin all the way around. But wait, there's more. The beer left in the can steams the chicken from the inside, producing moist, succulent meat. The key for that is to have less than one-third of the beer in the can; otherwise, the beer doesn't get hot enough to steam.

1 Pour out at least two-thirds of the beer, poke a couple of extra holes in the top of the can, season the chicken, and lower the hollow cavity of the chicken onto the can.

2 Tuck the wing tips behind the back of the chicken. Transfer the chicken on the beer can to the grill's cooking grate, balancing it on its two legs and the can, like a tripod.

3 Grill over indirect medium heat until done. For a smoked beer can chicken, add soaked and drained wood chips to the charcoal or to the smoker box of a gas grill once or twice during the first half of the cooking time. For a full recipe, see page 208.

When Is It Done?

As a chicken overcooks, the meat loses its flavor and gradually shrivels to a chalky texture. To avoid that, take your chicken off the grill just in time.

As long as you have a reliable instant-read thermometer, the "temperature test" works perfectly. Insert the sensor of the thermometer into the deepest part of the thigh, not touching the bone. The temperature there should be about 170°F. The meat is safe to eat above 160°F, but the dark meat is not really tender until it reaches 170°F. Ideally, the breast meat will be about 165°F.

If you don't have an instant-read thermometer, cut through the skin between a leg and the rest of the body. Bend that leg away from the body to expose the thigh joint. When the chicken is done, the meat at the joint should be opaque and the juices should run clear with no trace of pink.

CHICKEN UNDER BRICKS
WITH WHITE BARBECUE SAUCE

SERVES: 4 | PREP TIME: 20 minutes | GRILLING TIME: 40–50 minutes

SPECIAL EQUIPMENT: poultry shears, 2 foil-wrapped bricks or a cast-iron skillet, instant-read thermometer

SAUCE
1¼ cups mayonnaise
¼ cup cider vinegar
2 teaspoons prepared horseradish
2 teaspoons Dijon mustard
2 teaspoons granulated sugar
1 teaspoon fresh lemon juice
1 teaspoon freshly ground black pepper
¾ teaspoon kosher salt
¼ teaspoon hot pepper sauce or ground cayenne pepper

RUB
1 teaspoon prepared chili powder
1 teaspoon garlic powder
1 teaspoon ground cumin
1 teaspoon kosher salt
¼ teaspoon ground cayenne pepper

1 whole chicken, 4–5 pounds, spatchcocked (see page 203)
2 tablespoons extra-virgin olive oil

1. Prepare the grill for indirect cooking over high heat (450° to 550°F).

2. Whisk the sauce ingredients. Cover and refrigerate until ready to serve.

3. Combine the rub ingredients.

4. Brush the chicken on both sides with the oil and season evenly with the rub. Place the chicken, skin side down, over *indirect high heat*, and put two foil-wrapped bricks or a cast-iron skillet on top of the chicken. Close the lid and grill until golden around the edges, 20 to 25 minutes. Remove the bricks or skillet and, using a large spatula, carefully turn the chicken over, being careful not to tear the skin. Replace the bricks or skillet and continue cooking, with the lid closed, until the juices run clear and an instant-read thermometer inserted into the thickest part of the thigh (not touching the bone) registers 160° to 165°F, 20 to 25 minutes more. Remove from the grill and let rest for 10 to 15 minutes (the internal temperature will rise 5 to 10 degrees during this time). Cut into serving pieces and serve warm with the sauce.

SERVES: 4 | PREP TIME: 20 minutes | BRINING TIME: 8–24 hours | GRILLING TIME: 1¾–2 hours

SPECIAL EQUIPMENT: butcher's twine, large disposable foil pan, instant-read thermometer

BRINE
1½   quarts buttermilk
 1   medium yellow onion, finely chopped
 ¼   cup kosher salt
 ¼   cup granulated sugar
 2   tablespoons hot pepper sauce
 6   medium garlic cloves, minced or pushed through a press
 1   tablespoon ground coriander
 ½   teaspoon ground cayenne pepper

 1   whole chicken, 5½–6 pounds, neck, giblets, wing tips, and excess fat removed
 2   tablespoons extra-virgin olive oil

1. In a nonreactive pot or container just wide enough to hold the chicken, whisk the brine ingredients.

2. Submerge the chicken in the brine, breast side down, and refrigerate for 8 to 24 hours.

3. Prepare the grill for indirect cooking over medium heat (350° to 450°F).

4. Remove the chicken from the pot and discard the brine. Pat the chicken dry with paper towels and tie the drumsticks together with butcher's twine (see page 206). Place the chicken in a large disposable foil pan and drizzle with the oil.

5. Grill the chicken in the pan over *indirect medium heat*, with the lid closed, until the juices run clear and an instant-read thermometer inserted into the thickest part of the thigh (not touching the bone), registers 160° to 165°F, 1¾ to 2 hours, basting the chicken with the pan juices and rotating the pan occasionally. Remove the pan and the chicken from the grill and let the chicken rest for 10 to 15 minutes (the internal temperature will rise 5 to 10 degrees during this time). Cut the chicken into serving pieces. Serve warm.

SUMMER HERB-ROASTED CHICKEN

SERVES: 4 | PREP TIME: 15 minutes | GRILLING TIME: 1¼–1½ hours

SPECIAL EQUIPMENT: butcher's twine, instant-read thermometer

BUTTER

- 2 tablespoons unsalted butter, softened
- 2 tablespoons fresh thyme leaves
- 1 tablespoon finely chopped fresh chives
- 1 teaspoon finely grated lemon zest
- 1 garlic clove, minced or pushed through a press
- ⅛ teaspoon kosher salt
- ⅛ teaspoon freshly ground black pepper

- 1 whole chicken, 4–5 pounds, neck, giblets, and any excess fat removed
- 1 lemon, cut into quarters
- 3 sprigs fresh thyme
- 2 garlic cloves, smashed

1. Prepare the grill for indirect cooking over medium heat (350° to 450°F).

2. Mix the butter ingredients. Gently lift the skin from the chicken breast meat and the thighs, taking care not to cause any tears. Distribute half of the butter under the skin on the breast and thigh meat and the other half over the skin.

3. Insert the lemon quarters into the chicken's cavity, squeezing them gently as you do, along with the thyme and the garlic. Tie the drumsticks together with butcher's twine (see below). Fold the wings tips behind the chicken's back.

4. Grill the chicken over *indirect medium heat*, with the lid closed, until the juices run clear and an instant-read thermometer inserted into the thickest part of the thigh (not touching the bone) registers 160° to 165°F, 1¼ to 1½ hours. Remove from the grill and let rest for 10 to 15 minutes (the internal temperature will rise 5 to 10 degrees during this time). Cut the chicken into serving pieces. Serve warm.

1 Wrap a piece of butcher's twine under and around the drumsticks, cross it in the middle, and pull the ends to draw the drumsticks together.

2 Cross the twine above the drumsticks and tie a knot. This will hold the chicken in a compact shape and will help the meat cook more evenly.

HICKORY-SMOKED BEER CAN CHICKEN

SERVES: 4 | PREP TIME: 15 minutes | DRY-BRINING TIME: 2 hours | GRILLING TIME: 1¼–1½ hours

SPECIAL EQUIPMENT: 4 large handfuls hickory or oak wood chips, church key–style can opener, instant-read thermometer

- 1   whole chicken, 4–5 pounds, neck, giblets, and any excess fat removed
- 2   tablespoons kosher salt

RUB
- 2   teaspoons granulated onion
- 2   teaspoons paprika
- 1   teaspoon packed golden brown sugar
- ½   teaspoon freshly ground black pepper

- 1   tablespoon extra-virgin olive oil
- 1   can (12 ounces) beer, at room temperature

SMOKE SIGNALS

Near and dear to the griller's heart—right up there with a really great pair of tongs and bacon-wrapped anything—is smoke. Simple, hard working, and dependable, smoke is the duct tape of grilling. Sure, smoke adds flavor, and sometimes a little flair, but did you know it can clue you in on what's going on under the lid?

The color of the smoke can tell you a lot about how things are going. Seeing gray smoke shimmying from the fire is a good thing. It means juices from the meat are hitting the hot coals or the Flavorizer® bars, flashing and creating flavor. Everything is fine. Good even. But seeing black, sooty smoke frantically waving its arms at you means trouble is at hand and it's time to spring into action.

Black smoke signals that you might have a grease fire. This happens when fatty meats are placed over coals or burners that are too hot, or when the grill needs cleaning. To extinguish the flames when cooking on a charcoal grill, carefully remove the lid, shielding your face from the fire. Remove the meat using long-handled tongs and insulated barbecue mitts. Replace the lid with the damper closed. On a gas grill, turn off the burners and slowly lift the lid. Remove the meat, assess the situation, let the fire burn out, pledge to clean your grill, and offer smoke some thanks. It's got your back. It always does.

1. Sprinkle the salt evenly over the meaty parts of the chicken and inside the cavity (but not on the back). The chicken will be coated with a visible layer of salt. Cover with plastic wrap and refrigerate for 2 hours.

2. Combine the rub ingredients.

3. Soak the wood chips in water for at least 30 minutes.

4. Prepare the grill for indirect cooking over medium heat (350° to 450°F). Keep the temperature as close to 400°F as possible throughout the cooking time.

5. Rinse the chicken with cold water, inside and outside, to remove the salt, and then pat dry with paper towels. Brush the chicken with the oil and season all over, including inside the cavity, with the rub. Fold the wing tips behind the chicken's back.

6. Open the can of beer and pour out about two-thirds. Using a church key–style can opener, make two more holes in the top of the can. Place the can on a solid surface and then lower the chicken cavity over the can.

7. Drain and add two handfuls of wood chips to the charcoal or to the smoker box of a gas grill, following manufacturer's instructions, and close the lid. When the wood begins to smoke, transfer the chicken-on-a-can to the grill, balancing it on its two legs and the can like a tripod. Cook the chicken over *indirect medium heat*, with the lid closed, until the juices run clear and an instant-read thermometer inserted into the thickest part of the thigh (not touching the bone), registers 160° to 165°F, 1¼ to 1½ hours. After the first 15 minutes of cooking time, drain and add the remaining wood chips to the charcoal or to the smoker box. If using a charcoal grill, replenish the charcoal as needed to maintain a steady temperature, adding 6 to 10 unlit briquettes after 45 minutes. Leave the lid off the grill for about 5 minutes to help the new briquettes light.

8. Carefully remove the chicken-on-a-can from the grill (do not spill the contents of the beer can, which will be very hot). Let the chicken rest for 10 to 15 minutes (the internal temperature will rise 5 to 10 degrees during this time) before lifting it from the beer can and carving it into serving pieces. Serve warm.

BEER-BRINED TURKEY

SERVES: 4 | PREP TIME: 25 minutes | BRINING TIME: 12–14 hours | GRILLING TIME: 2½–3 hours

SPECIAL EQUIPMENT: sturdy plastic bag; 10-quart or larger stockpot; butcher's twine; 2 large disposable foil pans; 6 large handfuls hickory wood chips; instant-read thermometer

BRINE

- 4 bottles (each 12 ounces) lager
- 1 cup packed golden brown sugar
- ¾ cup kosher salt
- 3 tablespoons smoked paprika
- 1½ tablespoons dried thyme
- 1 tablespoon coarsely cracked black peppercorns
- 1 tablespoon granulated garlic
- 1 tablespoon granulated onion
- ½ teaspoon ground cayenne pepper
- 3 quarts ice water

- 1 whole turkey, 12–14 pounds, thawed if frozen
- 4 yellow onions, about 1¾ pounds total, coarsely chopped, divided
- 4 sprigs fresh thyme
- 3 tablespoons unsalted butter, melted
- 1 quart low-sodium chicken broth

1. About 14 hours before grilling, in a very large bowl combine all of the brine ingredients, except the ice water, and whisk until the salt and sugar are dissolved. Stir in the ice water. The brine should be very cold.

2. Remove the giblets, neck, and lumps of fat from the turkey and reserve (discard the liver). Place in a bowl, cover, and refrigerate until ready to grill. If the turkey has a plastic truss or a pop-up timer, remove and discard it. Place the turkey inside a sturdy plastic bag and put it in a 10-quart or larger stockpot. Pour enough of the brine into the bag to cover the turkey as much as possible when the bag is closed and tightly tied. Discard any extra brine. Seal the bag. Refrigerate the turkey for at least 12 hours and no longer than 14 hours.

3. Remove the turkey from the bag and discard the brine. Rinse the turkey under cold water and pat it dry inside and outside with paper towels. Put one-third of the chopped onions and all of the thyme sprigs into the body cavity. Tuck the wing tips behind the turkey's back and loosely tie the drumsticks together with butcher's twine (see page 206). Brush the turkey all over with the melted butter. Place one large disposable foil pan inside of the other to create a single pan of double thickness. Put the remaining onions into the pan and place the turkey, breast side down, on top of the onions. Allow the turkey to stand at room temperature for 1 hour before grilling.

4. Soak the wood chips in water for at least 30 minutes. Prepare the grill for indirect cooking over medium-low heat (about 350°F).

5. Place the reserved giblets, neck, and lumps of fat in the roasting pan and pour in the chicken broth. Drain and add two handfuls of the wood chips to the charcoal or to the smoker box of a gas grill, following manufacturer's instructions, and close the lid. When the wood begins to smoke, cook the turkey over *indirect medium-low heat*, with the lid closed, for 1 hour, keeping the grill's temperature as close to 350°F as possible. If using a charcoal grill, replenish the charcoal as needed to maintain a steady temperature, adding 8 to 10 unlit briquettes every 45 minutes to 1 hour. Leave the lid off the grill for about 5 minutes to help the new briquettes light.

6. After 1 hour, turn the turkey over so that the breast faces up. Drain and add two handfuls of wood chips to the charcoal or to the smoker box. Cook the turkey for another 45 minutes, and then drain and add the remaining two handfuls of wood chips to the charcoal or to the smoker box. Continue cooking the turkey, with the lid closed, until an instant-read thermometer inserted into the thickest part of the thigh (not touching the bone), registers 170°F, 45 minutes to 1¼ hours more.

7. Remove the pan with the turkey from the grill. Tilt the turkey so the juices run out of the body cavity and into the pan. Transfer the turkey to a cutting board and let rest for 20 to 30 minutes (the internal temperature will rise 5 to 10 degrees during this time). Save the pan juices to make the gravy (see recipe on the opposite page).

8. Carve the turkey and serve with the warm gravy.

1 Remove each half of the turkey breast by cutting lengthwise along each side of the breastbone.

2 Pull the first half of the breast away from the breastbone, using a knife to carefully release the meat from the rib cage, and transfer to a cutting board.

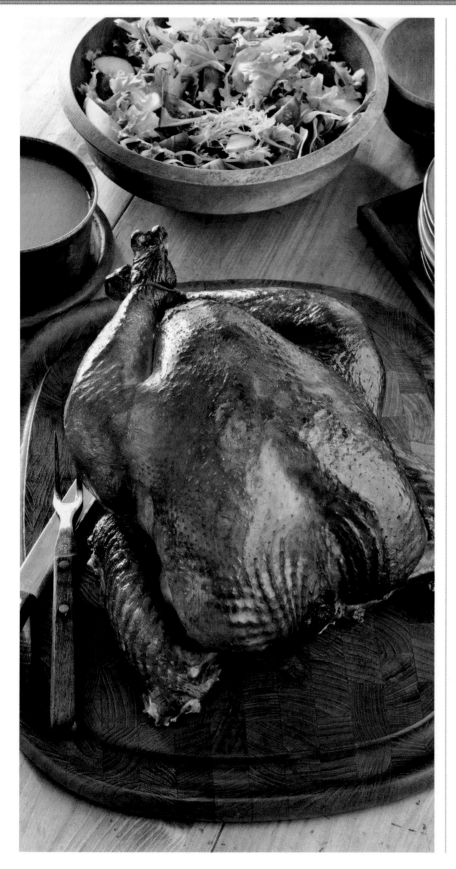

PREP TIME: 25 minutes

SPECIAL EQUIPMENT:
gravy separator

GRAVY

	Low-sodium chicken broth, as needed
	Melted unsalted butter, as needed
½	cup all-purpose flour
½	cup lager
1	teaspoon chopped fresh thyme leaves
	Kosher salt
	Freshly ground black pepper

1. Strain the pan juices into a gravy separator. Let stand until the fat rises to the surface, about 3 minutes. Pour the pan juices into a 1-quart measuring cup, reserving the fat. If necessary, add chicken broth to the 1-quart measuring cup so that you have 1 quart of liquid.

2. Measure the reserved fat. If necessary, add melted butter to make ½ cup. In a medium saucepan heat the fat (and butter) over medium heat. Whisk in the flour and let it bubble for 1 minute, whisking constantly. Whisk in the pan juices and the lager. Bring the gravy to a simmer, whisking frequently. Reduce the heat to medium-low, stir in the thyme, and simmer until slightly thickened, 3 to 5 minutes. Remove from the heat and season with salt and pepper, if desired (the salt and pepper in the brine may have provided enough seasoning already). Serve warm.

SERVES: 4–6 | PREP TIME: 15 minutes | MARINATING TIME: 1–4 hours | GRILLING TIME: 5–7 minutes

MARINADE

¼ cup extra-virgin olive oil
1 tablespoon Dijon mustard
1 tablespoon chopped fresh rosemary leaves
3 large garlic cloves, finely chopped
1 teaspoon kosher salt
¼ teaspoon freshly ground black pepper

8 turkey cutlets, each about 4 ounces and ¾ inch thick

RELISH

2 cups fresh or frozen cranberries
1 cup 100% cranberry juice (no sugar added)
⅓ cup packed golden brown sugar
¼ cup dried tart cherries, roughly chopped
¼ teaspoon kosher salt

1. In a large bowl whisk the marinade ingredients. Place the cutlets in the bowl and turn to coat. Cover and refrigerate for 1 to 4 hours.

2. Prepare the grill for direct cooking over medium heat (350° to 450°F).

3. In a medium saucepan over high heat, combine the relish ingredients and bring to a boil. Lower the heat to a simmer and cook until the cranberries are soft, 4 to 6 minutes, stirring and crushing the cranberries against the side of the saucepan often. Remove the saucepan from the heat, transfer the relish to a bowl, and let cool to room temperature.

4. Grill the cutlets over *direct medium heat,* with the lid closed, until the meat is firm to the touch and no longer pink in the center, 5 to 7 minutes, turning once after 3 to 4 minutes. Remove from the grill and serve warm with the relish.

SERVES: 4 | PREP TIME: 15 minutes | GRILLING TIME: 8–10 minutes

PATTIES

10	sun-dried tomato halves packed in oil, drained
10	large fresh basil leaves
1½	pounds ground turkey thigh meat
¾	teaspoon kosher salt
½	teaspoon dried oregano
¼	teaspoon freshly ground black pepper

¼	cup mayonnaise
2	teaspoons finely grated lemon zest
	Extra-virgin olive oil
4	slices fresh mozzarella cheese, each about ¼ inch thick (about 4 ounces)
4	ciabatta rolls, split
1	cup tightly packed baby arugula

1. Prepare the grill for direct cooking over medium heat (350° to 450°F).

2. Chop the sun-dried tomatoes and basil together as finely as possible to make a paste (you should have about ¾ cup). Gently mix the remaining patty ingredients with the paste. With wet hands, form four loosely packed patties of equal size, each about ¾ inch thick. Don't compact the meat too much or the patties will be tough. With your thumb or the back of a spoon, make a shallow indentation about 1 inch wide in the center of each patty. This will help the patties cook evenly and prevent them from puffing on the grill.

3. Combine the mayonnaise and the lemon zest, and set aside.

4. Lightly brush the patties on both sides with oil. Grill the patties over *direct medium heat*, with the lid closed, until fully cooked but still juicy, 8 to 10 minutes, turning once when the patties release easily from the grate without sticking. During the last 1 to 2 minutes of grilling time, top each patty with a slice of cheese to melt, and toast the rolls, cut side down, over direct heat. Remove from the grill and build the burgers with arugula and lemon mayonnaise. Serve warm.

POULTRY

213

SPICE-RUBBED DUCK BREASTS
WITH ORANGE-CUMIN SAUCE

SERVES: 4 | PREP TIME: 20 minutes | GRILLING TIME: about 8 minutes

RUB
- 2 teaspoons ground cumin
- 1 teaspoon ground coriander
- 1 teaspoon ground cardamom
- 1 teaspoon kosher salt
- 1 teaspoon freshly ground black pepper

- 4 boneless duck breast halves, each about 6 ounces, skin removed, patted dry
  Extra-virgin olive oil

SAUCE
- 1 cup fresh orange juice
- ¼ cup balsamic vinegar
- 1 tablespoon packed golden brown sugar
- 1 teaspoon ground cumin
- 1 teaspoon kosher salt
- ½ teaspoon ground cardamom
- ⅛ teaspoon freshly ground black pepper
- 2 teaspoons cornstarch dissolved in 1 tablespoon fresh orange juice

1. Combine the rub ingredients.

2. Lightly brush the duck breasts on both sides with oil and season evenly with the rub. Set aside at room temperature while you prepare the grill and make the sauce.

3. Prepare the grill for direct cooking over medium heat (350° to 450°F).

4. In a small saucepan whisk the orange juice, vinegar, brown sugar, cumin, salt, cardamom, and pepper. Bring to a boil over medium-high heat and cook until the liquid is reduced by one-third, about 10 minutes, stirring often. Reduce the heat to medium and whisk in the cornstarch mixture. Bring the sauce back to a simmer and simmer until the sauce thickens slightly, about 1 minute, stirring constantly. Remove from the heat.

5. Grill the duck breasts over *direct medium heat*, with the lid closed, until cooked to your desired doneness, about 8 minutes for medium rare, turning once. Remove from the grill and let rest for 3 to 5 minutes. Meanwhile, rewarm the sauce over low heat. Cut the duck breasts crosswise into ⅓-inch slices. Serve the duck warm with the sauce.

DUCK BREAST SALAD
WITH HOISIN DRESSING

SERVES: 4 | PREP TIME: 15 minutes | GRILLING TIME: about 8 minutes

4 boneless duck breast halves (with skin), each about 6 ounces, patted dry
1 teaspoon Chinese five spice
1 teaspoon kosher salt

DRESSING
⅔ cup vegetable oil
¼ cup rice vinegar
2 tablespoons toasted sesame oil
2 tablespoons water
1 tablespoon plus 1 teaspoon hoisin sauce
1 tablespoon peeled, minced fresh ginger
1 tablespoon sesame seeds
1 garlic clove, roughly chopped

4 cups loosely packed mixed baby greens
3 scallions (white and light green parts only), thinly sliced
12 ounces fresh raspberries
½ cup slivered almonds, preferably toasted

1. Prepare the grill for direct cooking over medium heat (350° to 450°F).

2. Score the skin of each duck breast on the diagonal in a crisscross pattern (do not cut through the breast meat). Season evenly with the Chinese five spice and the salt.

3. In a blender combine the dressing ingredients and puree until smooth.

4. Grill the duck breasts, skin side down first, over *direct medium heat*, with the lid closed, until the skin is browned and the meat is cooked to your desired doneness, about 8 minutes for medium rare, turning once (if flare-ups occur, move the breasts temporarily over indirect heat). Remove from the grill and let rest for 3 to 5 minutes. Cut the meat crosswise into ⅓-inch slices.

5. In a large bowl toss the mixed greens, scallions, raspberries, and almonds with ½ cup of the dressing. Divide the salad and duck evenly among four plates. Serve with the remaining dressing on the side.

POULTRY

215

SEAFOOD

7

GRILLING SEAFOOD

TYPE	THICKNESS / WEIGHT	APPROXIMATE GRILLING TIME
Fish, fillet or steak: halibut, red snapper, salmon, sea bass, swordfish, and tuna	½ inch thick	**6–8 minutes** direct high heat
	1 inch thick	**8–10 minutes** direct high heat
	1–1¼ inches thick	**10–12 minutes** direct high heat
Fish, whole	1 pound	**15–20 minutes** indirect medium heat
	2–2½ pounds	**20–30 minutes** indirect medium heat
	3 pounds	**30–45 minutes** indirect medium heat
Clam (discard any that do not open)	2–3 ounces	**6–8 minutes** direct high heat
Lobster tail	6 ounces	**7–11 minutes** direct medium heat
Mussel (discard any that do not open)	1–2 ounces	**5–6 minutes** direct high heat
Oyster	3–4 ounces	**5–7 minutes** direct high heat
Scallop	1½ ounces	**4–6 minutes** direct high heat
Shrimp	1½ ounces	**2–4 minutes** direct high heat

The types, thicknesses, weights, and grilling times are meant to be guidelines rather than hard and fast rules. Cooking times are affected by such factors as altitude, wind, outside temperature, and desired doneness. The general rule of thumb for grilling fish: 8 to 10 minutes per 1-inch thickness.

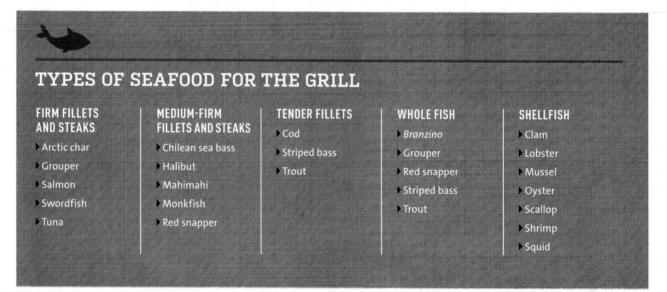

TYPES OF SEAFOOD FOR THE GRILL

FIRM FILLETS AND STEAKS
▸ Arctic char
▸ Grouper
▸ Salmon
▸ Swordfish
▸ Tuna

MEDIUM-FIRM FILLETS AND STEAKS
▸ Chilean sea bass
▸ Halibut
▸ Mahimahi
▸ Monkfish
▸ Red snapper

TENDER FILLETS
▸ Cod
▸ Striped bass
▸ Trout

WHOLE FISH
▸ *Branzino*
▸ Grouper
▸ Red snapper
▸ Striped bass
▸ Trout

SHELLFISH
▸ Clam
▸ Lobster
▸ Mussel
▸ Oyster
▸ Scallop
▸ Shrimp
▸ Squid

SEARED SCALLOPS AND GRITS

SERVES: 4 | PREP TIME: 30 minutes | GRILLING TIME: 4–6 minutes

7 tablespoons unsalted butter, divided
⅓ cup *panko* bread crumbs
1 garlic clove, minced or pushed through a press
2 teaspoons finely chopped fresh thyme leaves
Kosher salt

GRITS
3½ cups whole milk, plus more if needed
2 garlic cloves, minced or pushed through a press
¾ cup quick-cooking grits
4 ounces grated extra-sharp white cheddar cheese
Freshly ground black pepper

16 sea scallops, each about 2 ounces
1¼ teaspoons Cajun seasoning
4 scallions, ends trimmed
Hot pepper sauce
1 tablespoon finely chopped fresh Italian parsley leaves

1 Before grilling, remove any tough, little side muscle that may be still attached to the scallop.

2 Pinch one end of the muscle between your thumb and your index finger, and peel it off gently.

1. In a skillet over medium heat, melt the butter. Pour 5 tablespoons of the butter into a bowl; set aside. Add the *panko* and the garlic to the remaining 2 tablespoons butter in the skillet and cook until the *panko* is crisp and golden, 3 to 4 minutes, stirring often. Stir in the thyme and ⅛ teaspoon salt. Remove from the heat.

2. Prepare the grill for direct cooking over high heat (450° to 550°F).

3. In a saucepan combine 3½ cups milk, the garlic, and ¾ teaspoon salt. Bring to a simmer over medium-high heat. Gradually whisk in the grits. Reduce the heat to low and continue cooking until the mixture thickens and the grits are very tender, 6 to 9 minutes, whisking often and adding water ¼ cup at a time if the mixture seems too thick. Stir in the cheese and season with pepper. Remove from the heat and cover to keep warm.

4. Pat the scallops dry. Remove and discard the small, tough side muscle that might be left on each one. In a bowl combine the scallops, Cajun seasoning, ½ teaspoon salt, and ¼ teaspoon pepper. Turn the scallops in the seasonings, and then add 2 tablespoons of the melted butter and toss to coat.

5. Grill the scallops over *direct high heat*, with the lid closed, until they are lightly browned and just opaque in the center, 4 to 6 minutes, turning once or twice. During the last minute of grilling time, grill the scallions over *direct high heat*, turning once. Transfer the scallops to a clean bowl. Add the remaining 3 tablespoons melted butter and 1 tablespoon hot pepper sauce, or to taste; toss to coat. Roughly chop the scallions.

6. If the grits have solidified, loosen with a few tablespoons of water or milk and then warm through. Divide the grits among four plates. Top the grits with the scallions, scallops, and bread crumbs. Garnish with parsley and serve right away with more hot pepper sauce, if desired.

SERVES: 4 | PREP TIME: 15 minutes | GRILLING TIME: about 6 minutes

SPECIAL EQUIPMENT: metal or bamboo skewers

BREADING
 1   cup fresh bread crumbs
 1   tablespoon finely chopped fresh Italian parsley leaves
 1   teaspoon dried oregano
 ½   teaspoon smoked paprika
 ½   teaspoon freshly ground black pepper
 1   medium garlic clove, minced or pushed through a press
 ¼   teaspoon kosher salt

     Extra-virgin olive oil
12   large shrimp (21/30 count), peeled and deveined, tails removed
12   sea scallops, each 1–1½ ounces
 1   lemon, cut into wedges

1. If using bamboo skewers, soak in water for at least 30 minutes.

2. Prepare the grill for direct cooking over high heat (450° to 550°F).

3. In a shallow dish combine the breading ingredients, including 1 tablespoon oil.

4. Pat the scallops dry. Remove and discard the small, tough side muscle that might be left on each scallop. Thread the shrimp and scallops on their own skewers. Lightly brush the shellfish on both sides with oil and then press them into the breading mixture to coat, patting the crumbs firmly to help them adhere. Let stand for 5 minutes to allow the breading to set.

5. Grill the skewers over direct high heat, with the lid closed, until the shellfish is just opaque in the center and the crumbs are golden brown, turning once or twice (some of the crumbs may become slightly charred). The scallops will take about 6 minutes, and the shrimp will take about 4 minutes. Remove from the grill and serve immediately with the lemon wedges.

Serve the skewers with a grilled pepper medley. Cut four bell peppers into thin slices. Coat them lightly with oil and season with salt. Spread them in a single layer on a preheated perforated grill pan and grill over direct medium heat until crisp-tender, 4 to 6 minutes, turning occasionally.

SERVES: 4 | **PREP TIME: 50 minutes** | **GRILLING TIME: 3–5 minutes**

SPECIAL EQUIPMENT: metal or bamboo skewers

¾	cup roughly chopped fresh Italian parsley leaves
¼	cup roughly chopped fresh tarragon leaves
¼	cup shelled unsalted pistachios
5	teaspoons fresh lemon juice
1	garlic clove, peeled and smashed
	Kosher salt
	Freshly ground black pepper
	Extra-virgin olive oil
1	tablespoon water
32	large shrimp (21/30 count), peeled and deveined, tails left on
24	grape tomatoes
2	small zucchini, each halved lengthwise and cut crosswise into 24 half-moons
1	large yellow bell pepper, cut into 24 pieces
12	scallions (white and light green parts only), cut into 24 pieces
	Lemon wedges

1. If using bamboo skewers, soak in water for at least 30 minutes.

2. In a food processor combine the parsley, tarragon, pistachios, lemon juice, garlic, ¼ teaspoon salt, and ¼ teaspoon pepper. Process until the mixture is finely ground, 30 seconds to 1 minute. With the motor running, slowly pour ½ cup oil through the feed tube and process until smooth, scraping down the sides of the bowl once or twice. Transfer ⅓ cup of the pesto to a bowl for brushing on the kabobs. Transfer the remaining pesto to another bowl and stir in the water to loosen the pesto slightly. Set aside for serving.

3. Prepare the grill for direct cooking over high heat (450° to 550°F).

4. Thread the shrimp, tomatoes, zucchini, bell pepper, and scallions alternately onto skewers. Brush the ingredients with oil, and then brush them evenly with the reserved ⅓ cup pesto. Lightly season with salt and pepper. Grill the kabobs over *direct high heat*, with the lid closed, until the shrimp are just firm to the touch and opaque in the center, 3 to 5 minutes, turning once or twice. The vegetables will be crisp-tender. Remove from the grill. Drizzle the remaining pesto over the kabobs and squeeze the lemon on top.

LEMON RISOTTO
WITH GRILLED ASPARAGUS AND SHRIMP

SERVES: 6–8 | PREP TIME: about 20 minutes, plus 30–40 minutes for the risotto | GRILLING TIME: 6–8 minutes

1 pound asparagus
Extra-virgin olive oil
Kosher salt
18 extra-large shrimp (16/20 count), peeled and deveined, tails removed
1 tablespoon fresh lemon juice

RISOTTO
6 cups low-sodium chicken broth
3 tablespoons unsalted butter, divided
2 tablespoons extra-virgin olive oil
½ cup finely chopped yellow onion
1 teaspoon kosher salt, divided
2 cups arborio rice
½ cup dry white wine
½ cup finely grated Parmigiano-Reggiano® cheese, divided
1 tablespoon finely grated lemon zest
¼ cup fresh lemon juice
2 tablespoons finely chopped fresh Italian parsley leaves
1 tablespoon finely chopped fresh mint leaves
Freshly ground black pepper

1. Prepare the grill for direct cooking over medium heat (350° to 450°F).

2. Remove and discard the tough bottom of each asparagus spear by grasping each end and bending it gently until it snaps at its natural point of tenderness, usually about two-thirds of the way down the spear. Place the asparagus on a plate and drizzle with oil, turning to coat. Season with salt.

3. Brush the shrimp with oil and lightly season with salt.

4. Grill the asparagus (perpendicular to the bars on the cooking grate) over *direct medium heat*, with the lid closed, until browned in spots and crisp-tender, 6 to 8 minutes, turning occasionally. At the same time, grill the shrimp over *direct medium heat* until slightly firm on the surface and opaque in the center, 3 to 5 minutes, turning once. Remove from the grill as they are done. Toss the shrimp with the lemon juice. When the asparagus and shrimp are cool enough to handle, cut them into 1-inch pieces. Set aside.

5. In a medium saucepan over high heat, bring the broth to a simmer. Keep warm.

6. In a large saucepan over medium heat, melt 2 tablespoons of the butter with the oil. Add the onion and ½ teaspoon of the salt. Sauté until the onion is softened but not browned, 3 to 4 minutes. Add the rice and cook until the grains are coated with the butter mixture and turn opaque, about 2 minutes, stirring frequently. Add the wine and stir until evaporated, about 1 minute. Add 1 cup of the warm broth. Simmer until the rice has absorbed nearly all of the liquid, stirring occasionally. Add the remaining broth ½ cup at a time, stirring until nearly all of the liquid is absorbed before adding the next addition, 25 to 30 minutes in all. At this point the risotto should be creamy and the grains should be plump and tender, yet firm to the bite.

7. Remove the risotto from the heat and stir in the remaining 1 tablespoon butter, ¼ cup of the cheese, the lemon zest and juice, and the remaining ½ teaspoon salt. Fold in the asparagus, shrimp, parsley, and mint and season with pepper. Divide the risotto among serving bowls, garnish with the remaining ¼ cup cheese, and serve immediately.

SHRIMP AND CHORIZO TACOS
WITH FIRE-ROASTED CORN SALSA

SERVES: 4 | PREP TIME: 25 minutes | GRILLING TIME: 20–27 minutes

3 ears fresh corn, husked
   Extra-virgin olive oil
2 medium jalapeño chile peppers
1 Hass avocado, cut into ¼-inch pieces
¼ cup finely chopped red onion
2 tablespoons chopped fresh cilantro leaves
5 teaspoons fresh lime juice
   Kosher salt
   Freshly ground black pepper
24 large shrimp (21/30 count), peeled and deveined, tails removed
¾ teaspoon prepared chili powder
3 links fresh chorizo sausage, about 12 ounces total or 2 links hot linguica, about 13 ounces total
8 corn or flour tortillas (6–8 inches)

1. Prepare the grill for direct cooking over medium heat (350° to 450°F).

2. Lightly brush the corn all over with oil. Grill the corn and the jalapeños over *direct medium heat*, with the lid closed, until the corn is browned in spots and tender and the jalapeños are blackened and blistered, turning as needed. The corn will take 10 to 15 minutes and the jalapeños will take 7 to 9 minutes. Remove from the grill as they are done; let cool. Cut the corn kernels off the cobs. Scrape off and discard the loosened skin, and remove and discard the stems and seeds from the jalapeños; finely chop the jalapeños. Combine the corn, jalapeños, avocado, onion, cilantro, lime juice, ½ teaspoon salt, and ⅛ teaspoon pepper.

3. Brush the shrimp on both sides with 1 tablespoon oil and season with the chili powder, ¼ teaspoon salt, and ⅛ teaspoon pepper. Grill the chorizo over *direct medium heat*, with the lid closed, until cooked through, 10 to 12 minutes, turning occasionally. At the same time, grill the shrimp over *direct medium heat* until they are firm to the touch and opaque in the center, 3 to 5 minutes, turning once. During the last minute of grilling time, warm the tortillas over direct heat, turning once or twice. Remove everything from the grill and cut the chorizo into ¼-inch slices. Serve the shrimp, chorizo, and salsa in warm tortillas.

SERVES: 4 | PREP TIME: 25 minutes | MARINATING TIME: 1 hour | GRILLING TIME: 2–4 minutes

MARINADE

¼ cup minced yellow onion
¼ cup fresh lemon juice
2 tablespoons chopped fresh dill
1 tablespoon Dijon mustard

Extra-virgin olive oil
Kosher salt
Freshly ground black pepper
24 large shrimp (21/30 count), peeled and deveined, tails removed

DRESSING

2 tablespoons fresh lemon juice
1 tablespoon red wine vinegar
1 small garlic clove, minced or pushed through a press

SALAD

1½ cups cherry tomatoes, each cut in half
1 cup pitted kalamata olives
4 ounces crumbled feta cheese
1 small red bell pepper, thinly sliced
½ cup thinly sliced red onion
½ cup fresh Italian parsley leaves

1. Whisk the marinade ingredients, including ¼ cup oil, ½ teaspoon salt, and ½ teaspoon pepper. Place the shrimp in a large, resealable plastic bag and pour in the marinade. Press the air out of the bag and seal tightly. Turn the bag to distribute the marinade, place in a bowl, and refrigerate for 1 hour.

2. Prepare the grill for direct cooking over high heat (450° to 550°F).

3. Whisk the dressing ingredients. Add ¼ cup oil in a steady stream, whisking constantly to emulsify. Season with ½ teaspoon salt and ½ teaspoon pepper.

4. Remove the shrimp from the bag and discard the marinade. Grill the shrimp over *direct high heat*, with the lid closed, until they are firm to the touch and just turning opaque in the center, 2 to 4 minutes, turning once. Remove from the grill.

5. In a large bowl combine the salad ingredients. Drizzle half of the dressing over the salad and toss to coat. Divide the salad among four serving plates and top with the shrimp. Drizzle with additional dressing and serve immediately.

SEAFOOD

SHRIMP ROLLS
WITH LEMON-CHIVE MAYO

SERVES: 6 | PREP TIME: 25 minutes | GRILLING TIME: 3–5 minutes

SPECIAL EQUIPMENT: perforated grill pan

MAYO

½ cup mayonnaise
2 tablespoons finely chopped fresh chives
1 tablespoon finely chopped fresh tarragon leaves
1 tablespoon finely chopped fresh dill
½ teaspoon finely grated lemon zest
1 teaspoon fresh lemon juice

    Kosher salt
    Freshly ground black pepper
6 tablespoons (¾ stick) unsalted butter
2 garlic cloves, minced or pushed through a press
32 large shrimp (21/30 count), peeled and deveined, tails removed
6 hot dog buns, cut vertically from the top, sides trimmed
1½ cups thinly sliced romaine lettuce
1 large tomato, seeded and diced
    Hot pepper sauce
    Lemon wedges

1. Combine the mayo ingredients, including ¼ teaspoon salt and ¼ teaspoon pepper. Set aside.

2. Prepare the grill for direct cooking over high heat (450° to 550°F) and preheat a perforated grill pan.

3. In a saucepan over medium-low heat, melt the butter with the garlic. Remove from the heat. Pat the shrimp dry and put in a bowl. To the bowl with the shrimp add 2 tablespoons of the garlic butter, ¼ teaspoon salt, and ½ teaspoon pepper. Turn to coat. Brush the remaining garlic butter on the cut sides (outside only) of the buns.

4. Spread the shrimp in a single layer on the grill pan and grill over *direct high heat*, with the lid closed, until they are firm to the touch and just turning opaque in the center, 2 to 4 minutes, turning once or twice. Remove from the grill to cool. Toast the buns, buttered sides only, over *direct high heat*, about 1 minute, turning once.

5. Roughly chop the shrimp, add to the mayo, and stir to combine. Open the buns and add lettuce and the shrimp mixture. Top with tomatoes and serve immediately with hot pepper sauce and lemon wedges.

SERVES: 4 | PREP TIME: 30 minutes | GRILLING TIME: 6–8 minutes

SPECIAL EQUIPMENT: oyster knife

RÉMOULADE

½   cup mayonnaise
¼   cup finely chopped scallions (white and light green parts only)
1½ teaspoons Dijon mustard
½   teaspoon finely grated lemon zest
1½ teaspoons fresh lemon juice
¼   teaspoon hot pepper sauce
¼   teaspoon paprika
¼   teaspoon garlic powder
¼   teaspoon kosher salt

32 large, fresh oysters in the shell, each about 3 inches long
 4 soft French rolls, each about 6 inches long, split
 3 tablespoons extra-virgin olive oil
 2 cups shredded romaine lettuce
 3 medium tomatoes, cut into slices
16 dill pickle chips
½   cup French fried onions

1. Combine the rémoulade ingredients.

2. Prepare the grill for direct cooking over high heat (450° to 550°F).

3. Grill the oysters over *direct high heat*, with the lid closed, until they open ¼ to ½ inch, 5 to 7 minutes. Using tongs, carefully remove the oysters from the grill, place on a sheet pan, and cover tightly with aluminum foil. Discard any oysters that are not open.

4. Use an oyster knife to open the shells. Carefully cut each oyster loose from the top shell and then from the bottom shell by running the oyster knife carefully under the body. Cover the shucked oysters with foil to keep them warm.

5. Brush the cut side of each roll with the oil. Grill the rolls, cut side down, over *direct high heat* until lightly toasted, 30 seconds to 1 minute.

6. Spread the bottom half of each roll with rémoulade and top with lettuce, tomatoes, pickles, oysters, and French fried onions. Serve immediately.

SEAFOOD

229

LOBSTER TAILS
WITH BASIL-LEMON BUTTER

SERVES: 4 | PREP TIME: 10 minutes | GRILLING TIME: 7–11 minutes

SPECIAL EQUIPMENT: kitchen shears

BUTTER

1¼ cups (2½ sticks) unsalted butter
2   tablespoons finely chopped fresh basil leaves
1   tablespoon finely grated lemon zest
1   tablespoon fresh lemon juice
½   teaspoon hot pepper sauce
½   teaspoon kosher salt

4   frozen lobster tails, each 6–10 ounces, thawed

1 Use kitchen shears to cut through the hard back shell all the way to the fins.

2 Turn the lobster tail over, and cut through the center of the shell on the underside.

3 Use a sharp, heavy knife to cut each tail in half lengthwise, passing through the openings you already made.

1. Prepare the grill for direct cooking over medium heat (350° to 450°F).

2. In a small saucepan over low heat, melt the butter, swirling the saucepan occasionally. When the butter is melted, skim off the foam and discard. Stir in the remaining butter ingredients and heat for 1 minute. Remove from the heat. Pour off ¼ cup of the butter to use for grilling the lobster. Cover the saucepan to keep the remaining butter warm for serving.

3. Using kitchen shears, cut along the center of the top (rounded) side of one of the lobster shells, cutting from the wider end to the tail. Turn the lobster tail over and make the same cut, again starting at the wider end and cutting toward the tail. Using a knife, cut through the meat and the tail to divide the tail lengthwise into two pieces. Repeat with the remaining lobster tails.

4. Brush the meat side of the lobster with some of the butter reserved for grilling. Grill the lobster tails, meat side down, over *direct medium heat*, with the lid closed, for 2 to 3 minutes, depending on their size. Brush the tops of the shells with a little more of the butter, turn them over, and grill just until the meat is white and firm but not dry, 5 to 8 minutes more. Remove from the grill and serve the lobster warm with the reserved butter.

Tip

Be sure to allow the lobster tails, which are sold frozen, to thaw gently. Don't attempt to rush the process in a microwave oven, or the delicate meat will turn tough.

CIOPPINO WITH GRILLED SHELLFISH
AND GARLIC CROUTONS

SERVES: 4–6 | PREP TIME: 40 minutes | GRILLING TIME: 8–10 minutes

Extra-virgin olive oil
1 cup finely chopped yellow onion
1 medium fennel bulb, cored and thinly sliced
3 garlic cloves, smashed
1 small red bell pepper, cut into ¼-inch dice
1 teaspoon dried oregano
¼ teaspoon crushed red pepper flakes
1 can (28 ounces) Italian plum tomatoes in juice
4 cups low-sodium chicken broth
1 tablespoon tomato paste
1 bay leaf
Kosher salt
Freshly ground black pepper
24 large shrimp (21/30 count), peeled and deveined, tails left on
12 large sea scallops, each about 1½ ounces
1 large garlic clove, finely grated, minced, or pushed through a press
½ loaf ciabatta or other Italian bread, cut into 1½ inch cubes (12–16 pieces)
24 live mussels, about 1 pound total, scrubbed and debearded
¼ cup finely chopped fresh Italian parsley leaves

Tip

Cioppino, a fisherman's stew originating in San Francisco, typically includes shellfish that are gently poached in a tomato-based stock. In this recipe, shrimp and scallops are grilled separately and then added near the end, bringing charred, smoky flavors to the stew. The garlic croutons require some vigilance to avoid burning, but it's worth the trouble because the crunchy bread does a great job of soaking up the amazing broth.

1. In a large pot over medium heat, warm 2 tablespoons oil. Add the onion and the fennel and sauté until the vegetables begin to soften, about 5 minutes. Add the smashed garlic, bell pepper, oregano, and red pepper flakes and sauté for 2 minutes. Add the tomatoes and their juice (crushing the tomatoes with your hands before adding them to the pot), the broth, tomato paste, bay leaf, 1 teaspoon salt, and ¼ teaspoon pepper. Bring to a boil, reduce the heat to medium-low, and simmer, partially covered, for 30 minutes, stirring occasionally.

2. While the stew is simmering, prepare the grill for direct cooking over high heat (450° to 550°F).

3. Rinse the shrimp and the scallops under cold water and pat dry. Remove the small, tough side muscle that might be left on each scallop. Brush the shellfish on all sides with oil and lightly season with salt and pepper.

4. Combine 2 tablespoons oil, the finely grated garlic, and the bread cubes and toss to coat.

5. Grill the shrimp and the scallops over *direct high heat*, with the lid closed, until they are just opaque in the center, turning once. The shrimp will take 2 to 4 minutes and the scallops will take 4 to 6 minutes. Remove from the grill as they are done.

6. Lower the temperature of the grill to medium heat (350° to 450°F). Grill the bread cubes over *direct medium heat*, with the lid closed, until lightly browned on all sides, about 4 minutes, turning several times.

7. Just before serving, return the stew to a vigorous simmer over medium heat. Add the mussels, cover the pot, and cook until the mussels open, 3 to 5 minutes (discard any unopened mussels). Stir in the scallops and shrimp. Ladle the stew into wide soup bowls. Top with the parsley, garnish with the croutons, and serve warm.

gr▮ll SKILLS:
PERFECT FISH

Choose Wisely

1 Fresh fish have a firm, shiny flesh that bounces back a bit when you touch it. If the fish has started to separate, or if it's discolored, don't buy it.

2 High-quality fish smells like the ocean, not like cooked fish.

3 For whole fish, look for clear, bright eyes. If a fish has eyes that have clouded over, it's way past its prime.

4 The scales of whole fish should be smooth. Breaks or cracks in the scaling pattern indicate poor handling or age.

Filleting a Whole Fish

Begin by scaling and rinsing the fish in the sink. Then remove the head by making a diagonal cut just behind the small fin at the base of the head. Cut all the way through the bones.

Using a very sharp knife with a flexible blade, begin a cut about ½ inch deep just above the backbone near the tail end. Continue the cut along the length of the back until you reach the other end of the fish.

Then go back and make the cut deeper and deeper with each gentle stroke, keeping the blade of the knife as close to the bones as possible. Gently lift the top fillet with one hand so you can see where your knife is cutting.

Lay the fillet back in place and cut through the tail end, always moving the blade of the knife away from you in case the knife slips. Turn the fish over and repeat the process on the other side.

Firm Fillets

Salmon and halibut are good choices for grilling because their flesh is firm. Look for fillets that are at least one inch thick from end to end. Thinner fillets cook too quickly and tend to break apart.

Preventing Sticking

The first step is to get your cooking grate hot and clean enough that it will dry the watery surface of the fillets quickly so they can brown. Once they begin to brown on a clean grate, they begin to release.

Oil is a natural lubricant that will prevent sticking, so brush it evenly and generously over the fillets. But don't overdo it. If the fish is dripping with oil, you will probably get flare-ups.

Don't touch any fillet until it is browned and ready to turn. It is often a good idea to grill the first side a little longer than the second side. An extra few minutes on the first side (with the lid closed) will help the fillet to release from the grates more easily.

When Is It Done?

PEEK TEST

When the flesh turns from translucent to opaque all the way to the center and just begins to flake around the edges, the fish is done. This typically happens when the internal temperature reaches 125° to 130°F.

SKEWER TEST

If you don't have an instant-read thermometer, insert a metal skewer into the thickest part of the fish for a few seconds and then touch the skewer on a sensitive part of your skin.

If the skewer feels cold to an area like the base of your thumb, the fish is underdone. If the skewer feels warm, the fish is cooked. If the skewer feels hot, the fish is overcooked.

Using a Perforated Grill Pan

If you are concerned about turning your fillets on the grill, just set them on a preheated grill pan over indirect high heat. There is no need to turn them. They will roast fairly evenly on both sides, but the side touching the pan should develop a nice golden crust.

235

HALIBUT
WITH ROASTED VEGETABLES AND BASIL

SERVES: 4 | PREP TIME: 30 minutes | GRILLING TIME: 26–28 minutes

SPECIAL EQUIPMENT: perforated grill pan

2 cups loosely packed fresh basil leaves
2 tablespoons fresh lemon juice, divided
¼ teaspoon crushed red pepper flakes
  Kosher salt
  Extra-virgin olive oil
1 teaspoon dried thyme
½ teaspoon dried oregano
  Freshly ground black pepper
2 large red bell peppers, cut into ½-inch strips
2 medium red onions, cut crosswise into
  ½-inch slices and separated into rings
3 garlic cloves, finely chopped
1 pint cherry or grape tomatoes
18 oil-cured black olives, pitted and halved
4 halibut fillets (with skin), each 6–8 ounces
  and about 1 inch thick

1. In a food processor combine the basil, 1 tablespoon of the lemon juice, the red pepper flakes, and ½ teaspoon salt. Pulse a few times to roughly chop the basil. With the motor running, add ¼ cup oil in a steady stream and process until the mixture forms a chunky sauce. Transfer to a bowl and press a piece of plastic wrap onto the surface to prevent discoloring.

2. Prepare the grill for direct cooking over medium heat (350° to 450°F) and preheat a perforated grill pan.

3. In a large bowl whisk ¼ cup oil, the thyme, oregano, 1 teaspoon salt, and ½ teaspoon pepper. Add the bell peppers, onions, garlic, and tomatoes and toss to coat. Spread the vegetables in a single layer on the grill pan and grill over *direct medium heat*, with the lid closed, until the vegetables have softened and the tomatoes have begun to break down, about 20 minutes, stirring occasionally. Transfer the vegetables to a heatproof bowl. Stir in the olives. Keep warm. Increase the temperature of the grill to medium-high heat (400° to 500°F).

4. Brush the flesh side of the halibut fillets with oil and season evenly with 1 teaspoon salt and ½ teaspoon pepper. Grill the fillets over *direct medium-high heat*, with the lid closed, until the flesh just begins to flake when poked with the tip of a knife, 6 to 8 minutes, turning once. Remove from the grill. Remove the skin from the fillets. Divide the vegetables among four serving plates. Nestle a fillet in the center of the vegetables. Drizzle with the remaining 1 tablespoon lemon juice, and then spoon the sauce over the fish. Serve right away.

SERVES: 4 | PREP TIME: 30 minutes | GRILLING TIME: 6–8 minutes

RÉMOULADE

- ⅓ cup mayonnaise
- 2 scallions, ends trimmed, minced
- 1 tablespoon minced fresh chives
- 1 tablespoon capers, rinsed and chopped
- 1½ teaspoons finely chopped fresh Italian parsley leaves
- 1½ teaspoons fresh lemon juice
- 1 teaspoon minced garlic
- ¼ teaspoon freshly ground black pepper

    Kosher salt
- 2¼ cups shredded green cabbage, about ½ pound
- 1 carrot, cut into small dice
- 1 scallion (white and light green parts only), cut into thin strips about 2 inches long

MARINADE

- ¼ cup peanut oil
- 3 tablespoons chopped fresh basil leaves
- 2 tablespoons fresh lemon juice
- 2 teaspoons finely chopped fresh ginger
- ½ teaspoon crushed red pepper flakes
- ½ teaspoon ground cayenne pepper
- ¼ teaspoon ground turmeric

- 4 skinless halibut fillets, each about 6 ounces and 1 inch thick

1. Combine the rémoulade ingredients. Season with salt, if desired. In a large bowl combine the cabbage, carrot, and scallion. Add the rémoulade and toss until mixed.

2. Prepare the grill for direct cooking over high heat (450° to 550°F).

3. Whisk the marinade ingredients, including ¾ teaspoon salt. Pat the halibut fillets dry with a paper towel, place them in a shallow baking dish, and brush them thoroughly with some of the marinade. Reserve the remaining marinade.

4. Grill the fillets over *direct high heat*, with the lid closed, until they release from the cooking grate without sticking, 4 to 5 minutes. Carefully turn the fillets over and brush with the reserved marinade. Discard any remaining marinade. Continue cooking until the fish just begins to flake when poked with the tip of a knife, 2 to 3 minutes more. Remove from the grill and serve warm with the slaw.

HALIBUT AND SHRIMP PATTIES
WITH GRILLED VEGETABLE SALAD

SERVES: 4 | PREP TIME: 20 minutes | CHILLING TIME: 30 minutes–1 hour | GRILLING TIME: 10–12 minutes

SPECIAL EQUIPMENT: perforated grill pan

PATTIES

- 1 pound skinless halibut fillets
- 8 ounces shrimp, peeled and deveined, tails removed
- 3 tablespoons minced fresh chives
- 1½ tablespoons minced fresh dill
- 1 tablespoon Dijon mustard
- 1 tablespoon fresh lemon juice

  Kosher salt
  Freshly ground black pepper
  Extra-virgin olive oil
- 2 medium zucchini, cut crosswise into ½-inch slices
- 2 medium Japanese eggplants, cut crosswise into ½-inch slices
- 2 medium red bell peppers, cut into bite-sized pieces
- 6 cups shredded romaine lettuce
  Homemade or store-bought ranch dressing

Tip

Pureed shrimp takes the place of the egg or bread crumbs used in other recipes to bind all the ingredients together.

1. In a food processor combine the patty ingredients, including ½ teaspoon salt and ½ teaspoon pepper, and pulse until the mixture forms a chunky paste, scraping down the sides of the bowl once or twice. With wet hands, gently form four loosely packed patties of equal size, each about 4 inches in diameter, and place them on a baking sheet. Refrigerate for 30 minutes to 1 hour.

2. Prepare the grill for direct cooking over medium heat (350° to 450°F) and preheat a perforated grill pan.

3. Brush the patties on both sides with oil. Brush the zucchini, eggplants, and bell peppers with oil and season evenly with salt and pepper.

4. Spread the vegetables in a single layer on the grill pan and grill over *direct medium heat*, with the lid closed, until crisp-tender, 6 to 8 minutes, turning once or twice. At the same time, grill the patties on the cooking grates over *direct medium heat* until fully cooked, 10 to 12 minutes, turning once or twice. Remove from the grill as they are done.

5. Place 1½ cups of the lettuce on each of four serving plates. Top with grilled vegetables and a patty. Drizzle with the ranch dressing and serve immediately.

FRESH TUNA SANDWICHES
WITH RED PEPPER MAYO AND CUCUMBER SALAD

SERVES: 4 | PREP TIME: 15 minutes | GRILLING TIME: 3–4 minutes

SALAD
- 1 English cucumber, about 12 ounces, very thinly sliced
- ½ large sweet onion, thinly sliced
- ¼ cup seasoned rice vinegar
- 1 teaspoon ground coriander

- ½ roasted red bell pepper (from a jar), drained
- ½ cup mayonnaise
- 4 tuna fillets, each about 6 ounces and 1 inch thick
- 1 tablespoon extra-virgin olive oil
- ½ teaspoon kosher salt
- ¼ teaspoon paprika
- ⅛ teaspoon freshly ground black pepper
- 4 small ciabatta rolls, split
- 1 cup baby arugula

1. Prepare the grill for direct cooking over high heat (450° to 550°F).

2. Combine the salad ingredients and toss thoroughly. Set aside at room temperature until ready to serve, stirring occasionally.

3. In a food processor or a blender combine the bell pepper and the mayonnaise and puree until fairly smooth, scraping down the sides of the bowl as needed.

4. Lightly brush the tuna fillets on both sides with the oil and season evenly with the salt, paprika, and pepper. Grill the fillets over *direct high heat*, with the lid open, until cooked to your desired doneness, 3 to 4 minutes for medium rare, turning once. During the last minute of grilling time, toast the rolls, cut side down, over direct heat. Remove the tuna and the rolls from the grill. Cut the tuna into thin slices.

5. Spread the cut side of the rolls generously with the red pepper mayo and top with tuna and arugula. Drain any excess liquid from the cucumber salad and serve with the warm sandwiches.

If you have a mandoline or a food processor equipped with a slicing blade, use it to slice the cucumber and the onion as thinly as possible.

SERVES: 6 | PREP TIME: 15 minutes | GRILLING TIME: 2–3 minutes

TAPENADE

¼ cup finely chopped dried figs
½ cup medium-dry sherry
1 cup store-bought black olive or mixed olive tapenade
¼ cup finely chopped fresh mint leaves
Finely grated zest of 1 lemon
1 tablespoon fresh lemon juice
¼ teaspoon freshly ground black pepper

Extra-virgin olive oil

RUB

½ teaspoon paprika
½ teaspoon kosher salt
¼ teaspoon freshly ground black pepper

6 ahi tuna steaks, each about 8 ounces and 1 inch thick

1. In a small bowl stir the figs and sherry thoroughly and let stand for 10 minutes. Drain, discarding any remaining sherry. Combine the figs with the tapenade, mint, lemon zest and juice, and pepper. If, after combining the ingredients, the tapenade seems too dry, add up to 2 tablespoons oil until it reaches your desired consistency. Set aside until serving.

2. Prepare the grill for direct cooking over high heat (450° to 550°F).

3. Combine the rub ingredients. Lightly brush the tuna steaks on both sides with oil and season evenly with the rub. Grill the steaks over *direct high heat*, with the lid open, until cooked to rare doneness, 2 to 3 minutes, turning once. Remove from the grill and serve right away with the tapenade spooned on top.

For medium-rare doneness, grill the tuna for 3 to 4 minutes, turning once.

For medium doneness, grill the tuna for about 5 minutes, turning once.

SEAFOOD

241

SEARED SPICY TUNA AND AVOCADO ROLLS

SERVES: 4 | **PREP TIME: 45 minutes** | **GRILLING TIME: 1½–2 minutes**

SPECIAL EQUIPMENT: bamboo sushi mat

2	cups raw sushi rice
¼	cup seasoned rice vinegar
4	teaspoons honey
¾	teaspoon kosher salt
½	cup mayonnaise
1	tablespoon plus 4 teaspoons toasted sesame oil, divided
4	teaspoons wasabi paste
1	tuna steak, about 1 pound and 1 inch thick
8	sheets nori, each about 7½ by 8 inches
1	Hass avocado, halved and cut crosswise into 24 slices
4	teaspoons sesame seeds, toasted
½	cup low-sodium soy sauce
1	tablespoon hot chili-garlic sauce, such as Sriracha Pickled ginger (optional)

1. Cook the rice according to package directions. Cool thoroughly. Combine the vinegar, honey, and salt and whisk until the salt is dissolved. Pour the mixture over the cooled rice and mix gently but thoroughly.

2. Prepare the grill for direct cooking over high heat (450° to 550°F).

3. Combine the mayonnaise, 4 teaspoons of the oil, and the wasabi paste. Reserve ¼ cup for serving.

4. Coat the tuna steak on both sides with the remaining 1 tablespoon oil. Grill over *direct high heat*, with the lid open, until the tuna is browned on the outside and just barely warm but still red in the center, 1½ to 2 minutes, turning once. Remove from the grill and cool completely. Cut the steak lengthwise into eight ½-inch slices.

5. Arrange the sushi mat with the slats running horizontally. Place one sheet of nori, shiny side down, on the mat, lining up a long edge with the edge of the mat nearest you. With wet hands, spread ½ cup of rice onto the nori in a thin, even layer, leaving a ½-inch border on the long end opposite you. Spread 2 teaspoons of the mayonnaise mixture in a horizontal stripe about ¾ inch wide across the rice, 2 inches from the side nearest you. Put one slice of the tuna on top of the mayonnaise and then three slices of avocado over the tuna. Top with ½ teaspoon sesame seeds.

6. Beginning with the edge nearest you, lift up the nori and fold the bottom up and over the filling, tightly rolling the sushi into a thick cylinder, using the mat to assist in rolling. Once rolled, wrap the sushi in the mat and gently squeeze to shape and seal. If the ½-inch border of nori doesn't stick, moisten lightly with water and press to seal securely. Repeat with remaining nori and filling.

7. Combine the soy sauce and the hot chili-garlic sauce. Transfer the rolls, seam side down, to a cutting board. Dip a sharp, thin knife into water and shake off any excess. Using a sawing motion, cut the rolls crosswise into six to eight equal pieces. Serve with the soy sauce mixture, the reserved mayonnaise, and the pickled ginger, if using.

1 Buy sushi-grade tuna and sear it quickly over high heat, leaving the center raw.

2 Arrange the tuna in a line on the mayonnaise, followed by the avocado and the sesame seeds.

3 Lift up the nori and fold the bottom up and over the filling, rolling the sushi into a tight cylinder.

4 Roll the mat outside the cylinder to help create a nice round, compact shape.

Tip

To make spreading the mayonnaise over the rice easier, put the mixture in a resealable plastic bag, cut off a corner, and squeeze the mixture out of the bag.

OPEN-FACED SALMON BURGERS
WITH WASABI MAYO

SERVES: 4 | PREP TIME: 35 minutes | CHILLING TIME: 1–2 hours | GRILLING TIME: 6–7 minutes

PATTIES

1	skinless salmon fillet, about 1½ pounds, pin bones removed, cut into 1-inch chunks
6	tablespoons *panko* bread crumbs
2	tablespoons cottage cheese
1	large egg, lightly beaten
3	scallions (white and light green parts only), finely chopped
1	tablespoon peeled, grated fresh ginger
	Finely grated zest of 1 large lime
½	teaspoon kosher salt
¼	teaspoon freshly ground black pepper

6	tablespoons mayonnaise
1	teaspoon prepared wasabi paste
	Olive oil cooking spray
2	English muffins, split
1	Hass avocado, cut lengthwise into thin slices
8	slices tomato

1. In a food processor combine the patty ingredients. Pulse until the salmon chunks are evenly chopped, four to six pulses, being careful not to puree the mixture.

2. With wet hands and handling the mixture as little as possible, gently form four patties of equal size, each about ¾ inch thick. Place the patties on a large plate, cover loosely with plastic wrap, and refrigerate for at least 1 hour or up to 2 hours.

3. Prepare the grill for direct cooking over high heat (450° to 550°F).

4. Whisk the mayonnaise and the wasabi. Cover and refrigerate until ready to serve.

5. Lightly coat the salmon patties with olive oil spray on both sides. Grill the patties over *direct high heat*, with the lid closed, for about 4 minutes (do not move the patties during this time or they may fall apart). Using a metal spatula, carefully turn the patties over and continue cooking until they are firm and cooked through, 2 to 3 minutes more. During the last minute of grilling time, lightly toast the muffins, cut side down, over direct heat. Remove the patties and the muffins from the grill.

6. Place the muffins, cut side up, on a platter. Fan one-quarter of the avocado slices on top of each muffin half, and place a salmon patty on the avocado. Top each patty with two slices of tomato and a dollop of wasabi mayo. Serve immediately.

SERVES: 4 | **PREP TIME:** 20 minutes | **GRILLING TIME:** 12–15 minutes

SPECIAL EQUIPMENT: 1 untreated cedar plank,
12–15 inches long and about 7 inches wide

1	salmon fillet (with skin), about 2 pounds and 1–1½ inches thick, pin bones removed
	Kosher salt
	Freshly ground black pepper
2	tablespoons Dijon mustard
2	tablespoons packed golden brown sugar
1	pound broccolini, stem ends trimmed and split lengthwise ½ inch below the florets (see photo below)
2½	tablespoons extra-virgin olive oil
1½	teaspoons finely grated orange zest

1. Soak the cedar plank in water for at least 1 hour.

2. Prepare the grill for direct cooking over medium heat (350° to 450°F).

3. Carefully cut the salmon fillet crosswise into four equal pieces and generously season the salmon with salt and pepper. Stir the mustard and the brown sugar into a paste. Spread the paste all over the salmon. Toss the broccolini with the oil, ¾ teaspoon salt, and ½ teaspoon pepper.

4. Place the soaked cedar plank over *direct medium heat* and close the lid. After 5 to 10 minutes, when the plank begins to smoke and char, turn the plank over. Place the fillets, skin side down, in a single layer on the plank, leaving a little room between the fillets, and place the broccolini perpendicular to the bars on the cooking grates. Grill the fillets and the broccolini over *direct medium heat,* with the lid closed, until the salmon is cooked to your desired doneness and the broccolini is crisp-tender, 12 to 15 minutes, turning the vegetables and checking the salmon for doneness every 5 minutes. The broccolini will char a little on the floret ends. Remove the fillets from the plank and transfer the broccolini to a large bowl. Add the orange zest to the broccolini and toss to combine. Serve right away.

Splitting the broccolini stems in half means they will cook faster.

Char the cedar plank on one side before adding the salmon.

SEAFOOD

245

SALMON AND VEGETABLE KABOBS
WITH LEMON-HERB VINAIGRETTE

SERVES: 4 | **PREP TIME:** 30 minutes | **GRILLING TIME:** 8–10 minutes

SPECIAL EQUIPMENT: 8 metal or bamboo skewers

VINAIGRETTE
¼ cup fresh lemon juice
3 tablespoons minced fresh cilantro leaves
3 tablespoons minced fresh Italian parsley leaves
4 garlic cloves, minced or pushed through a press
1½ teaspoons paprika
¾ teaspoon ground cumin
¼ teaspoon ground cayenne pepper

  Kosher salt
  Extra-virgin olive oil
1½ pounds skinless center-cut salmon fillet, cut into
    1¼-inch cubes, pin bones removed
2 medium zucchini, cut into 1-inch-thick half-moons
2 medium yellow squash, cut into 1-inch-thick half-moons
½ large red onion, cut lengthwise into quarters, each
    quarter cut crosswise into 2 pieces
  Freshly ground black pepper
1 lemon, quartered

1. If using bamboo skewers, soak in water for at least 30 minutes.

2. Prepare the grill for direct cooking over medium-high heat (400° to 500°F).

3. Combine the vinaigrette ingredients, including 1 teaspoon salt. Gradually add ½ cup oil, whisking constantly until emulsified. Set aside until ready to serve.

4. Thread the salmon cubes onto four skewers. Thread the zucchini, squash, and onion alternately onto four more skewers. Generously brush the salmon and the vegetables all over with oil and season evenly with salt and pepper.

5. Grill the kabobs over *direct medium-high heat*, with the lid closed, until the vegetables are crisp-tender and the salmon is crusty and golden outside and beginning to turn opaque in the center but still moist, 8 to 10 minutes, turning four times. Remove the kabobs from the grill and serve immediately with the vinaigrette and the lemon quarters.

SERVES: 4 | **PREP TIME: 25 minutes** | **MARINATING TIME: 30 minutes** | **GRILLING TIME: 18–24 minutes**

MARINADE

- 1 can (15 ounces) unsweetened coconut milk
- 2 tablespoons fresh lime juice
- 1 tablespoon canola oil
- 1½ teaspoons Thai red curry paste

- 4 salmon fillets (with skin), each 6–8 ounces and about 1 inch thick, pin bones removed
- 1 large red bell pepper
- 1 garlic clove, minced or pushed through a press
- 1 tablespoon peeled, grated fresh ginger
- 1 teaspoon kosher salt
- ¼ cup finely chopped fresh cilantro leaves

1. Combine the marinade ingredients. Place the salmon fillets in a large, resealable plastic bag and pour in the marinade. Press the air out of the bag and seal tightly. Turn the bag to distribute the marinade, place on a plate, and marinate at room temperature for 30 minutes, turning occasionally.

2. Prepare the grill for direct cooking over high heat (450° to 550°F).

3. Grill the bell pepper over *direct high heat*, with the lid closed, until blackened and blistered all over, 10 to 12 minutes, turning occasionally. Put the pepper in a bowl and cover with plastic wrap to trap the steam. Let stand for about 10 minutes. Peel away and discard the charred skin. Cut off and discard the stem and seeds, then roughly chop the pepper. Transfer the pepper to a food processor.

4. Remove the fillets from the bag and pour the marinade into the food processor with the pepper. Add the garlic, ginger, and salt and process until smooth. Transfer to a saucepan and bring to a boil over medium-high heat. Reduce the heat to a simmer and cook for 2 to 3 minutes. Keep warm.

5. Grill the fillets, flesh side down first, over *direct high heat*, with the lid closed, until you can lift the fillets off the cooking grates without sticking, 6 to 8 minutes. Turn the fillets over and continue to cook to your desired doneness, 2 to 4 minutes more for medium rare. Slip a spatula between the skin and the flesh and transfer the fillets to serving plates. Serve the salmon warm with the sauce, and garnish with the cilantro.

RECIPE REMIX:
Then and Now

What do you get when you soak salmon steaks in a bath of lime juice and oil for six long hours? A pretty mushy mix of fragrant fish. We've learned through the years that salmon is plenty rich and flavorful on its own. Marinating it for a long time is usually unnecessary; eventually a marinade's acidic elements will wreak havoc on the delicate texture of fish. Salmon is at its best when paired with bright, sweet, and clean flavors, like the freshly grilled salsa we've added in our Remix. Our contemporary tastes prefer a balance of flavors—sweet and salty, heavy and light. The result is special enough for company, but easy enough to do on a weeknight.

The Original

Lime-Seasoned Salmon
Recipe from *Weber® Grill Out!* ©1990

Charcoal: Direct
Gas: Indirect/Medium Heat

4 fresh or frozen salmon, whitefish, tuna, or sea bass steaks, cut 1 inch thick (about 1 pound)
1/4 cup salad oil
1/4 cup lime juice
1 tablespoon water
1 tablespoon soy sauce
2 teaspoons sesame oil
2 teaspoons honey
4 cups shredded mixed greens
1/2 cup shredded radishes
1/2 cup alfalfa sprouts
1 tablespoon toasted sesame seed
1 canned green chili pepper, rinsed, seeded, and chopped (optional)

Thaw fish, if frozen. Place the fish in a plastic bag set into a shallow dish.

For marinade, in a small mixing bowl combine salad oil, lime juice, water, soy sauce, sesame oil, and honey; pour over the fish. Close bag. Marinate in refrigerator 6 hours, turning bag occasionally to distribute marinade.

In a large mixing bowl toss together mixed greens, radishes, alfalfa sprouts, sesame seed, and, if desired, chili pepper. Transfer to a serving platter. Set aside.

Drain fish, reserving marinade. Transfer marinade to a small aluminum pan.

Lightly grease cooking grill. Place fish on the cooking grill. Grill 10 to 12 minutes or till fish flakes when tested with a fork, turning once halfway through grilling time. After turning, place pan of marinade on the cooking grill beside the fish. Grill marinade till bubbly.

To serve, pour hot marinade over greens on serving platter; toss to wilt slightly. Top with grilled fish. Makes 4 servings.

248

SALMON FILLETS
WITH ROASTED CORN, SWEET TOMATO, AND AVOCADO SALSA

SERVES: 6 | PREP TIME: 30 minutes | GRILLING TIME: 16–24 minutes

2   ears fresh corn, husked
     Extra-virgin olive oil
     Kosher salt
     Freshly ground black pepper
¼   teaspoon prepared chili powder
2   cups cherry tomatoes, red, yellow,
     or a mixture, each cut into quarters
1   cup roughly chopped arugula
2   scallions (white and light green
     parts only), finely chopped
2   tablespoons fresh lime juice
1   large Hass avocado, finely diced
6   salmon fillets (with skin), each
     6–8 ounces and about 1 inch thick,
     pin bones removed
1   lime, cut into 6 wedges

1. Prepare the grill for direct cooking over high heat (450° to 550°F).

2. Lightly brush the corn all over with oil and season evenly with ¼ teaspoon salt, ¼ teaspoon pepper, and the chili powder.

3. Grill the corn over *direct high heat*, with the lid closed, until charred in spots and tender, 8 to 12 minutes, turning occasionally. Remove from the grill and let cool. Working over a large bowl, cut the kernels from the cobs. To the bowl with the corn, add the tomatoes, arugula, scallions, 2 tablespoons oil, the lime juice, ½ teaspoon salt, and ¼ teaspoon pepper. Fold in the avocado.

4. Generously coat the flesh side of the salmon fillets with oil and season evenly with salt and pepper. Grill the fillets, flesh side down first, over *direct high heat*, with the lid closed, until you can lift the fillets off the cooking grates without sticking, 6 to 8 minutes. Turn the fillets over and continue to cook to your desired doneness, 2 to 4 minutes more for medium rare. Slip a spatula between the skin and the flesh and transfer the fillets to serving plates. Serve warm with the salsa and the lime wedges.

SERVES: 4 | PREP TIME: 30 minutes | GRILLING TIME: 6–7 minutes

RELISH

- 3 large plum tomatoes, seeded and finely diced (about 1½ cups)
- ½ cup black olives, such as kalamata, each cut in half
- ½ cup green olives, such as *Cerignola*, each cut in half (or quartered if large)
- 3 tablespoons extra-virgin olive oil
- 2 tablespoons capers, rinsed and drained
- 1 tablespoon white balsamic vinegar
- 2 anchovy fillets packed in olive oil, drained and minced
- 2 medium garlic cloves, minced or pushed through a press
- ½ teaspoon crushed red pepper flakes
- ¼ teaspoon freshly ground black pepper

- 4 arctic char fillets, each 6–8 ounces and about ½ inch thick
- 1 tablespoon extra-virgin olive oil
- ¾ teaspoon kosher salt
- ½ teaspoon freshly ground black pepper
- ½ cup chopped fresh basil leaves

1. Combine the relish ingredients. Set aside at room temperature until ready to serve.

2. Prepare the grill for direct cooking over high heat (450° to 550°F).

3. Brush the arctic char fillets on both sides with the oil and season evenly with the salt and pepper. Grill the fillets over *direct high heat*, with the lid closed, until you can lift them off the cooking grates without sticking, about 4 minutes. Turn the fillets over and continue cooking to your desired doneness, 2 to 3 minutes more for medium rare. Remove from the grill.

4. Stir the basil into the relish. Generously spoon the relish over the fillets and serve immediately.

If you can't find arctic char, substitute salmon, halibut, or swordfish. The relish is also great served over chicken.

BASIL- AND CITRUS-STUFFED WHOLE FISH
WITH PESTO

SERVES: 4 | **PREP TIME:** 20 minutes | **GRILLING TIME:** 30–40 minutes

SPECIAL EQUIPMENT: butcher's twine

- 2 tablespoons extra-virgin olive oil
- 2 whole *branzino* or striped bass, each 1½–2 pounds, gutted, scaled, and fins removed
- ¾ teaspoon kosher salt
- ½ teaspoon freshly ground black pepper
- 3 large lemons
- 2 medium navel oranges, divided
- ⅓ cup store-bought pesto
- 30 fresh basil leaves

1. Prepare the grill for indirect cooking over medium heat (350° to 450°F).

2. Rub the oil evenly on the inside and outside of each fish, and season evenly inside and outside with the salt and pepper. Set aside.

3. Grate the zest of one of the lemons and one of the oranges into the pesto. Add the juice from one lemon half into the pesto and stir to combine. Cut the remaining 2½ lemons and both oranges into slices ¼ inch thick, discarding the ends. Cut four of the lemon slices in half and two of the orange slices into quarters. Fill each fish cavity with four of the halved lemon slices, four of the quartered orange slices, and fifteen basil leaves.

4. Cut four 18-inch lengths of butcher's twine. Place two pieces of twine parallel and about 1½ inches apart from each other. Put one orange and one lemon slice in the center of each piece of twine. Place one fish on top of the fruit slices, then put another orange and lemon slice side by side on top of the fish. Wrap each piece of twine around the fish and tie, securing the fruit to the fish. Repeat with the other fish.

5. Grill the fish over *indirect medium heat*, with the lid closed, until the flesh is opaque near the bone but still juicy, 30 to 40 minutes, turning once. Remove from the grill and let rest for about 2 minutes.

6. Arrange the remaining lemon and orange slices on a small serving platter. Remove the twine from each fish, discard the grilled fruit slices, and then cut off the head and tail. Cut along the backbone and then open the fish like a book. Remove the basil, the lemon and orange slices, and the bones. Lift the flesh off the skin. Place the filleted fish on the prepared serving platter and drizzle with 2 tablespoons of the pesto. Serve the fish warm with the remaining pesto.

SEAFOOD

SWORDFISH
WITH ROASTED TOMATOES AND OLIVES

SERVES: 4 | PREP TIME: 20 minutes | GRILLING TIME: 14–18 minutes

2 pounds plum tomatoes
Extra-virgin olive oil
Kosher salt
1 large garlic clove, minced or pushed through a press
¼ teaspoon crushed red pepper flakes, or to taste
½ cup kalamata olives, cut in half lengthwise
2 teaspoons fresh thyme leaves *or* 1 teaspoon dried thyme
4 swordfish steaks, each about 8 ounces and 1 inch thick
Freshly ground black pepper

1. Prepare the grill for direct cooking over medium heat (350° to 450°F).

2. Core the tomatoes and cut them in half lengthwise. Scoop out the seeds and discard. Toss the tomatoes with 2 tablespoons oil and lightly season with salt. Grill the tomatoes, cut side down first, over *direct medium heat*, with the lid closed, until blackened and blistered in spots, 6 to 8 minutes, turning once or twice. Transfer the tomatoes to a bowl. When the tomatoes are cool enough to handle, remove and discard the skin. Coarsely chop the tomato flesh and return to the bowl.

3. In a large saucepan over medium heat, warm 1 tablespoon oil. Add the garlic and red pepper flakes and sauté until fragrant without letting the garlic brown, about 1 minute. Add the tomatoes along with any oil left in the bowl and then add the olives and thyme. Simmer until thickened, about 20 minutes, stirring occasionally.

4. Lightly brush the swordfish steaks on both sides with 1 tablespoon oil and season evenly with salt and pepper. Grill the steaks over *direct medium heat*, with the lid closed, until they are just opaque in the center but still juicy, 8 to 10 minutes, turning once. Serve warm with the sauce spooned over the top.

SERVES: 4 | PREP TIME: 20 minutes | GRILLING TIME: 4–5 minutes

DRESSING

5	scallions (white and light green parts only), thinly sliced
1½	tablespoons seasoned rice vinegar
1½	tablespoons mirin (sweet rice wine)
1½	tablespoons fish sauce
1	tablespoon low-sodium soy sauce
2	teaspoons fresh lemon juice
1	teaspoon toasted sesame oil
¼	teaspoon crushed red pepper flakes

1	English cucumber, seeded and cut into large matchsticks
	Canola oil
1	tablespoon finely chopped fresh cilantro leaves
4	center-cut swordfish steaks, each about 6 ounces and ¾ inch thick
½	teaspoon kosher salt
¼	teaspoon freshly ground black pepper

1. In a small bowl whisk the dressing ingredients. Transfer half of the dressing (about ¼ cup) to a medium bowl. If time allows, refrigerate the medium bowl, covered, for up to 1 hour (if the dressing is chilled, the cucumber salad will be crisper). Set aside the remaining dressing in the small bowl for the swordfish.

2. Prepare the grill for direct cooking over high heat (450° to 550°F).

3. Add the cucumber, 1 tablespoon canola oil, and the cilantro to the medium bowl. Toss to coat thoroughly with the dressing.

4. Lightly brush the swordfish steaks on both sides with canola oil and season evenly with the salt and pepper. Grill the steaks over *direct high heat,* with the lid closed, for 2 minutes without moving them, then turn the steaks and continue cooking until the flesh is just opaque in the center but still juicy, 2 to 3 minutes more. Swordfish dries out quickly, so be careful not to overcook it. Remove the steaks from the grill and let rest for about 2 minutes. Transfer the steaks to serving plates and mound some of the cucumber salad on the side. Spoon a little of the reserved dressing over the top of each steak and serve immediately.

DIJON AND GARLIC SWORDFISH KABOBS
WITH LEMON VINAIGRETTE

SERVES: 4 | PREP TIME: 20 minutes | MARINATING TIME: 30 minutes | GRILLING TIME: 6–8 minutes

SPECIAL EQUIPMENT: 8 metal or bamboo skewers

MARINADE

3 tablespoons Dijon mustard
   Grated zest of 1 lemon
2 teaspoons chopped fresh rosemary leaves
2 garlic cloves, minced or pushed through a press
¾ teaspoon kosher salt
¼ teaspoon freshly ground black pepper

   Extra-virgin olive oil
4 swordfish steaks, each about 8 ounces and 1 inch thick, cut into 1-inch pieces
2 bell peppers, each about 8 ounces, preferably 1 red and 1 green, cut into 1-inch squares

VINAIGRETTE

2 tablespoons fresh lemon juice
1 teaspoon Dijon mustard
½ teaspoon kosher salt
¼ teaspoon freshly ground black pepper

3 cups cooked rice

1. If using bamboo skewers, soak them in water for at least 30 minutes.

2. Prepare the grill for direct cooking over medium heat (350° to 450°F).

3. In a medium bowl whisk the marinade ingredients, including ¼ cup oil. Place the swordfish pieces in the bowl, turn to coat, cover, and marinate at room temperature for 30 minutes. In another bowl toss the bell pepper squares with 2 teaspoons oil.

4. Whisk the vinaigrette ingredients, including ¼ cup oil.

5. Thread the swordfish and the peppers alternately onto the skewers. Discard any remaining marinade. Grill the kabobs over *direct medium heat*, with the lid closed, until the swordfish is just opaque in the center but still juicy, 6 to 8 minutes, turning several times. Remove from the grill. Divide the rice among four plates and place two kabobs on each serving of rice. Drizzle the swordfish and the rice with the vinaigrette and serve immediately.

Mild and versatile, swordfish has a firm, meaty flesh that absorbs marinades nicely. The texture also holds up well on kabobs, but be careful about adding a lot of other ingredients to the skewers. Cubes of swordfish and squares of bell pepper are perfectly grilled in the same amount of time, but if you try adding a bunch of other seafood or vegetables, you are bound to wind up with some pieces that are either undercooked or overcooked. When in doubt, separate the ingredients so that each skewer has only one ingredient that you have cut into even pieces. That way, every ingredient can get just the right time and temperature it needs.

FISH TACOS
WITH PINEAPPLE AND RADISH SALSA

SERVES: 4 | PREP TIME: 30 minutes | GRILLING TIME: 7–9 minutes

SALSA
- 1½ cups diced fresh pineapple
- 8 medium radishes, grated on the large holes of a box grater (1 cup)
- ¼ cup fresh lime juice
- 1 serrano chile pepper, seeded and minced, or to taste
- 2 tablespoons minced fresh chives
- ½ teaspoon ground cumin
- ½ teaspoon kosher salt

PASTE
- 2 tablespoons extra-virgin olive oil
- 2 tablespoons prepared chili powder
- 2 teaspoons ground cumin

- 4 skinless cod fillets, each about 6 ounces and ½ inch thick
- 8 corn tortillas (6 inches)

1. Prepare the grill for direct cooking over high heat (450° to 550°F).

2. Combine the salsa ingredients.

3. Whisk the paste ingredients. Spread the paste evenly on both sides of the cod fillets.

4. Wrap four tortillas in each of two foil packets.

5. Grill the fillets over **direct high heat**, with the lid closed, for 4 minutes. Using a metal spatula, turn the fillets over and continue cooking until the flesh barely begins to flake when poked with the tip of a knife, 2 to 4 minutes more. Remove from the grill. Break the fillets into large chunks.

6. Warm the tortilla packets over **direct high heat** for about 1 minute, turning once. Remove from the grill and divide the tortillas among four serving plates. Fill the tortillas with cod and salsa and serve immediately.

SERVES: 4 | **PREP TIME: 10 minutes** | **GRILLING TIME: about 6 minutes**

SPECIAL EQUIPMENT: grill-proof griddle or cast-iron skillet

SAUCE

- ⅔ cup mayonnaise
- 3 tablespoons sweet pickle relish
- 2 tablespoons finely chopped shallot
- 1 tablespoon capers, rinsed, drained, and chopped
- 2 teaspoons fresh lemon juice
- ¼ teaspoon dried tarragon

- 4 skinless cod fillets, each 6–7 ounces and ¾ inch thick
  Extra-virgin olive oil
- ½ teaspoon kosher salt
- ¼ teaspoon freshly ground black pepper

1. Prepare the grill for direct cooking over high heat (450° to 550°F) and preheat a grill-proof griddle for about 10 minutes.

2. Whisk the sauce ingredients. Cover and refrigerate until ready to use.

3. Lightly brush both sides of the fillets with oil and season evenly with the salt and pepper. Place the fillets on the griddle and cook over *direct high heat*, with the lid closed, until the fish just begins to flake when poked with the tip of a knife, about 6 minutes, carefully turning with a spatula after 4 minutes. Remove the fillets from the griddle and serve warm with the tartar sauce.

Using a grill-proof griddle on your grill is a great way to get a nice crust on fish fillets. One of the keys to success when making this dish is allowing the griddle plenty of time to preheat. Once it is thoroughly heated, cook the fish a little longer on the first side than on the second side.

SEAFOOD

CRISPY TROUT
WITH HERB SALAD AND SHALLOT-LEMON VINAIGRETTE

SERVES: 4 | PREP TIME: 30 minutes | GRILLING TIME: about 10 minutes

VINAIGRETTE
½   cup minced shallots
2½ tablespoons white balsamic vinegar
2   teaspoons finely grated lemon zest
2   tablespoons fresh lemon juice
½   cup extra-virgin olive oil
1   teaspoon kosher salt
¾   teaspoon freshly ground black pepper
¾   teaspoon granulated sugar

1   cup fresh basil leaves
1   cup fresh Italian parsley leaves
1   cup fresh mint leaves
¼   cup small fresh dill sprigs
½   cup *panko* bread crumbs
1   tablespoon finely grated lemon zest
4   large trout fillets (with skin), each 6–8 ounces
2   teaspoons ground fennel
1   teaspoon kosher salt
1   teaspoon freshly ground black pepper

1. Whisk the shallots, vinegar, lemon zest, and lemon juice. Add the oil in a steady stream, whisking constantly to emulsify. Whisk in the salt, pepper, and sugar.

2. Combine the basil, parsley, mint, and dill. Cover and refrigerate while preparing the trout.

3. Prepare the grill for indirect cooking over high heat (450° to 550°F).

4. Combine the *panko* and the lemon zest. Coat the flesh side of each trout fillet with 1 tablespoon of the vinaigrette and season evenly with the fennel, salt, and pepper. Press the *panko* mixture evenly onto the flesh side of each fillet.

5. Grill the fillets, skin side down, over **indirect high heat**, with the lid closed, until the flesh is opaque in the center, the skin is lightly charred, and the *panko* is crisp and golden brown, about 10 minutes (do not turn). Transfer the fillets to serving plates.

6. Toss the herb salad with enough of the vinaigrette to coat lightly. Divide the herb salad among serving plates, spoon any remaining vinaigrette over the fillets, and serve immediately.

SERVES: 6 | PREP TIME: 30 minutes | GRILLING TIME: about 10 minutes

1½ cups tightly packed fresh basil leaves
1 cup extra-virgin olive oil

SALSA
3 cups finely diced seedless watermelon (about 1 pound)
2 tablespoons minced shallot
2 tablespoons minced fresh mint leaves
1 tablespoon balsamic vinegar
½ teaspoon coarsely ground black pepper
¼ teaspoon kosher salt

6 large trout fillets (with skin), each 6–8 ounces

1. Prepare a bowl of ice water and spread paper towels on a work surface. Bring a large saucepan of water to a boil over high heat. Add the basil leaves to the saucepan and blanch for 10 seconds. Using a slotted spoon, transfer the leaves to the ice water to stop them from cooking. Using your hands, gently squeeze the basil to remove any excess water, place them on the paper towels, and blot dry.

2. In a food processor or blender combine the basil leaves and the oil and puree until smooth. Transfer to a small, covered container. (The basil oil can be kept for up to 2 weeks, covered, in the refrigerator. Bring to room temperature before using.)

3. Prepare the grill for indirect cooking over high heat (450° to 550°F).

4. Gently combine the salsa ingredients.

5. Brush 1 tablespoon of the basil oil on the flesh side of each trout fillet. Grill the fillets, skin side down, over *indirect high heat*, with the lid closed, until the flesh is opaque in the center and the skin is lightly charred, about 10 minutes (do not turn). Transfer the fillets to serving plates. Serve warm with the salsa and a drizzle of the basil oil over each fillet.

SEAFOOD

8

VEGETABLES AND SIDES

GRILLING VEGETABLES

TYPE	THICKNESS / SIZE	APPROXIMATE GRILLING TIME
Artichoke hearts	whole	**14–18 minutes:** boil 10–12 minutes; cut in half and grill 4–6 minutes direct medium heat
Asparagus	½-inch diameter	**6–8 minutes** direct medium heat
Beet (6 ounces)	whole	**1–1½ hours** indirect medium heat
Bell pepper	whole	**10–12 minutes** direct medium heat
Carrot	1-inch diameter	**7–11 minutes:** boil 4–6 minutes, grill 3–5 minutes direct high heat
Corn, husked		**10–15 minutes** direct medium heat
Corn, in husk		**20–30 minutes** direct medium heat
Eggplant	½-inch slices	**8–10 minutes** direct medium heat
Garlic	whole	**45 minutes–1 hour** indirect medium heat
Mushroom, button or shiitake		**8–10 minutes** direct medium heat
Mushroom, portabello		**8–12 minutes** direct medium heat
Onion	halved	**35–40 minutes** indirect medium heat
	½-inch slices	**8–12 minutes** direct medium heat
Potato, new	halved	**15–20 minutes** direct medium heat
Potato, russet	whole	**45 minutes–1 hour** indirect medium heat
	½-inch slices	**9–11 minutes** direct medium heat
Potato, sweet	whole	**45 minutes–1 hour** indirect high heat
	½-inch slices	**12–15 minutes** direct medium heat
Scallion	whole	**3–4 minutes** direct medium heat
Squash, acorn (1½ pounds)	halved	**40 minutes–1 hour** indirect medium heat
Tomato, garden or plum	whole	**8–10 minutes** direct medium heat
	halved	**6–8 minutes** direct medium heat
Zucchini	½-inch slices	**4–6 minutes** direct medium heat

Just about everything from artichoke hearts to zucchini tends to cook best over direct medium heat. The temperature on the grill's thermometer should be somewhere between 350° and 450°F.

SERVES: 4 | PREP TIME: 10 minutes | GRILLING TIME: 10–15 minutes

SPREAD

- 3 tablespoons mayonnaise
- 1–2 tablespoons sour cream
- 1 tablespoon fresh lime juice

TOPPING

- 3 tablespoons grated *cotija* or Parmigiano-Reggiano® cheese
- ¾ teaspoon prepared chili powder
- ¼ teaspoon chipotle chile powder

- 4 ears fresh corn, husked

Try the recipe with butter and lime juice instead of the spread. Here's how:

In a small bowl combine ¼ cup plus 1 tablespoon melted unsalted butter with 1 tablespoon fresh lime juice. Lightly brush the corn all over with about half of the butter mixture. Grill the corn as directed in step 3. Remove from the grill and brush the corn all over with the remaining butter mixture. Sprinkle the corn evenly with the topping.

1. Prepare the grill for direct cooking over medium heat (350° to 450°F).

2. In a small bowl combine the spread ingredients. In another bowl combine the topping ingredients.

3. Grill the corn over *direct medium heat*, with the lid closed, until the kernels are browned in spots and tender, 10 to 15 minutes, turning occasionally.

4. Remove from the grill, brush the corn all over with the spread, and then season evenly with the topping. Serve right away.

CORN ON THE COB

It's summer's sweetest gift—a crunchy, juicy, silk-wrapped side often more celebrated than the main course. And just when you think it can't get any better, you introduce it to the grill.

This grain-in-vegetable's-clothing is naturally sweet, thanks to its abundance of the plant-based sugar dextrose. The starchy compound gives corn its sublime flavor, but also its potential to burn. Luckily, fresh corn needs only a few minutes over a fire to achieve perfection.

There are several great methods for grilling corn. The first two call for pulling the husks back but not off, stripping off the silk, replacing the husks, and then securing them shut with either a piece of butcher's twine or a sliver of husk. Soak the cobs in their husks in cold water (optional), and then do one of two things: place them over direct medium heat with the lid closed for twenty to thirty minutes, or nestle them in the hot embers of a charcoal fire for about ten minutes. The latter method requires frequent turning and undivided attention, but the kernels caramelize rather than steam, producing that coveted sweet-savory flavor.

The third method happens to be our favorite (and the easiest). Shuck the corn completely, lightly oil the cobs, and place over a direct fire for ten to fifteen minutes with the lid closed. A tasty, caramelized char dapples the kernels, thanks to direct exposure to the heat. Beyond tasting fantastic, it looks impressive, and your guests aren't stuck shucking a piping hot corncob over their dinner.

A little butter and salt is plenty of adornment, but we love the style of street vendors in Mexico: with a squeeze of lime and a sprinkle of chile powder.

ROASTED CORN AND RED PEPPER SALAD

SERVES: 4–6 | PREP TIME: 20 minutes | GRILLING TIME: 14–17 minutes

3 tablespoons unsalted butter, melted
1 tablespoon finely chopped fresh basil leaves
⅛ teaspoon hot pepper sauce *or* ground cayenne pepper
  Kosher salt
  Freshly ground black pepper
2 ears fresh corn, white or yellow, husked
2 large red bell peppers
3 tablespoons extra-virgin olive oil
4 teaspoons fresh lime juice
1 tablespoon mayonnaise
1½ teaspoons spicy brown mustard
1 cup roughly chopped green cabbage
1 cup loosely packed baby arugula
½ cup loosely packed fresh basil leaves
4 scallions (white and light green parts only), finely chopped

1. Prepare the grill for direct cooking over high heat (450° to 550°F).

2. Whisk the butter, basil, hot pepper sauce, ¼ teaspoon salt, and ⅛ teaspoon pepper. Place both ears of corn on one sheet of aluminum foil, about 15 inches long, and brush the corn all over generously with the butter mixture. Wrap up the corn, crimping the edges of the foil tightly to trap the steam and prevent the packet from leaking.

3. Grill the corn packet and the bell peppers over *direct high heat,* with the lid closed, until the peppers are blackened and blistered all over, 10 to 12 minutes, turning occasionally. Remove the corn packet from the grill after 10 minutes. Put the peppers in a bowl and cover with plastic wrap to trap the steam. Let stand for about 10 minutes. Meanwhile, carefully unwrap the corn and return to the grill over *direct high heat* until browned in spots and tender, 4 to 5 minutes. Remove from the grill.

4. When the peppers are cool enough to handle, peel away and discard the charred skin. Cut off and discard the stems and seeds, then cut the peppers into ¼-inch dice. Cut the kernels off the cobs into a large bowl.

5. To the bowl with the corn, add the oil, lime juice, mayonnaise, mustard, ¼ teaspoon salt, and ¼ teaspoon pepper. Toss to combine evenly. Fold in the red peppers, cabbage, arugula, basil, and scallions. Serve warm or at room temperature.

SUMMER CORN, TOMATO, AND AVOCADO SALAD

SERVES: 4 | PREP TIME: 15 minutes | GRILLING TIME: 10–15 minutes

2 ears fresh corn, husked
   Extra-virgin olive oil
   Kosher salt
2 tablespoons fresh lime juice
½ teaspoon ground cumin
   Freshly ground black pepper
1 large Hass avocado, cut into ½-inch dice
1½ cups halved cherry or grape tomatoes
½ cup finely chopped red onion
¼ cup chopped fresh Italian parsley leaves

Tip

This versatile salad can be varied in many ways. Try replacing the parsley with cilantro and serving it as a salsa alongside chicken or fish. For a more substantial salad, spoon the vegetables over a bed of mixed greens. Select a firm but ripe avocado for this recipe, so that the pieces will maintain their shape when tossed with the other ingredients.

1. Prepare the grill for direct cooking over medium heat (350° to 450°F).

2. Brush the corn all over with oil and lightly season with salt. Grill over *direct medium heat,* with the lid closed, until browned in spots and tender, 10 to 15 minutes, turning occasionally. Remove from the grill. When the corn is cool enough to handle, cut the kernels from the cobs into a large bowl.

3. Whisk 3 tablespoons oil, the lime juice, cumin, ½ teaspoon salt, and ¼ teaspoon pepper. Set the dressing aside.

4. To the bowl with the corn, add the avocado, tomatoes, onion, and parsley. Pour the dressing on top. Toss gently to combine and season with more salt and pepper, if desired. Serve immediately.

VEGETABLES AND SIDES

267

CHARRED CARROT SALAD
WITH SPINACH AND PARMESAN

SERVES: 6 | PREP TIME: 15 minutes | MARINATING TIME: 30 minutes–2 hours | GRILLING TIME: 8–10 minutes

SPECIAL EQUIPMENT: perforated grill pan

1½ pounds medium carrots, peeled and cut diagonally
    into slices about 2 inches long and ½ inch thick
3   tablespoons extra-virgin olive oil, divided
    Kosher salt
    Freshly ground black pepper
1   teaspoon Dijon mustard
3   tablespoons red wine vinegar
1   bag (6 ounces) fresh baby spinach leaves
2   tablespoons chopped fresh chives
1   chunk Parmigiano-Reggiano® cheese, about 2 ounces,
    shaved into strips with a vegetable peeler

1. Toss the carrots with 1 tablespoon of the oil. Lightly season with salt and pepper and set aside at room temperature for at least 30 minutes or up to 2 hours.

2. Prepare the grill for direct cooking over medium heat (350° to 450°F) and preheat a perforated grill pan.

3. Remove the carrots from the bowl and let the excess oil drip back into the bowl. Spread the carrots in a single layer on the grill pan and grill over *direct medium heat*, with the lid closed, until crisp-tender and lightly charred, 8 to 10 minutes, turning once or twice. Remove from the grill.

4. In a small bowl whisk the mustard and the vinegar. Add the remaining 2 tablespoons oil in a steady stream, whisking constantly to emulsify. Season with salt and pepper.

5. Put the spinach, chives, and carrots in a bowl and toss with the vinaigrette. Top the salad with the cheese and serve immediately.

To make the salad a little more complex, toss in
a handful of pine nuts or toasted walnuts.

SERVES: 6 | PREP TIME: 20 minutes | GRILLING TIME: 45 minutes–1 hour

6 golden or red beets, 1½–2 pounds total, leafy tops
   and root ends removed
   Extra-virgin olive oil

DRESSING
2 tablespoons fresh lemon juice
1 tablespoon red wine vinegar
1 teaspoon honey
½ teaspoon kosher salt
½ teaspoon freshly ground black pepper

5 ounces baby arugula (about 8 cups)
4 ounces crumbled goat cheese (about 1 cup)
3 tablespoons roughly chopped fresh tarragon leaves
½ cup shelled roasted, salted pistachios

We love homemade salad dressing, but preparing it does pose a too-many-tasks-not-enough-hands problem. By wrapping a kitchen towel around the base of the bowl, it stays put while you whisk with one hand and pour the oil with the other. Problem solved.

1. Prepare the grill for indirect cooking over medium heat (350° to 450°F).

2. Scrub the beets under cold water, and then lightly brush them all over with oil. Grill the beets over *indirect medium heat*, with the lid closed, until they are tender but not too soft when pierced with the tip of a knife, 45 minutes to 1 hour, turning once or twice. Remove from the grill and put them in a bowl. Cover with plastic wrap and let stand at room temperature until cool enough to handle.

3. Whisk the dressing ingredients. Add ¼ cup oil in a steady stream, whisking constantly to emulsify. Set aside.

4. Remove the beets from the bowl and, using a sharp paring knife, cut off the stem ends and remove the peel. Cut each beet in half horizontally, and then cut each half into quarters or eighths. Put the beets in a bowl, drizzle with ¼ cup of the dressing, and gently toss to coat. Put the arugula in another bowl, drizzle with just enough of the remaining dressing to coat the leaves very lightly, 3 to 4 tablespoons, and toss to combine. Arrange the arugula on a platter or on individual plates. Spoon the beets over the arugula. Top with the goat cheese, tarragon, and pistachios. Serve immediately.

VEGETABLES AND SIDES

GRILLED VEGETABLE GRATIN
WITH RICOTTA AND BASIL

SERVES: 4–6 | PREP TIME: 45 minutes | GRILLING TIME: 43–52 minutes

SPECIAL EQUIPMENT: 7-by-10½-inch or 8-inch-square grill-proof baking dish or 9-inch cast-iron skillet

- 2 large red bell peppers
- 2 small globe eggplants, about 1 pound total, ends trimmed, cut crosswise into ¼-inch slices
  Extra-virgin olive oil
- 3 medium zucchini, about 1 pound total, cut crosswise into ¼-inch slices
- 3 medium yellow squash, about 1 pound total, cut crosswise into ¼-inch slices
  Kosher salt
  Freshly ground black pepper
- 1 large egg
- 12 ounces whole-milk ricotta cheese (1½ cups)
- ¼ cup plus 2 tablespoons chopped fresh basil leaves, divided
- 1 garlic clove, minced or pushed through a press
- ½ cup finely grated Parmigiano-Reggiano® cheese

Tip

Grilled summer vegetables are the stars of this cheesy gratin that's redolent of fresh basil. Choose zucchini, squash, and eggplant with similar diameters for the prettiest dish. If the eggplant is wider, cut each slice in half or in quarters after grilling.

1. Prepare the grill for direct and indirect cooking over medium heat (350° to 450°F).

2. Grill the bell peppers over *direct medium heat*, with the lid closed, until blackened and blistered all over, 10 to 12 minutes, turning occasionally. Put the peppers in a bowl and cover with plastic wrap to trap the steam. Let stand for about 10 minutes. Remove the peppers from the bowl and peel away and discard the charred skin. Cut off and discard the stems and seeds, and cut each pepper into four pieces.

3. Generously brush the eggplant on both sides with oil. Lightly brush the zucchini and the squash on both sides with oil. Season the vegetables evenly with ½ teaspoon salt and ¼ teaspoon pepper. Grill the vegetables over *direct medium heat*, with the lid closed, until nicely marked and tender but not too soft, 8 to 10 minutes for the eggplant, and 4 to 6 minutes for the zucchini and the squash, turning once or twice.

4. Lightly oil a 7-by-10½-inch grill-proof baking dish. In a medium bowl whisk the egg, ricotta, ¼ cup of the basil, the garlic, ½ teaspoon salt, and ½ teaspoon pepper. Using half of the vegetables, arrange a layer of eggplant, then squash, then zucchini, then bell peppers, overlapping the slices slightly. Spread half of the ricotta mixture over the vegetables in an even layer and top with half of the cheese. Repeat with the remaining vegetables, ricotta mixture, and cheese. Cook over *indirect medium heat*, with the lid closed, until the cheese is melted and bubbly, rotating the dish occasionally, 25 to 30 minutes. Remove from the grill and let cool slightly. Serve warm or at room temperature, garnished with the remaining 2 tablespoons basil.

GLOBE EGGPLANT
WITH SUN-DRIED TOMATO VINAIGRETTE

SERVES: 4 | PREP TIME: 15 minutes | GRILLING TIME: 8–10 minutes

VINAIGRETTE

- 4 sun-dried tomato halves packed in oil, drained and minced
- 2 tablespoons balsamic vinegar
- 1 tablespoon minced shallot
- 1 teaspoon dried oregano
- 1 teaspoon honey

  Kosher salt
  Freshly ground black pepper
  Extra-virgin olive oil
- 2 globe eggplants, each about 1 pound, ends trimmed

1. Prepare the grill for direct cooking over medium heat (350° to 450°F).

2. Whisk the vinaigrette ingredients, including ¼ teaspoon salt and ⅛ teaspoon pepper. Add ⅓ cup oil in a steady stream, whisking constantly to emulsify. Set aside.

3. Cut the eggplants crosswise into ½-inch slices. Brush both sides of each slice with oil and season evenly with ¼ teaspoon salt and ¼ teaspoon pepper. Grill over *direct medium heat*, with the lid closed, until well marked and tender, 8 to 10 minutes, turning once or twice. Place the slices on a platter. Immediately spoon the vinaigrette over the top. Serve warm or at room temperature.

SERVES: 4–6 | PREP TIME: 15 minutes | GRILLING TIME: 6–8 minutes

SAUCE

- 1 cup mayonnaise
- 2 tablespoons minced fresh basil leaves
  Finely grated zest of 1 lime
- 2 teaspoons fresh lime juice
- 1 garlic clove, minced or pushed through a press
- ⅛ teaspoon ground cayenne pepper

- 2 pounds asparagus
- 2 tablespoons extra-virgin olive oil
- ½ teaspoon kosher salt
- ½ teaspoon freshly ground black pepper

1. Whisk the sauce ingredients. Transfer to a small serving bowl and refrigerate, covered, until ready to serve.

2. Prepare the grill for direct cooking over medium heat (350° to 450°F).

3. Remove and discard the tough bottom of each asparagus spear by grasping each end and bending it gently until it snaps at its natural point of tenderness, usually about two-thirds of the way down the spear. Brush the asparagus with the oil and season evenly with the salt and pepper.

4. Grill the asparagus over *direct medium heat*, with the lid closed, until nicely marked and crisp-tender, 6 to 8 minutes, rolling occasionally. Remove from the grill and serve warm with the sauce.

SERVES: 4; 8 as a side dish | PREP TIME: 40 minutes | GRILLING TIME: 20–30 minutes

Extra-virgin olive oil
1 pound ground chuck (80% lean)
1 cup finely chopped yellow onion
3 large garlic cloves, minced or pushed through a press
2 plum tomatoes, seeded and finely diced (about 1 cup)
1 jalapeño chile pepper, seeded and minced
¼ cup tomato paste
1 teaspoon kosher salt
1 teaspoon paprika
1 teaspoon ground cumin
½ teaspoon freshly ground black pepper
½ teaspoon ground coriander
2 cups steamed long- or medium-grain white rice
6 ounces crumbled feta cheese, divided (about 1½ cups)
¼ cup plus 2 tablespoons finely chopped fresh Italian parsley leaves, divided
¼ cup finely chopped fresh mint leaves
4 large red bell peppers, each cut in half lengthwise, seeds and ribs removed, stems left on

1. In a large skillet over medium heat, warm 1 tablespoon oil. Crumble the ground chuck into the skillet and cook until browned, 6 to 8 minutes, stirring to break up any clumps. Using a slotted spoon, transfer to a bowl. Pour off the fat from the skillet and wipe clean. Add 1 tablespoon oil and the onion to the skillet and sauté over medium heat until the onion is softened, 5 to 7 minutes. Add the garlic, tomatoes, and jalapeño and cook for 1 minute, stirring frequently. Return the meat to the skillet. Add the tomato paste, salt, paprika, cumin, pepper, and coriander. Cook until the flavors are blended, about 1 minute, stirring often. Remove from the heat. Gently stir in the rice, 1 cup of the feta, ¼ cup of the parsley, and the mint.

2. Prepare the grill for indirect cooking over medium heat (350° to 450°F).

3. Firmly pack the filling into the pepper halves, mounding it about ½ inch above the rim. Top evenly with the remaining ¼ cup feta. Grill the stuffed peppers over *indirect medium heat*, with the lid closed, until the peppers are tender and the filling is hot, 20 to 30 minutes. Transfer to a platter. Drizzle the peppers with a little oil and garnish with the remaining 2 tablespoons of parsley. Serve warm.

SERVES: 4; 8 as a side dish | PREP TIME: 20 minutes | GRILLING TIME: 40–45 minutes

4 large russet potatoes, each about 8 ounces, unpeeled, scrubbed, halved horizontally, and pierced with a fork
8 ounces large button mushrooms, stems removed
1 tablespoon extra-virgin olive oil
2 scallions, ends trimmed, finely chopped, dark green tops reserved
½ cup sour cream
4 ounces sharp cheddar cheese, grated
   Kosher salt
   Freshly ground black pepper

1. Prepare the grill for indirect cooking over medium heat (350° to 450°F).

2. Brush the potato halves and the mushrooms all over with the oil. Grill the potato halves over *indirect medium heat*, with the lid closed, until they are just tender when pierced with a fork, 25 to 30 minutes, turning occasionally. At the same time, grill the mushrooms over *indirect medium heat* until tender, about 15 minutes, turning once. Remove from the grill as they are done.

3. When cool enough to handle, scoop out the interior of each potato half, leaving a shell about ½ inch thick. Place the potato flesh in a medium bowl and coarsely mash with a fork. Add the white and light green parts of the scallions, the sour cream, and the cheese. Roughly chop the mushrooms, add to the potato mixture, and stir to combine. Season with salt and pepper. Stuff each of the potato skins with an equal amount of the potato mixture. (At this point the potatoes can be covered loosely with plastic wrap and kept at room temperature for up to 2 hours.)

4. Grill the stuffed potatoes over *indirect medium heat*, with the lid closed, until the cheese is melted and the potatoes are heated through, about 15 minutes. Garnish with the reserved dark green scallion tops and serve right away.

VEGETABLES AND SIDES

275

SPANISH FRITTATA
WITH BABY POTATOES AND PEPPERS

SERVES: 4; 8 as a side dish | **PREP TIME:** 30 minutes | **GRILLING TIME:** 25–31 minutes

SPECIAL EQUIPMENT: 9-inch cast-iron skillet

8   large eggs
    Kosher salt
    Freshly ground black pepper
2   tablespoons extra-virgin olive oil
8   ounces baby Yukon gold potatoes, unpeeled, scrubbed, and thinly sliced (about 2 cups)
½   large red onion, thinly sliced (about 1¼ cups)
1   medium red bell pepper, cut into thin strips
2   teaspoons smoked paprika, divided
1   cup frozen petite peas, thawed
2   medium garlic cloves, minced or pushed through a press
2½ ounces soft garlic-and-herb cheese, broken into small pieces
2   tablespoons finely chopped fresh Italian parsley leaves
2   tablespoons capers, rinsed and drained

Tip

The Italian version of an omelet, a frittata, is usually made in a skillet on top of the stove and then finished in the oven to lightly brown the eggs on the top. This version, which is cooked in a skillet on the grill from beginning to end, gets its Spanish flavor from the combination of potatoes, peppers, smoked paprika, and capers. It is substantial enough to serve four as a simple supper, with two generous wedges per person. A green salad tossed with a sherry vinaigrette and some grilled country-style bread would be fitting side dishes.

1. Prepare the grill for direct cooking over medium heat (350° to 450°F) and preheat a 9-inch cast-iron skillet.

2. Whisk the eggs with ½ teaspoon salt and ¼ teaspoon pepper.

3. Add the oil to the skillet and then add the potatoes, onion, and bell pepper. Cook over *direct medium heat*, with the lid closed, for 1 minute, stirring occasionally. Season evenly with 1 teaspoon salt, ½ teaspoon pepper, and 1½ teaspoons of the paprika and stir to combine. Continue cooking, with the lid closed, until the potatoes are tender when pierced with a fork and the vegetables are lightly browned, 13 to 15 minutes, stirring frequently so that the vegetables cook evenly and don't stick to the skillet. Add the peas and the garlic and cook for 1 to 2 minutes more.

4. Spread the vegetables evenly in the skillet. Pour the eggs on top of the vegetables and then add the cheese. Cook over *direct medium heat*, with the lid closed, until the eggs are puffed and just firm in the center, 10 to 13 minutes, lowering the heat if needed to prevent the frittata from getting too brown on the bottom. Wearing insulated barbecue mitts, remove the skillet from the grill. Top evenly with the parsley, the remaining ½ teaspoon paprika, and the capers. Serve the frittata from the skillet, either warm or at room temperature.

GRILLED POTATO PLANKS
WITH LEMON AIOLI

SERVES: 6–8 | PREP TIME: 15 minutes | GRILLING TIME: 9–11 minutes

AIOLI

1   cup mayonnaise
2   tablespoons fresh lemon juice
1   tablespoon minced garlic

   Freshly ground black pepper
   Kosher salt
6   tablespoons extra-virgin olive oil
1   teaspoon minced garlic
6   russet potatoes, each about 6 ounces, unpeeled, scrubbed, and cut lengthwise into ½-inch planks
1   tablespoon finely chopped fresh Italian parsley leaves

1. Prepare the grill for direct cooking over medium heat (350° to 450°F).

2. Combine the aioli ingredients, including ⅛ teaspoon pepper. Set aside at room temperature for about 15 minutes to allow the flavors to blend. Taste and add salt, if desired.

3. Stir together the oil and the garlic. Brush the potato planks on both sides with the garlic oil, making sure to distribute the garlic bits evenly, and season with ½ teaspoon salt and ½ teaspoon pepper.

4. Grill the potato planks over *direct medium heat*, with the lid closed, until they are tender when pierced with a fork, 9 to 11 minutes, turning once after 5 to 6 minutes. If some of the potatoes start to become too dark before they are done, move them to a cooler part of the grill. Remove from the grill, top with the parsley, and serve warm with the lemon aioli.

SERVES: 4 | PREP TIME: 15 minutes | GRILLING TIME: 12–15 minutes

SPECIAL EQUIPMENT: perforated grill pan

CHILI SOUR CREAM
- 1 cup sour cream
- 2 tablespoons finely chopped fresh cilantro leaves
- 1 tablespoon fresh lime juice
- 1 teaspoon hot chili-garlic sauce, such as Sriracha
- 1 teaspoon kosher salt
- 1 large garlic clove, finely chopped

SEASONING
- 2 teaspoons paprika
- 2 teaspoons kosher salt
- 1 teaspoon freshly ground black pepper
- 1 teaspoon ground cumin
- ½ teaspoon ground coriander
- ½ teaspoon ground cayenne pepper, or to taste

- 2 sweet potatoes, each about 1 pound, peeled
- 2 tablespoons extra-virgin olive oil

1. Prepare the grill for direct cooking over medium heat (350° to 450°F) and preheat a perforated grill pan.

2. Whisk the chili sour cream ingredients.

3. Combine the seasoning ingredients. Scrub the potatoes under cold water and then dry them with paper towels. Cut the potatoes into 4-by-½-by-½-inch sticks. Toss the potatoes thoroughly with the oil and the seasoning.

4. Spread the potatoes in a single layer on the grill pan and grill over *direct medium heat*, with the lid closed, until they are tender when pierced with a knife, 12 to 15 minutes, turning occasionally to brown all sides. Remove from the grill and serve warm with the chili sour cream.

SWEET POTATOES
WITH HONEY-CASHEW BUTTER

SERVES: 4–6 | **PREP TIME:** 10 minutes | **GRILLING TIME:** 45 minutes–1 hour

4   sweet potatoes, each about 8 ounces
3   tablespoons unsalted butter, softened
1   tablespoon honey
⅓   cup roughly chopped unsalted cashews, toasted
½   teaspoon kosher salt
¼   teaspoon chipotle chile powder

Tip

Choose cylindrical potatoes of a similar size
and thickness so they cook evenly.

1. Prepare the grill for indirect cooking over high heat (450° to 550°F).

2. Scrub the potatoes under cold water, and then dry them with paper towels. Wrap the potatoes individually in sheets of aluminum foil. Grill over *indirect high heat*, with the lid closed, until they are soft when squeezed with a pair of tongs, 45 minutes to 1 hour. Remove from the grill and let cool for about 5 minutes.

3. While the potatoes are grilling, make the honey-cashew butter: Using a rubber spatula, mash the butter and the honey together. Stir in the cashews, salt, and chile powder. Set aside.

4. Remove the potatoes from the foil, and then slip off and discard the skins. Cut the potatoes into ½-inch slices, put in a serving bowl, and dollop the honey-cashew butter all over. Serve warm.

SOUTHWEST GRILLED RED POTATO SALAD
WITH CHORIZO

SERVES: 4–6 | PREP TIME: 15 minutes | GRILLING TIME: 27–35 minutes

SPECIAL EQUIPMENT: perforated grill pan

1 large red onion, cut crosswise into ½-inch slices
1 large green bell pepper
  Extra-virgin olive oil
2 fresh chorizo sausages or 3 hot Italian sausages, about 8 ounces total
2 pounds red potatoes, 1½–2 inches in diameter, unpeeled, scrubbed, each cut into quarters
  Kosher salt

DRESSING
¼ cup mayonnaise
2 tablespoons chopped fresh cilantro leaves
1 tablespoon fresh lime juice
¼ teaspoon prepared chili powder
¼ teaspoon ground cumin
⅛ teaspoon chipotle chile powder

1. Prepare the grill for direct cooking over medium heat (350° to 450°F).

2. Lightly brush the onion and the bell pepper all over with oil. Grill the onion, bell pepper, and sausages over *direct medium heat*, with the lid closed, until the onions are tender, the bell pepper is blackened and blistered all over, and the sausages are fully cooked, 12 to 15 minutes, turning occasionally. Remove the vegetables and the sausages from the grill. Place the bell pepper in a bowl and cover with plastic wrap to trap the steam. Let stand for about 10 minutes. Preheat a perforated grill pan over *direct medium heat* for about 10 minutes.

3. Remove the bell pepper from the bowl and peel away and discard the charred skin, cut off the stem, and remove the seeds. Cut the bell pepper, onion, and sausages into small pieces. Toss the potatoes with 2 tablespoons oil and ½ teaspoon salt.

4. Spread the potatoes in a single layer on the grill pan and grill over *direct medium heat*, with the lid closed, until they are tender inside and crispy outside, 15 to 20 minutes, turning occasionally. Meanwhile, combine the dressing ingredients.

5. Remove the potatoes from the grill. To the bowl with the dressing, add the potatoes, onion, bell pepper, and sausages; toss to coat evenly. Season with salt. Serve at room temperature.

RECIPE REMIX:
Then and Now

Once upon a time, vegetables were second-class citizens, afterthoughts, nothing but vehicles for a heavy cheese sauce. Consider this broccoli casserole, with its hefty butter content and 8 ounces of cheese spread as evidence. Yikes. Thankfully, we've come to appreciate vegetables for both their flavor and their nutrition and we'll gussy them up just to the point of embellishment but not disguise. Broccoli gains a crunchy, caramelized quality when it's grilled, flavor that is further enhanced with a sprinkling of wonderfully crisp *panko* bread crumbs and salty Parmigiano-Reggiano® cheese. The Remix retains the cheese and bread elements of the original, but it also lets the broccoli shine. And that's just the point, isn't it?

The Original

Broccoli Casserole
Recipe from *Weber Recipe and Instruction Book*, ©1968

1/4 onion, finely chopped
6 tablespoons butter
2 tablespoons flour
1/2 cup water
1 jar (8 ounces) cheese spread
2 packages frozen chopped broccoli, thawed and well drained
3 eggs, well beaten
1/2 cup bread crumbs

USE INDIRECT METHOD
Sauté onion in 4 tablespoons butter, stir in flour and add water. Cook over low heat stirring until mixture thickens and comes to a boil; blend in cheese. Combine sauce, broccoli, and eggs; mix gently until blended. Pour into 1-1/2 quart oven-proof casserole or foil pan and cover with crumbs; dot with remaining butter. Place casserole on cooking grate and cook for 30 minutes.

GRILLED BROCCOLI
WITH TOASTED BREAD CRUMBS AND PARMESAN

SERVES: 6 | PREP TIME: 15 minutes | GRILLING TIME: 6–7 minutes

SPECIAL EQUIPMENT: perforated grill pan

- 1 pound fresh broccoli
- 3 tablespoons extra-virgin olive oil, divided
- 3 medium garlic cloves, finely chopped
- ¼ teaspoon kosher salt
- 1 teaspoon fresh lemon juice

BREAD CRUMBS
- ¼ cup *panko* bread crumbs
- 1 tablespoon extra-virgin olive oil
- ½ teaspoon crushed red pepper flakes
- ¼ teaspoon kosher salt
- ¼ teaspoon ground pepper

- 2 tablespoons freshly grated Parmigiano-Reggiano® cheese

1. Cut the broccoli crown into florets, cut any large florets into bite-sized pieces, and cut the stalk crosswise into ½-inch slices. This should yield about 6 cups of broccoli. In a large saucepan of rapidly boiling, salted water, blanch the broccoli until barely tender, 2 to 3 minutes. Drain and then plunge into a large bowl of ice water to stop the cooking. When the broccoli is cool, drain well. If desired, set aside at room temperature for up to 30 minutes, or in the refrigerator for 1 hour, covered.

2. Prepare the grill for direct cooking over medium heat (350°F to 450°F) and preheat a perforated grill pan.

3. Combine the broccoli with 2 tablespoons of the oil. Mince the chopped garlic with the salt and then drag the side of a knife over the garlic to smash it into a paste. Add the paste and the lemon juice to the broccoli. Toss to coat evenly.

4. Blend the bread crumb ingredients.

5. Spread the broccoli in a single layer on the grill pan and grill over *direct medium heat*, with the lid closed, for 3 minutes, tossing the broccoli once or twice. Scatter the bread crumb mixture over the broccoli and continue to grill until the broccoli is golden brown in parts but still mostly bright green and crisp-tender, 3 to 4 minutes more. Serve the broccoli warm with the grated cheese on top.

BLACK BEAN BURGERS
WITH CHIPOTLE CREAM AND AVOCADO

SERVES: 4 | PREP TIME: 20 minutes | CHILLING TIME: 2–24 hours | GRILLING TIME: 8–10 minutes

PATTIES

Extra-virgin olive oil
¾ cup finely chopped red onion
¾ cup finely chopped red bell pepper
2 garlic cloves, minced or pushed through a press
2 cans (each 15 ounces) black beans, rinsed, drained, and patted dry
¾ cup crushed salted tortilla chips
1 large egg
1 canned chipotle chile pepper in adobo sauce, minced, with 1 teaspoon of the adobo sauce
3 tablespoons chopped fresh cilantro leaves
1 tablespoon tomato paste
1 teaspoon ground cumin
½ teaspoon kosher salt

CHIPOTLE CREAM

½ cup sour cream
2 teaspoons adobo sauce from the canned chipotle chile
Finely grated zest of ½ lime
1 teaspoon fresh lime juice

4 hamburger buns, split
1 large Hass avocado, mashed
4 leaves lettuce
8 slices tomato

1. In a nonstick skillet over medium heat, warm 1 tablespoon oil. Add the onion, bell pepper, and garlic and cook until tender, 3 to 5 minutes, stirring occasionally. Add the black beans and cook just until any excess moisture from the beans is evaporated, about 2 minutes, stirring occasionally. Remove from the heat and let cool for 10 minutes. Transfer the bean mixture to a food processor. Add the remaining patty ingredients and pulse 10 to 12 times until the beans are coarsely pureed. Let stand for 5 minutes. With wet hands, gently form four patties, each about 4 inches in diameter and ¾ inch thick. Place on a wax paper-lined sheet pan and cover with plastic wrap. Refrigerate for at least 2 hours or up to 24 hours. It is important to chill the patties or they will be too soft to turn on the grill.

2. Mix the chipotle cream ingredients. Cover and refrigerate.

3. Prepare the grill for direct cooking over medium heat (350° to 450°F).

4. Brush the patties on both sides with oil. Grill over *direct medium heat*, with the lid closed, until heated through, 8 to 10 minutes, turning once. During the last minute of grilling time, toast the buns, cut side down, over direct heat. Spread the top bun halves with avocado. Top the bottom bun halves with lettuce, tomato, a patty, and chipotle cream. Serve warm.

SMOKY VEGETARIAN CHILI
WITH PINTO BEANS

SERVES: 6 | PREP TIME: 30 minutes | GRILLING TIME: about 50 minutes

SPECIAL EQUIPMENT: 1 large handful mesquite wood chips, Dutch oven

3   medium zucchini, trimmed and cut in half lengthwise
2   large portabello mushrooms, stems and gills removed
    Extra-virgin olive oil
3   ears fresh corn, husked
3   large red bell peppers
1½ cups finely chopped white onion
2   garlic cloves, minced or pushed through a press
1   medium jalapeño chile pepper, seeded and minced
2   tablespoons smoked paprika
1½ teaspoons ground cumin
½   teaspoon chipotle chile powder
1   can (28 ounces) Italian plum tomatoes in juice, roughly chopped, juice reserved
1   cup tomato-vegetable juice
1   can (15 ounces) pinto beans, rinsed and drained
    Kosher salt
    Freshly ground black pepper
    Grated cheddar cheese

1. Soak the wood chips in water for at least 30 minutes. Prepare the grill for direct cooking over medium heat (350° to 450°F).

2. Brush the zucchini and the mushrooms on both sides with oil. Grill the zucchini, mushrooms, corn, and bell peppers over *direct medium heat,* with the lid closed, turning as needed. The zucchini will take 4 to 6 minutes, the mushrooms will take 6 to 8 minutes, the corn will take about 8 minutes, and the bell peppers will take 10 to 12 minutes. Remove from the grill as they are done. Put the bell peppers in a bowl and cover with plastic wrap to trap the steam. Let stand for about 10 minutes. Peel away and discard the charred skin from the bell peppers. Cut off and discard the stems and seeds. Cut the bell peppers, zucchini, and mushrooms into ½-inch dice. Cut the corn kernels off the cobs.

3. In a large Dutch oven over *direct medium heat,* warm 2 tablespoons oil. Add the onion, garlic, and jalapeño and cook, with the lid closed, until the onion is softened, about 3 minutes. Stir in the paprika, cumin, and chile powder. Add the canned tomatoes and juice, the tomato-vegetable juice, zucchini, mushrooms, corn, and bell peppers. Drain and add the wood chips to the charcoal or to the smoker box of a gas grill, following manufacturer's instructions. Simmer the chili, uncovered, with the grill lid closed, until the juices are thickened, about 30 minutes, stirring occasionally. If the chili is cooking too quickly, move over indirect heat. During the last 5 minutes, stir in the beans and season with salt and pepper. Serve the chili warm, topped with cheese.

SPINACH AND RICOTTA CALZONES

SERVES: 4–6 | PREP TIME: 25 minutes | RISING TIME: 1½–1¾ hours | GRILLING TIME: 16–20 minutes

SPECIAL EQUIPMENT: pizza stone

DOUGH

- 3 cups all-purpose flour, plus more as needed
  Extra-virgin olive oil
- 1¾ teaspoons kosher salt
- 1½ teaspoons instant, quick-rising yeast
- 1 cup very warm water (115°–120°F)

FILLING

- 1 medium zucchini, ends trimmed, cut lengthwise into ½-inch slices
- 6 ounces fresh spinach, coarsely chopped
- ½ teaspoon granulated garlic
- ⅔ cup ricotta cheese
- ½ cup freshly grated Parmigiano-Reggiano® cheese
- ½ cup grated sharp provolone cheese
- 1 plum tomato, 4–5 ounces, cored, seeded, and chopped
- ¼ cup chopped fresh basil leaves
- ½ teaspoon dried oregano
- ¼ teaspoon kosher salt
- ¼ teaspoon freshly ground black pepper

  Yellow cornmeal
  Tomato sauce (optional)

1. In a food processor combine the flour, 1 tablespoon oil, the salt, and the yeast. With the motor running, add the warm water through the feed tube to make a ball of dough that is soft but not sticky and rides on top of the blade (there will be some crumbles of dough, too). If the dough is too moist, dust with 1 tablespoon of flour. If it is too dry, sprinkle with 1 teaspoon water. Process briefly, check the dough again, and repeat until the dough is the correct texture.

2. Coat a medium bowl with oil. Shape the dough into a ball, put it in the bowl, and turn to coat with the oil. Cover the bowl with plastic wrap and let stand in a warm, draft-free place until the dough is doubled in volume, 1¼ to 1½ hours.

3. Prepare the grill for direct cooking over medium heat (350° to 450°F).

4. Brush the zucchini on both sides with 1 teaspoon oil and grill over *direct medium heat*, with the lid closed, until grill marks appear and the zucchini is crisp-tender, 4 to 6 minutes, turning once. Coarsely chop and put the pieces in a medium bowl. In a large sauté pan over medium-high heat, warm 2 teaspoons of oil. Add the spinach and granulated garlic and cook until the spinach is wilted, 2 to 3 minutes, stirring occasionally. Add the spinach and the remaining filling ingredients to the bowl with the zucchini, and stir to combine.

5. Turn the dough out onto a lightly floured work surface and divide it into four equal pieces. Shape each into a ball. Working with one ball of dough at a time, press it into a 4-inch disk, then use a rolling pin to roll it into an 8-inch round, dusting the work surface lightly with flour and turning the dough as needed. Repeat with the remaining dough balls. Loosely cover the rounds with plastic wrap and let stand for 10 minutes. During this resting time the gluten in the dough will relax, making the dough easier to work with. The dough rounds may also shrink slightly.

6. Preheat a pizza stone following manufacturer's instructions for at least 15 minutes. Some stones need to be placed on a cold grill before they are heated. If this is the case, place the pizza stone on the grill when preheating it to cook the zucchini.

7. Sprinkle a large baking sheet with a light coating of cornmeal. Reroll one piece of dough, if necessary, so that it forms an 8-inch round again. Place a quarter of the filling on half of the round, spreading it out but leaving a ½- to ¾-inch border uncovered. Moisten the border with water and fold the unfilled half of the dough over the filling to make a half-moon shape. Lightly press on the top of the calzone to press out any air, then firmly twist and crimp the edges with your fingers to seal. Place the calzone on the baking sheet and repeat with the remaining dough and the remaining filling. Cover the calzones with plastic wrap and let stand for 15 to 20 minutes until very slightly puffy.

8. Brush the tops and the crimped edges of the calzones with oil. Carefully place them on the pizza stone at least 1 inch apart. Grill over *direct medium heat*, with the lid closed, until the dough is lightly browned and crisp, 12 to 14 minutes. Remove from the grill and immediately brush the calzones with more oil. Let stand for 3 minutes. Serve with tomato sauce, if using.

Tip

The dough for this recipe, which is made using instant yeast and a food processor, couldn't be simpler, but 1½ pounds of premade pizza dough could be substituted. If you like, have your favorite homemade or store-bought tomato sauce warmed and ready for dipping.

BUTTERMILK-CHEDDAR CORN BREAD

SERVES: 8 | PREP TIME: 15 minutes | GRILLING TIME: 30–35 minutes

SPECIAL EQUIPMENT: 10-inch cast-iron skillet

- 1 tablespoon vegetable oil
- 2 cups all-purpose flour
- 1 cup yellow cornmeal
- ½ cup granulated sugar
- 2 teaspoons baking powder
- 1 teaspoon baking soda
- 1 teaspoon kosher salt
- 1½ cups buttermilk
- 2 large eggs
- ½ cup (1 stick) plus 2 tablespoons unsalted butter, melted and cooled, divided
- 2 cups grated cheddar cheese
- ¾ cup finely chopped chives

1. Prepare the grill for indirect cooking over medium-high heat (about 425°F).

2. Add the oil to a 10-inch cast-iron skillet, and place the skillet over *indirect medium-high heat* for 5 minutes while the grill preheats. Wearing insulated barbecue mitts, swirl the skillet so that the oil coats the bottom and sides.

3. In a large bowl whisk the flour, cornmeal, sugar, baking powder, baking soda, and salt.

4. In a medium bowl whisk the buttermilk, eggs, and ½ cup of the melted butter until smooth. Stir in the cheese and the chives. Pour the wet ingredients over the dry ingredients all at once, and stir gently with a rubber spatula just until blended. Pour the batter into the hot skillet and gently smooth the top.

5. Grill over *indirect medium-high heat*, with the lid closed, until the top is golden brown on the edges and a skewer or a toothpick inserted into the center comes out moist but not wet, 25 to 30 minutes. Wearing insulated barbecue mitts, remove the skillet from the grill, run a knife around the edges to loosen the corn bread, and carefully invert onto a cutting board. Flip the corn bread over and brush the top with the remaining 2 tablespoons of melted butter. Serve warm or at room temperature.

SERVES: 8–10 | **PREP TIME: 10 minutes** | **GRILLING TIME: 9–14 minutes**

½   cup sun-dried tomatoes packed in oil
8   garlic cloves, minced or pushed through a press
1   teaspoon dried oregano
¼   teaspoon crushed red pepper flakes
2   tablespoons unsalted butter, softened
1   loaf French or Italian bread, about 1 pound, cut
    crosswise in half, each half cut lengthwise to
    make 4 pieces
1½ cups grated Mexican-style cheese blend (6 ounces)

1. Prepare the grill for direct and indirect cooking over medium heat (350° to 450°F).

2. Drain the tomatoes, reserve 3 tablespoons of the oil, and chop the tomatoes. In a small skillet over medium heat, warm the reserved oil. Add the garlic, oregano, and red pepper flakes, and cook until the garlic just barely starts to brown, 2½ to 3 minutes, stirring occasionally. Remove from the heat and transfer to a medium bowl. Add the butter and stir until the butter is melted and the mixture is well combined.

3. Tear off two long sheets of aluminum foil and place two bread pieces, cut side up, on each piece. Brush with an equal amount of the butter mixture, and then close the bread like a sandwich, with the cut sides facing each other. Wrap the bread in the foil.

4. Grill the bread over *direct medium heat*, with the lid closed, until heated through, 5 to 8 minutes, turning every 2 minutes. Remove from the grill, open the foil, and set the bread halves, cut side up, next to each other on the foil. Top with the cheese and the sun-dried tomatoes. Return the bread to the grill, leaving the halves on top of the foil and unwrapped. Grill over *indirect medium heat*, with the lid closed, until the cheese melts, 4 to 6 minutes. Remove from the grill and cut into 2-inch pieces. Serve warm or at room temperature.

VEGETABLES AND SIDES

BEER AND CHEDDAR BREAD

SERVES: 8 | PREP TIME: 20 minutes | RISING TIME: about 2¼ hours | GRILLING TIME: 1¼–1½ hours

SPECIAL EQUIPMENT: stand mixer (optional), pizza peel (optional), pizza stone, spray bottle

- 1 bottle (12 ounces) dark beer, at room temperature
- 2 tablespoons granulated sugar
- 2 tablespoons unsalted butter, softened, plus more for the bowl
- 1 package (¼ ounce) instant, quick-rising yeast
- 1½ teaspoons table salt
- 1½ teaspoons dried thyme
- ½ teaspoon granulated garlic
- ½ teaspoon granulated onion
- ¼ teaspoon crushed red pepper flakes
- 4½ cups unbleached, all-purpose flour, plus more as needed
- 4 ounces sharp cheddar cheese, diced
  Extra-virgin olive oil

1 You can make the dough in a stand mixer fitted with a paddle beater first and then a dough hook for the final mixing. When you pull it out of the bowl, it should be smooth and elastic.

2 You can also make the dough entirely by hand, mixing it first in a bowl and then kneading it on a floured work surface. It is ready when the surface is completely smooth.

3 The little pieces of cheese that you scatter over the dough and roll inside of it will melt slowly and will ooze into the bread pockets.

4 As you slide your dough onto the pizza stone, spray the top with water, which will keep the surface moist and soft enough that the dough can rise fully.

1. MIXER METHOD: In the bowl of a stand mixer, mix the beer, sugar, 2 tablespoons butter, yeast, salt, thyme, granulated garlic, granulated onion, and red pepper flakes. Attach the bowl to the mixer and affix the paddle beater. With the mixer on low speed, gradually add enough of the flour to make a soft dough that does not stick to the bowl. Turn off the mixer, cover the bowl with a towel, and let stand for 10 minutes. Switch from the paddle to the dough hook. With the mixer on medium-low speed, knead the dough, adding more flour as needed to keep it from sticking, until the dough is smooth and elastic, about 8 minutes.

HAND METHOD: To make the dough by hand, in a large bowl using a wooden spoon, mix the beer, sugar, 2 tablespoons butter, yeast, salt, thyme, granulated garlic, granulated onion, and red pepper flakes. Gradually stir in enough of the flour as necessary to make a stiff dough that cannot be stirred anymore. Turn out onto a well-floured work surface. Knead by hand, adding more flour as needed, until the dough is smooth and elastic and does not stick to the work surface, about 10 minutes.

2. Grease a large bowl with butter. Shape the dough into a ball. Put the dough in the bowl, smooth side down, and then turn smooth side up, coating the dough with butter. Cover with plastic wrap and let stand in a warm, draft-free place until the dough is doubled in volume, about 1½ hours.

3. Place a 12-inch square of parchment paper on a pizza peel (or a rimless baking sheet). Set aside.

4. On a lightly floured surface, gently roll the dough into a 13-by-9-inch rectangle. Scatter the cheese over the dough. Starting at a short end, roll the dough to enclose the cheese. Tuck the ends of the dough underneath the mass, and shape the dough into a ball. Place the dough, smooth side up, on the parchment-lined pizza peel. Coat a large piece of plastic wrap with oil. Cover the dough loosely with the plastic wrap, oiled side down, and let stand in a warm, draft-free place until the loaf looks inflated, but not doubled, about 45 minutes. Remove the plastic wrap.

5. Prepare the grill for indirect cooking over medium heat (about 375°F) and preheat a pizza stone for about 15 minutes, following manufacturer's instructions.

6. Fill a spray bottle with water. Slide the loaf with the parchment paper onto the pizza stone. Quickly spray the surface of the loaf with water. Grill over *indirect medium heat*, with the lid closed, until the bread is golden brown and sounds hollow when tapped on the bottom, 1¼ to 1½ hours. (Some cheese may ooze onto the stone.) Remove the loaf from the stone, transfer to a wire cooling rack, and let cool for at least 30 minutes before cutting into slices.

PORTABELLO MUSHROOM AND CHEESE PANINI

SERVES: 4 | PREP TIME: 20 minutes | MARINATING TIME: 30 minutes–1 hour | GRILLING TIME: 10–16 minutes

SPECIAL EQUIPMENT: cast-iron grill press (optional)

MARINADE

- 1 cup extra-virgin olive oil
- ⅓ cup balsamic vinegar
- 2 tablespoons minced garlic
- 2 teaspoons dried oregano
- 1 teaspoon kosher salt
- ½ teaspoon crushed red pepper flakes
- ½ teaspoon freshly ground black pepper

- 8 portabello mushrooms, each about 4 inches in diameter, stems trimmed evenly with the bottoms
- 4 round crusty rolls, split
- 2 cups grated fontina or mozzarella cheese (7 ounces)
- 1 cup tightly packed baby arugula

Tip

Be sure to use sturdy rolls. The mushrooms give off deliciously dark juices, and a thin roll will get soggy.

1. Whisk the marinade ingredients. Spread the mushrooms in a single layer on a rimmed baking sheet and spoon the marinade over them. Turn to coat both sides generously. Let stand at room temperature for 30 minutes to 1 hour.

2. Prepare the grill for direct cooking over medium heat (350° to 450°F).

3. Grill the mushrooms over *direct medium heat*, smooth side facing up first, with the lid closed, until juicy and tender, 8 to 12 minutes, turning once or twice and brushing with the marinade left on the baking sheet. Remove from the grill.

4. Reduce the temperature of the grill to low heat (250° to 350°F).

5. Sprinkle the bottom half of each roll with ¼ cup of the cheese. Stack 2 mushrooms on each roll, then top the mushrooms with another ¼ cup of the cheese, ¼ cup of the arugula, and the top half of the roll. Press the top of the roll firmly to compress. Place the sandwiches over *direct low heat* and press them down, one at a time, with a grill press or a wide, sturdy spatula. Grill until the bread is toasted and the cheese is melted, 2 to 4 minutes, turning once and pressing them flat after turning. Remove from the grill, cut in half, and serve immediately.

SERVES: 4 | **PREP TIME: 15 minutes** | **GRILLING TIME: 3–5 minutes**

3 tablespoons extra-virgin olive oil
½ teaspoon dried oregano
½ teaspoon kosher salt
¼ teaspoon freshly ground black pepper
1½ pounds green and/or yellow zucchini, ends trimmed, cut lengthwise into ¼-inch slices
½ cup whipped cream cheese, softened
⅓ cup store-bought basil pesto
Finely grated zest of 1 lemon
5 fresh basil leaves, finely chopped (optional)
1 French baguette, about 8 ounces, cut crosswise into 4 pieces, each halved horizontally
8 ounces roasted red bell peppers (in a jar), drained and cut into flat strips
4 ounces smoked Gouda, provolone, or mozzarella cheese, cut into thin slices

1. In a baking dish whisk the oil, oregano, salt, and pepper. Add the zucchini and turn to coat evenly. Set aside at room temperature.

2. Combine the cream cheese, pesto, lemon zest, and basil (if using).

3. Prepare the grill for direct cooking over medium heat (350° to 450°F).

4. Grill the zucchini over *direct medium heat*, with the lid closed, until tender and nicely marked, 3 to 5 minutes, turning once or twice. During the last minute of grilling time, toast the baguette pieces, cut side down, over direct heat. Remove the zucchini and the baguette pieces from the grill.

5. Spread a thin layer of the cream cheese mixture over the cut side of each baguette piece. Build the sandwiches with equal amounts of the zucchini, bell peppers, and cheese. Serve warm.

9 DESSERTS

GRILLING FRUIT

TYPE	THICKNESS / SIZE	APPROXIMATE GRILLING TIME
Apple	whole	**35–40 minutes** indirect medium heat
	½-inch slices	**4–6 minutes** direct medium heat
Apricot	halved lengthwise	**4–6 minutes** direct medium heat
Banana	halved lengthwise	**3–5 minutes** direct medium heat
Nectarine	halved lengthwise	**6–8 minutes** direct medium heat
Peach	halved lengthwise	**6–8 minutes** direct medium heat
Pear	halved lengthwise	**6–8 minutes** direct medium heat
Pineapple	½-inch slices or 1-inch wedges	**5–10 minutes** direct medium heat
Plum	halved lengthwise	**6–8 minutes** direct medium heat
Strawberry	whole	**4–5 minutes** direct medium heat

Just about everything from apples to strawberries tends to cook best over direct medium heat. The temperature on the grill's thermometer should be somewhere between 350° and 450°F.

SPECIAL EQUIPMENT: 12-inch cast-iron skillet

- 6 tablespoons (¾ stick) unsalted butter, divided
- 7 firm but ripe pears, about 3 pounds total, peeled, halved, and cored
- ½ cup packed golden brown sugar
- ½ teaspoon kosher salt
- ¼ teaspoon ground cinnamon
- ¼ teaspoon ground ginger

BATTER

- 1¼ cups cake flour
- 1 teaspoon baking powder
- ¼ teaspoon baking soda
- ¼ teaspoon ground cinnamon
- ¼ teaspoon ground ginger
- ¼ teaspoon kosher salt
- ½ cup whole milk
- ½ cup sour cream
- 2 large eggs
- 2 teaspoons pure vanilla extract
- ½ cup (1 stick) unsalted butter, softened
- ⅓ cup granulated sugar

Lightly sweetened whipped cream

1. Prepare the grill for direct and indirect cooking over medium heat (350° to 450°F).

2. Melt 2 tablespoons of the butter. Brush the butter on both sides of the pear halves. Grill the pears over *direct medium heat*, with the lid closed, until nicely marked, 10 to 12 minutes, turning once. Remove from the grill and let cool.

3. In a 12-inch cast-iron skillet combine the remaining 4 tablespoons butter, the brown sugar, salt, cinnamon, and ground ginger. Close the lid and cook over *direct medium heat* until the sugar is melted and the liquid starts to bubble slightly around the edges, 2 to 3 minutes. Wearing insulated barbecue mitts, remove the skillet from the grill and place on a sheet pan. Arrange the pear halves in the skillet, flat side down and overlapping if necessary, starting at the edge of the skillet and working in toward the center. Set aside.

4. In a medium bowl combine the cake flour, baking powder, baking soda, cinnamon, ginger, and salt. In a small bowl whisk the milk, sour cream, eggs, and vanilla extract. In a large bowl using an electric mixer on medium-high speed, cream the butter and sugar until light and fluffy, 2 to 3 minutes. With the mixer on low, add the milk mixture and then the flour mixture. Blend until smooth, scraping down the sides of the bowl as necessary. Pour the batter evenly over the pears in the skillet, smoothing it with a rubber spatula, if necessary.

5. Bake the cake over *indirect medium heat*, with the lid closed, keeping the temperature as close to 350°F as possible, until the top is golden brown and a skewer or a toothpick inserted into the center comes out clean, 35 to 45 minutes. Wearing insulated barbecue mitts, remove the skillet from the grill and let cool for 10 minutes. (If the cake stays in the skillet longer than 10 minutes, the topping will begin to harden and it will be difficult for the cake to release.)

6. Remove the cake from the skillet by running a paring knife around the edge to loosen it. Place a serving platter large enough to hold the cake over the top of the skillet. Carefully invert the skillet and platter at the same time, and then slowly remove the skillet. If any pears have stuck to the bottom of the skillet, use a spatula to remove them, and replace them on top of the cake. Let the cake cool slightly before cutting it into wedges. Serve warm or at room temperature topped with whipped cream.

SERVES: 6 | PREP TIME: 10 minutes | GRILLING TIME: 6–8 minutes

⅓ cup sliced unblanched almonds
¾ cup sour cream
   Finely grated zest of 1 large lemon
1 tablespoon honey, or to taste
3 large, firm but ripe pears, halved and cored
1½ tablespoons balsamic vinegar
2 teaspoons packed golden brown sugar

1. Prepare the grill for direct cooking over medium heat (350° to 450°F).

2. In a small, dry skillet over medium heat, toast the almonds until golden brown, 2 to 3 minutes, stirring frequently and watching closely to avoid burning. Transfer to a cutting board and roughly chop.

3. Whisk the sour cream, lemon zest, and honey.

4. Grill the pear halves, cut side down, over *direct medium heat*, with the lid closed, until lightly charred, 4 to 5 minutes. Turn the pears cut side up, brush generously with the vinegar, and grill until warmed through and beginning to soften, 2 to 3 minutes more. Remove from the grill. Mound about 2 tablespoons of lemon cream into the center of each pear half, top evenly with the brown sugar and almonds, and serve immediately.

SERVES: 4 | PREP TIME: 10 minutes | MARINATING TIME: about 1 hour | GRILLING TIME: 8–10 minutes

6 tablespoons (¾ stick) unsalted butter, softened
2 tablespoons dark or spiced rum
1 tablespoon plus 2 teaspoons packed dark brown sugar, divided
3 tablespoons sweetened coconut flakes
1 pineapple, peeled, cut lengthwise into 8 spears, core removed
⅛ teaspoon kosher salt
⅛ teaspoon freshly ground black pepper

Tip

To choose a ripe pineapple, first press the base and lower sides of the pineapple. It should give slightly under pressure. Next, sniff the bottom of the fruit. If it is ripe, it will have a distinct pineapple smell. If either one of these signs is missing, keep looking.

1. Combine the butter, rum, and 1 tablespoon of the brown sugar. Beat with a wooden spoon or mix with an electric hand mixer on medium speed until smooth and fluffy and the rum is completely incorporated.

2. In a skillet over low heat, toast the coconut, about 3 minutes. Watch it closely, as it can burn quickly. Pour the coconut into a small bowl and set aside.

3. Put the pineapple spears in a nonreactive baking dish just large enough to hold them. Combine the remaining 2 teaspoons brown sugar, the salt, and the pepper and season the pineapple evenly with the sugar and spices. Allow the pineapple to stand at room temperature for 1 hour, brushing the liquid released from the pineapple over the spears once or twice.

4. Prepare the grill for direct cooking over medium heat (350° to 450°F).

5. Grill the spears over *direct medium heat*, with the lid closed, until nicely marked, 8 to 10 minutes, turning once or twice. Remove from the grill and immediately spoon the rum butter over the spears to melt. Top with the coconut and serve immediately.

1 pineapple, peeled, cut crosswise into ½-inch slices, core removed

2 large, ripe but slightly firm mangoes, peeled and cut into 8 slices

3 firm but ripe peaches, each cut in half

3 firm but ripe nectarines, each cut in half

3 firm but ripe plums, each cut in half
   Vegetable oil

DRESSING

2 tablespoons chopped fresh mint leaves

2 teaspoons finely grated lime zest

2 tablespoons fresh lime juice

2 tablespoons honey

1. Prepare the grill for direct cooking over medium heat (350° to 450°F)

2. Lightly brush the fruit all over with oil. Grill the fruit, placing the peaches, nectarines, and plums cut side down first, over *direct medium heat*, with the lid closed, until lightly charred and beginning to soften, 8 to 10 minutes for the pineapple; 6 to 8 minutes for the peaches, nectarines, and plums; and 4 to 6 minutes for the mangoes, turning once. Remove from the grill as they are done and let cool for 10 minutes. Cut the pineapple and mangoes into 1-inch pieces. Cut each peach, nectarine, and plum half into four wedges.

3. In a large bowl combine the dressing ingredients. Add the grilled fruit and toss gently to combine. Serve immediately or refrigerate for up to 4 hours before serving.

WHAT THE GRILL DOES FOR FRUIT

Think for a second about the difference between a marshmallow right out of the bag and one that you have just toasted over a campfire so that it is richly golden and lightly charred on the surface. It's as if the fire and smoke have wrapped the marshmallow in a warm, fragile crust that oozes with sweetness.

The difference between raw fruit and grilled fruit is like that, only better, because you start with something much more flavorful than a marshmallow. You start with a ripe piece of glistening fruit whose natural flavors have matured and deepened slowly on the tree or vine. When you grill that fruit, the juices sizzle and change almost immediately. They turn deliciously caramelized and intensely concentrated while the interior of the fruit warms and softens to the point that it nearly melts on your tongue. Now that's a difference worth grilling for.

SERVES: 6 | PREP TIME: 10 minutes | GRILLING TIME: about 8 minutes

SAUCE

⅓ cup maple syrup
2 tablespoons unsalted butter
¼ teaspoon ground cinnamon
¼ teaspoon kosher salt

6 firm but ripe peaches, each cut in half
1½ tablespoons vegetable oil
1 quart vanilla ice cream
⅓ cup chopped toasted pecans

1. Prepare the grill for direct cooking over medium-low heat (about 350°F).

2. In a saucepan combine the sauce ingredients. Cook over medium heat until the butter melts, 2 to 3 minutes, stirring constantly. Remove from the heat and set aside.

3. Brush the peach halves with the oil. Grill the peaches, cut side down, over *direct medium-low heat*, with the lid closed, until they are lightly charred and starting to soften, about 4 minutes. Turn the peaches over and brush with a little of the sauce. Continue to grill until the peaches are tender, about 4 minutes more. Transfer the peaches to a cutting board and let rest for 5 minutes. Cut the peaches into wedges.

4. To serve, scoop ice cream into six serving bowls. Divide the peaches evenly among the bowls and drizzle with the remaining sauce. Top with the toasted pecans.

SERVES: 4 | PREP TIME: 25 minutes | GRILLING TIME: 20–26 minutes

SPECIAL EQUIPMENT: grill-proof griddle or cast-iron skillet

1½   cups fresh blueberries
¾   cup maple syrup
     Finely grated zest of 1 lemon
2   tablespoons unsalted butter, melted
2   tablespoons granulated sugar, divided
4   firm but ripe peaches, each cut in half
4   large eggs
⅔   cup half-and-half
1   teaspoon pure vanilla extract
½   teaspoon ground cinnamon
¼   teaspoon kosher salt
     Unsalted butter
8   slices day-old challah, each about ¾ inch thick

1. Prepare the grill for direct cooking over medium heat (350° to 450°F).

2. In a saucepan over medium-high heat, combine the blueberries, syrup, and lemon zest and bring to a boil. Reduce the heat to low and simmer for 3 minutes. Remove from the heat. Keep warm, if desired.

3. Combine the melted butter and 1 tablespoon of the sugar and stir until the sugar is dissolved. Brush the peach halves all over with the butter mixture. Grill over *direct medium heat*, with the lid closed, until they are browned in spots and warm throughout, 8 to 10 minutes, turning every 3 minutes or so. Transfer to a cutting board. When cool enough to handle, cut into wedges.

4. Preheat a grill-proof griddle over *direct medium heat* for about 10 minutes. In a baking dish whisk the eggs, half-and-half, the remaining 1 tablespoon sugar, the vanilla extract, cinnamon, and salt until thoroughly combined. Working in batches, place the bread in the egg mixture, soak for 2 minutes, and turn once. Butter the griddle. Using tongs, remove the bread from the egg mixture, allowing any excess to drip back into the dish. Place the bread on the griddle and cook with the lid closed, until golden brown on both sides, 6 to 8 minutes, turning once. Remove from the griddle and keep warm. Repeat with the remaining bread. Serve the French toast topped with the grilled peaches and the blueberry syrup.

SAUCE

½ cup granulated sugar
2 tablespoons water
½ cup heavy whipping cream
¼ cup (½ stick) unsalted butter, softened
2 teaspoons fresh lemon juice

6 firm but ripe apricots, each cut lengthwise in half
1 tablespoon vegetable oil
1 tablespoon granulated sugar
1 pint vanilla gelato or ice cream
½ cup coarsely crushed amaretti cookies

1. In a small, heavy saucepan combine the sugar with the water. Without touching the sugar, allow it to melt and turn golden brown (but not burned) over medium heat, 9 to 11 minutes, occasionally swirling the saucepan by the handle to be sure all the sugar caramelizes evenly. Meanwhile, in another pan, bring the cream and the butter to a simmer over medium heat, and then remove it from the heat. When the sugar mixture is golden brown throughout, remove it from the heat. Add the cream mixture to the sugar mixture very slowly (it will bubble up). Then add the lemon juice and whisk the sauce until smooth. Let cool until just slightly warm. If necessary, warm the sauce again over very low heat.

2. Prepare the grill for direct cooking over medium heat (350° to 450°F).

3. Brush the apricots with the oil. Sprinkle with the sugar. Grill the apricots, cut side down, over *direct medium heat*, with the lid closed, until heated through, 4 to 6 minutes, turning once. (Cooking times will vary depending on the ripeness of the apricots.) Remove from the grill.

4. To serve, stack one apricot half, one scoop of gelato, some crushed cookies, and a spoonful of caramel sauce in each dessert dish. Repeat, and finish with an apricot half, a drizzle of sauce, and more crushed cookies. Serve immediately.

SERVES: 4 | PREP TIME: 15 minutes | GRILLING TIME: about 2 minutes

1 cup heavy whipping cream
2 teaspoons confectioners' sugar
½ teaspoon pure vanilla extract
4 large navel oranges
  Vegetable oil
  Store-bought chocolate sauce

1. Prepare the grill for direct cooking over medium heat (350° to 450°F).

2. In a medium bowl using an electric mixer on medium speed, beat the cream until the trail from the beaters is just visible, about 3 minutes. Add the confectioners' sugar and vanilla extract and continue to beat until soft peaks form. Cover and refrigerate until ready to use.

3. Cut away the skin and pith of the oranges, and then cut the oranges crosswise into ¼-inch slices. Lightly brush both sides of the orange slices with oil.

4. Grill the orange slices over *direct medium heat*, with the lid closed, until nicely marked on both sides, about 2 minutes, turning once.

5. Warm the chocolate sauce. Divide the orange slices among four serving bowls, overlapping the slices slightly. Top with a generous dollop of the whipped cream and drizzle with chocolate sauce. Serve immediately.

SERVES: 6 | PREP TIME: 10 minutes | GRILLING TIME: 7–9 minutes

SPECIAL EQUIPMENT: 10-inch cast-iron skillet

- 3 pints fresh strawberries, hulled and each cut vertically in half
- ⅓ cup granulated sugar
- ¼ cup dark rum
- 1 teaspoon pure vanilla extract
- 3 tablespoons unsalted butter
- 1 store-bought pound cake, 10–12 ounces, cut into 12 slices
- 1 quart strawberry ice cream

1. Combine the strawberries, sugar, rum, and vanilla extract. Set aside at room temperature, and stir occasionally.

2. Prepare the grill for direct cooking over medium-low heat (about 350°F) and preheat a 10-inch cast-iron skillet.

3. Add the butter to the skillet and stir with a long-handled spoon until the butter is melted. Add the strawberry mixture, close the lid, and cook over *direct medium-low heat* until the strawberries start to soften, 7 to 9 minutes, stirring occasionally. During the last 2 minutes of grilling time, grill the cake slices over direct heat until lightly marked, turning once. Remove the skillet and the cake from the grill.

4. Place two slices of the cake on each of six serving plates and top with an equal amount of the strawberry ice cream. Spoon the strawberries and any sauce in the skillet over the cake and the ice cream. Serve immediately.

RECIPE REMIX:
Then and Now

You've got to hand it to past generations. They sure did know how to take a cooking shortcut. Case in point: the canned cherry pie filling and yellow cake mix used in this Cherry Delight. While we do not doubt it was delightful, we know that preparing fresher flavors can be just as easy and considerably more delicious. This time around, we sauté fresh, pitted cherries with sugar and raspberry vinegar, and pour the mixture over vanilla ice cream. The addition of chocolate curls ups the fun and flavor antes, and dessert is served with the can opener remaining safely out of sight.

The Original

Cherry Delight

Recipe from *Barbecuing the Weber® Covered Way*, ©1972

1 can (1 pound) cherry pie filling
1 package (18-1/2 ounces) yellow cake mix
1/2 cup butter or margarine, melted
1 can (3-1/2 ounces) flaked coconut
1/2 cup chopped walnuts
1-1/2 to 2 pints vanilla ice cream, optional

Spread cherry pie filling evenly over bottom of 8 x 8 x 2-inch square pan. Sprinkle yellow cake mix evenly over fruit. Drizzle butter or margarine evenly over cake mix. Sprinkle top with coconut and nuts. Center on cooking grill; cover kettle and bake about 45 minutes or until done. Serve warm or chilled, plain or topped with ice cream.

Yield: 9 to 12 servings.

WARM CHERRIES AND CHOCOLATE
OVER VANILLA ICE CREAM

The Remix

SERVES: 4–6 | PREP TIME: 15 minutes

SAUCE

- 1 pound fresh cherries, each cut in half or 1 bag (1 pound) frozen sweet dark cherries, thawed and drained
- 6 tablespoons granulated sugar
- 2 tablespoons plus ¼ teaspoon red raspberry red vinegar, divided
- ¼ teaspoon almond extract
- 1 teaspoon cornstarch dissolved in 1½ teaspoons water
- ½ teaspoon finely grated orange zest

- 1 chunk semisweet, dark, or milk chocolate, about 2 ounces
- 1 quart vanilla ice cream
  Chopped pistachios

1. In a saucepan over medium heat, combine the cherries, sugar, and 2 tablespoons of the vinegar and bring to a simmer. Cook until the cherries are tender and the liquid has thickened very slightly, stirring occasionally. Stir in the almond extract and cook for 1 minute. Then add the cornstarch mixture. Bring to a boil, immediately reduce the heat to low, and cook until thickened, 1 minute, stirring occasionally. Remove from the heat and stir in the remaining ¼ teaspoon vinegar and the orange zest. Set aside at room temperature for up to 2 hours.

2. Use a vegetable peeler against the thick side of the chocolate to make curls.

3. After grilling your main course, reheat the cherry sauce in the saucepan over *direct medium heat* (350° to 450°F) on the cooking grate of your gas or charcoal grill, over medium heat on the side burner of your gas grill, or on your stovetop. Scoop ice cream in each of four to six bowls and top with some of the cherry sauce. Garnish with chocolate curls and pistachios. Serve immediately.

SERVES: 6 | PREP TIME: 15 minutes | GRILLING TIME: 3–5 minutes

SAUCE
½ cup granulated sugar
2 tablespoons water
½ cup heavy whipping cream
¼ cup (½ stick) unsalted butter, softened
2 tablespoons bourbon
2 teaspoons fresh lemon juice

1 tablespoon granulated sugar
¾ teaspoon ancho chile powder
3 firm but ripe bananas, each cut lengthwise in half
3 tablespoons unsalted butter, melted
1 pint vanilla ice cream
½ pint coconut sorbet
¼ cup unsweetened coconut flakes, toasted

Grill banana halves in their skins to hold the fruit together.

1. Prepare the grill for direct cooking over medium heat (350° to 450°F).

2. In a small, heavy saucepan combine the sugar with the water. Without touching the sugar, allow it to melt and turn golden brown (but not burnt) over medium heat, 9 to 11 minutes, occasionally swirling the saucepan by the handle to be sure all the sugar caramelizes evenly. Meanwhile, in another pan, bring the cream, butter, and bourbon to a simmer over medium heat, and then remove it from the heat. When the sugar mixture is golden brown throughout, remove it from the heat. Add the cream mixture to the sugar mixture very slowly (it will bubble up). Then add the lemon juice and whisk the sauce until smooth. Let cool until just slightly warm.

3. Combine the sugar and the chile powder. Brush the cut side of the bananas with the melted butter and season with the sugar mixture. Grill the bananas, cut side down, over *direct medium heat*, with the lid closed, until warm and nicely marked, 3 to 5 minutes (do not turn). Remove from the grill, peel the bananas, and cut them into ¾-inch pieces. If necessary, warm the sauce again over very low heat. Divide the ice cream and the sorbet evenly among six bowls. Top with bananas, sauce, and toasted coconut flakes. Serve immediately.

MAKES: 36 cookies | PREP TIME: 20 minutes | GRILLING TIME: about 45 minutes

SPECIAL EQUIPMENT: pizza stone

2½ cups all-purpose flour
1 teaspoon baking soda
¾ teaspoon table salt
½ cup (1 stick) unsalted butter, softened
½ cup all-natural peanut butter
¾ cup granulated sugar
¾ cup packed golden brown sugar
2 large eggs, at room temperature
2 teaspoons pure vanilla extract
12 ounces semisweet chocolate chips (2 cups)

Tip

You'll be happy to have a thermometer on your grill's lid for this recipe, as these cookies will be most successful if you keep a steady baking temperature of 350° to 375°F.

1. Sift the flour, baking soda, and salt into a large bowl.

2. In another large bowl combine the butter, peanut butter, and both sugars and beat until smooth. One at a time, beat in the eggs, followed by the vanilla. Gradually add in the flour mixture. Mix in the chocolate chips. Refrigerate the dough while you preheat the grill.

3. Prepare the grill for indirect cooking over medium-low heat (350° to 375°F) and preheat a pizza stone over indirect heat for at least 15 minutes, following manufacturer's instructions.

4. One heaping tablespoon at a time, scoop the dough into 36 balls. Arrange about 12 balls in even rows at least 2 inches apart on the pizza stone. Refrigerate the remaining balls until ready to grill. Bake the cookies over *indirect medium-low heat*, with the lid closed, until lightly browned around the edges, 12 to 15 minutes. Transfer the cookies to a wire cooling rack and let cool for 3 to 5 minutes. Repeat the process with the remaining dough. Serve the cookies warm.

SPECIAL EQUIPMENT: 12-well muffin pan

6½ tablespoons unsalted butter, divided
4 ounces top-quality bittersweet chocolate
2 large eggs
¼ cup granulated sugar
1 tablespoon all-purpose flour
½ cup cold whipped cream
1 cup fresh raspberries

Tip

Each muffin cup in the pan should measure
2¾ inches in diameter by 1¼ inches high, and
each should hold 4 ounces by volume.

1. Using ½ tablespoon of the butter, grease the four cups down the center of a 12-well muffin pan.

2. In a bowl set over a pan of barely simmering water, melt the chocolate and the remaining 6 tablespoons butter, stirring occasionally until smooth. In another bowl whisk the eggs and the sugar until light and fluffy, about 20 seconds. Add the warm chocolate mixture to the egg mixture and mix until smooth. Then add the flour and mix until you no longer see specks of flour.

3. Fill the four greased cups with the batter (almost to the top rim, but not all the way). If not ready to cook, refrigerate for as long as 3 hours.

4. Prepare the grill for indirect cooking over medium heat (ideally 400°F).

5. Place the muffin pan over *indirect medium heat* and bake, with the lid closed, until the cake tops no longer jiggle when you shake the pan, about 10 minutes (or as long as 14 minutes if the batter has been refrigerated). Remove from the grill and let rest for 5 to 10 minutes.

6. Run a knife around the outer rim of each cake to make sure it is not stuck to the pan. On top of the muffin pan place a cutting board or a platter that is slightly larger than the pan. Holding the pan and cutting board together, invert them so that the cakes fall out of the pan. Serve immediately with whipped cream and raspberries.

10

RUBS, BRINES, MARINADES, AND SAUCES

RUBS

MAKING RUBS

A rub is a mixture of spices, herbs, and other seasonings (often including sugar) that can quickly give a boost of flavors to foods before grilling. This page provides some mighty good examples, but dare to be different. One of the steps toward developing your own style at the grill is to concoct a signature rub recipe or two. Only you will know exactly what ingredients are blended in your special jar of "magic dust."

A word about freshness: Ground spices lose their aromas in a matter of months (eight to ten months maximum). If you have been holding on to a little jar of coriander for years, waiting to blend the world's finest version of curry powder, forget about it. Dump the old, tired coriander and buy some freshly ground. Better yet, buy whole coriander seeds and grind them yourself. Whatever you do, store your spices and spice rubs in airtight containers away from light and heat, to best preserve their flavors and fragrances.

BEEF RUB

MAKES: 2 tablespoons

- 2 teaspoons kosher salt
- 1 teaspoon granulated garlic
- 1 teaspoon freshly ground black pepper
- 1 teaspoon smoked paprika
- ½ teaspoon ground coriander
- ½ teaspoon ground cumin

LAMB RUB

MAKES: 2 tablespoons

- 2 teaspoons kosher salt
- 1 teaspoon paprika
- 1 teaspoon curry powder
- 1 teaspoon freshly ground black pepper
- ½ teaspoon granulated onion
- ½ teaspoon anise seed

PORK RUB

MAKES: about 1½ tablespoons

- 2 teaspoons kosher salt
- 1 teaspoon ground cumin
- ½ teaspoon freshly ground black pepper
- ½ teaspoon dried oregano
- ½ teaspoon packed golden brown sugar
- ¼ teaspoon chipotle chile powder

POULTRY RUB

MAKES: about 3 tablespoons

- 2 teaspoons kosher salt
- 2 teaspoons dried thyme
- 1 teaspoon dried oregano
- 1 teaspoon granulated onion
- 1 teaspoon ground coriander
- 1 teaspoon freshly ground black pepper
- ½ teaspoon prepared chili powder

SEAFOOD RUB

MAKES: about 2 tablespoons

- 2 teaspoons kosher salt
- 1 teaspoon prepared chili powder
- 1 teaspoon granulated garlic
- ½ teaspoon ground coriander
- ½ teaspoon celery seed
- ½ teaspoon freshly ground black pepper

VEGETABLE RUB

MAKES: 2 tablespoons

- 1 teaspoon mustard powder
- 1 teaspoon granulated onion
- 1 teaspoon paprika
- 1 teaspoon kosher salt
- ½ teaspoon granulated garlic
- ½ teaspoon ground coriander
- ½ teaspoon ground cumin
- ½ teaspoon freshly ground black pepper

HOW LONG?

If you leave a rub on for a long time, the seasonings intermix with the juices in the meat and produce more pronounced flavors as well as a crust. This is good to a point, but a rub with a lot of salt or sugar will draw moisture out of the meat over time, making the meat tastier, yes, but also drier. So how long should you use a rub? Here are some guidelines.

TIME	TYPES OF FOOD
Up to 15 minutes	Small foods, such as shellfish, cubed meat for kabobs, and vegetables
15–30 minutes	Thin cuts of boneless meat, such as chicken breasts, fish fillets, pork tenderloins, chops, and steaks
30 minutes–1½ hours	Thicker cuts of boneless or bone-in meat, such as leg of lamb, whole chickens, and beef roasts
2–8 hours	Big or tough cuts of meat, such as racks of ribs, whole hams, pork shoulders, and turkeys

MAKING BRINES

Good grillers love to brine, and for good reason. A nice, salty soak in a brine will ensure that meats, especially lean varieties, such as chicken breast and pork loin, stay moist and flavorful against the high heat and/or long cooking times of certain recipes. Brines penetrate meat's cellular structure to both break down the tough stuff and plump it all up, making your meat more tender, more flavorful, and much less likely to dry out. There's an art—and a science—to brining, starting with the ratios. You'll need ½ to 1 cup of kosher salt for every gallon of water. Meat likes balance, so it will absorb salt until it matches the levels in the brine. See the chart below for some guidelines.

HOW LONG?

TIME	TYPES OF FOOD
Up to 30 minutes	Small foods, such as shellfish, cubed meat for kabobs, and vegetables
30 minutes– 1 hour	Thin cuts of boneless meat, such as chicken breasts, fish fillets, pork tenderloins, chops, and steaks
2–4 hours	Thicker cuts of boneless or bone-in meat, such as leg of lamb, whole chickens, and beef roasts
4–12 hours	Big or tough cuts of meat, such as racks of ribs, whole hams, pork shoulders, and turkeys

BUTTERMILK BRINE

GOOD WITH: pork, chicken, turkey, game
MAKES: enough brine for 3 pounds of meat

- 2   cups buttermilk
- ¾   cup finely chopped onion
- 2   tablespoons granulated sugar
- 2   tablespoons kosher salt
- 3   fresh thyme sprigs
- 2   garlic cloves, peeled and smashed
- 2   fresh or dried bay leaves, torn
- 1   teaspoon black peppercorns

1. Combine the ingredients and whisk until the sugar and salt are dissolved. Before grilling, remove the meat from the brine and discard the brine. Rinse the meat and pat dry with paper towels, inside and outside the cavity, if using a whole bird. Refrigerate for at least one hour, uncovered, to dry thoroughly.

NORMANDY BRINE

GOOD WITH: pork, chicken, turkey
MAKES: enough brine for 3 pounds of meat

- 2   cups apple cider
- ⅓   cup packed dark brown sugar
- ⅓   cup kosher salt
- 4   fresh thyme sprigs
- 6   whole cloves, smashed
- 1   tablespoon yellow mustard seed
- 2   teaspoons black peppercorns
- 2   bay leaves, torn
- 2   cups water

1. In a medium saucepan over medium-low heat, combine all of the ingredients, except the water, whisking to dissolve the sugar and salt. Remove from the heat and add the water. Cool completely. Before grilling, remove the meat from the brine and discard the brine. Rinse the meat and pat dry with paper towels, inside and outside the cavity, if using a whole bird. Refrigerate for at least 1 hour, uncovered, to dry thoroughly.

ITALIAN BRINE

GOOD WITH: pork, chicken, turkey
MAKES: enough brine for 3 pounds of meat

- 2   cups water
- 1   orange, quartered
- 1   lemon, quartered
- 1   small yellow onion, quartered
- ¼   cup granulated sugar
- ¼   cup kosher salt
- 4   sprigs fresh oregano or thyme
- 2   teaspoons black peppercorns
- 4   fresh sage leaves
- 2   garlic cloves, peeled and smashed
- 2   bay leaves
- 2   cups dry white wine

1. Pour the water into a saucepan, and then add the orange and lemon quarters, simultaneously squeezing the juice into the water. Add the remaining brine ingredients except the wine. Heat over medium-low heat, stirring to dissolve the sugar and salt. Remove from the heat and add the wine. Cool completely. Before grilling, remove the meat from the brine and discard the brine. Rinse the meat and pat dry with paper towels, inside and outside the cavity, if using a whole bird. Refrigerate for at least 1 hour, uncovered, to dry thoroughly.

MARINADES

MAKING MARINADES

It's what's inside that counts—and that's flavor, where marinades are concerned. Letting food sit in a mixture of acidic liquid, oil, herbs, and seasonings does wonders to kick-start items that might need a little boost, like leaner cuts of meat and even vegetables, in addition to keeping them moist on the grill. Bold ingredients work best—think garlic, rosemary, or soy sauce—to maximize the marinade's effect, and the right combinations can give your meal a regional or ethnic flair.

MOROCCAN MARINADE

This potent marinade is commonly used with fish, but equally delicious with lamb, beef, chicken, shrimp, and hearty vegetables, such as eggplant and cauliflower. It will keep for up to 2 days refrigerated, but its flavor is freshest when used within 1 day. If refrigerating, pour a thin layer of olive oil over top before covering to prevent discoloration.

GOOD WITH: beef, lamb, chicken, fish, shrimp, vegetables
MAKES: about 1 cup

- ⅓ cup extra-virgin olive oil
- 2 teaspoons finely grated lemon zest
- ¼ cup fresh lemon juice
- ¼ cup roughly chopped fresh cilantro leaves
- ¼ cup roughly chopped fresh Italian parsley leaves
- 3 garlic cloves, minced or pushed through a press
- 2 teaspoons smoked paprika
- 1 teaspoon ground cumin
- 1 teaspoon ground coriander
- 1 teaspoon kosher salt

1. In a medium bowl whisk all of the ingredients.

INDIAN MARINADE

Cardamom and coriander infuse yogurt in this tandoori-inspired marinade. The yogurt acts as a tenderizer while creating a thick coating that boosts flavor during grilling. Be sure to use freshly ground spices. If they have been in your spice cabinet for one year or longer, then it's time to replace them.

GOOD WITH: chicken, fish, vegetables
MAKES: about 1 cup

- ½ cup whole-milk yogurt
- ¼ cup extra-virgin olive oil
- 2 tablespoons fresh lemon juice
- 1 tablespoon peeled, finely grated fresh ginger
- 2 teaspoons ground cardamom
- 3 large garlic cloves, minced or pushed through a press
- 1 teaspoon ground coriander
- 1 teaspoon kosher salt
- 1 teaspoon freshly ground black pepper

1. In a medium bowl whisk all of the ingredients.

HOW LONG?

The right length of time varies, depending on the strength of the marinade and the food you are marinating. If your marinade includes intense ingredients like soy sauce, hard liquor, or hot chiles and strong spices, don't overdo it. A fish fillet should still taste like fish, not like a burning-hot, salt-soaked piece of protein. Also, if an acidic marinade is left on meat or fish too long, it can turn the surface dry or mushy. Here are some guidelines to get you going.

TIME	TYPES OF FOOD
15–30 minutes	Small foods, such as shellfish, fish fillets, cubed meat for kabobs, and tender vegetables
1–3 hours	Thin cuts of boneless meat, such as chicken breasts, pork tenderloins, chops, steaks, and sturdy vegetables
2–6 hours	Thicker cuts of boneless or bone-in meat, such as leg of lamb, whole chickens, and beef roasts
6–12 hours	Big or tough cuts of meat, such as racks of ribs, whole hams, pork shoulders, and turkeys

FIESTA MARINADE

While this festive marinade is reminiscent of a margarita, be sure to save your best tequila for cocktails, and choose a lower-shelf option for the marinade.

GOOD WITH: beef, chicken, fish, shrimp
MAKES: about 1¼ cups

½	cup fresh orange juice
¼	cup fresh lime juice
¼	cup gold tequila
1	large jalapeño chile pepper, including seeds, finely chopped
3	tablespoons agave nectar
2	tablespoons soy sauce
2	teaspoons ground cumin
4	garlic cloves, minced or pushed through a press

1. In a medium bowl whisk all of the ingredients.

SWEET AND SIMPLE MARINADE

Classic barbecue sauce ingredients come together in this sweet and sharp marinade.

GOOD WITH: beef, pork, chicken
MAKES: about 1 cup

½	cup soy sauce
¼	cup bourbon or whiskey
¼	cup honey
2	tablespoons ketchup
2	tablespoons Dijon mustard
1	tablespoon cider vinegar
1	tablespoon extra-virgin olive oil
4	garlic cloves, minced or pushed through a press

1. In a medium bowl whisk all of the ingredients.

GO-TO FAVORITE MARINADE

A generous amount of grated onion with its juice adds the necessary sweetness to round out this simple marinade.

GOOD WITH: chicken, fish, shrimp, scallops, vegetables
MAKES: about 1¼ cups

1	small yellow onion, grated, with juice (about ½ cup)
¼	cup fresh lemon juice
3	tablespoons extra-virgin olive oil
3	tablespoons soy sauce
2	tablespoons Dijon mustard
1	teaspoon freshly ground black pepper

1. In a medium bowl whisk all of the ingredients.

SMOKY MARINADE

Chipotle chile peppers add smoke and heat to this feisty marinade, which is smoothed and sweetened with ketchup and brown sugar. This is a great marinade for flavoring and tenderizing tough cuts of meat, such as flank steak, skirt steak, and tri-tip.

GOOD WITH: beef, pork, chicken, shrimp
MAKES: about 1 cup

4	canned chipotle chile peppers in adobo sauce, minced (about ⅓ cup)
¼	cup fresh lime juice
3	tablespoons ketchup
2	tablespoons extra-virgin olive oil
1	tablespoon packed dark brown sugar
4	garlic cloves, minced or pushed through a press
2	teaspoons kosher salt
1	teaspoon ground cumin
1	teaspoon prepared chili powder

1. In a medium bowl whisk all of the ingredients.

CILANTRO: LOVE IT OR HATE IT

Cilantro has a secure home among the likes of black licorice, mayonnaise, and musical theater—in the "you either love it or you hate it" ranks.

"Cilantrophiles" cite the herb's fresh, vibrant flavor and unparalleled ability to tame the heat of spicy foods (hence its popularity in Asia and Latin America), while "cilantrophobes" will tell you that any food it has touched tastes drenched in dish soap, or even worse, bugs.

Oddly enough, there are scientific theories for this culinary schism. Some studies have shown that there is an anti-cilantro gene, and others found that the aroma of cilantro to have smelly cousins that are by-products of soaps and lotions and, yes, even some insects. Since taste and smell are strong triggers of memories, experiences with cleaning agents or with an infestation are likely not what you want to recall when diving into chips and guacamole.

For the lucky ones that don't have that strong reaction, a sprinkling of chopped cilantro leaves can lighten rich or heavy flavors and deliciously balance acidic ones. Try cilantro pesto as a fantastic alternative to the traditional basil variety. But if you're among the "forget it" crowd and are looking to substitute cilantro—also called coriander—in a recipe, some bright, lemony parsley can do the trick. Or just omit the herb part altogether.

If you are a lover of cilantro and want to cook with it for a crowd, wonderful. But don't say we didn't warn you.

MAKING SAUCES

No matter what you grill or what sorts of regional styles you prefer, chances are very good that you will brush, ladle, or drizzle some sort of sauce on your food. Without it, your meal could be missing an essential range of flavor, an important degree of texture, or a beautiful boost of color—or all three. Grilling sauces are usually pretty easy to make. Sometimes the prep is as simple as whisking a handful of ingredients, most of which are probably in your pantry or refrigerator already. Whichever type of sauce you choose, keep in mind the all-important principle of balance. Whether you are making a fresh salsa, a lively vinaigrette, or a sweet and smoky barbecue sauce, you should first understand some fundamentals about taste.

TASTE 101

SWEETNESS

As humans we are wired to like sweetness, even in savory sauces. It is a nice counterpoint to acidity or spiciness, as it rounds out the sharp edges. The right level of sweetness varies according to the particular sauce. For example, in barbecue sauces the sweetness is usually much higher than the acidity, but in an herb sauce like pesto, there is only a trace of sweetness. Sweet condiments include white and brown sugar, molasses, honey, maple syrup, ketchup, apple juice, and hoisin sauce. You can also add sweetness with fruits, sweet peppers, and corn.

SOURNESS

Sourness is the acidity that keeps sweetness in check and is also crucial for bringing some zip and tang to rich sauces that would otherwise taste flat. Imagine how boring and one-dimensional a vinaigrette would be if it had no acidity. Sour ingredients include vinegars (cider, wine, rice, balsamic), some citrus juices, mustards, yogurt, and sharp and tangy vegetables, such as tomatillos.

SALTINESS

Saltiness is absolutely critical. Salt itself is the single best ingredient for exciting our taste buds and amplifying other flavors. Even sweet sauces like caramel benefit from salt. But, of course, too much saltiness will disrupt the other features of any good sauce, so start with just a little and add more slowly. If a sauce actually tastes salty, you've gone too far. Your choice of ingredients includes, of course, kosher or sea salt, but also soy sauce, Worcestershire sauce, fish sauce, and capers.

BITTERNESS

A lot of us have bad associations with bitterness. It reminds us of extreme examples like burned brussels sprouts and liver, but keep in mind that a little bitterness is often an essential component of great wine, beer, coffee, and yes, even some sauces. It balances out sweetness and provides a little edginess. Delicious choices for bitterness (in small amounts) include cranberry juice, olives, and horseradish—but not all together.

SPICINESS

Spiciness is not really a taste. It is a combination of both flavor and sensation; that is, you taste it *and* you feel it. Depending on the type of sauce, your choice of spices can emphasize specific regions and ethnic traditions. Usually the spicier sauces are tempered with sweetness. Some of the most popular spicy ingredients include fresh ginger and garlic, chili powder, fresh chile peppers, and bottled hot sauces.

UMAMI

This is the taste that is as much fun to say (uuu-mam-ee) as it is to eat. Umami is the deep, rich savoriness that usually comes from concentrated, aged, or fermented ingredients like Parmesan cheese, bacon, and red wine. When a sauce seems a little thin or bland, try adding some umami. Other potent sources are Worcestershire sauce, beef broth, and sun-dried tomatoes.

BARBECUE SAUCES

The barbecue sauces hundreds of years ago were basting liquids, or "mops," made from just butter, vinegar, salt, and pepper, to add moisture and an extra touch of good taste to meat as it sizzled over a fire. Time and regional differences introduced additional ingredients, such as tomatoes, sugar, mustard, and mayonnaise, leading to a wide variety of traditions and flavor profiles—not to mention evangelizing followers. Today you will find a nearly endless assortment of barbecue sauces, yet they all share some elements. Whether it's a vinegar- or mustard-based Carolina sauce, a tomato-enriched Kansas City sauce, or a soy-and-ginger Asian-inspired sauce, all good barbecue sauces find a balance of sweetness, sourness, spiciness, and saltiness—and the best ones have a good dose of umami from something like Worcestershire sauce.

CLASSIC RED BARBECUE SAUCE

Ketchup provides the base flavor and the smooth, thick body of this sauce. Apple juice and molasses bump up the sweetness quite a bit, while cider vinegar provides the required acidity.

MAKES: about 1¼ cups

¾ cup apple juice
½ cup ketchup
3 tablespoons cider vinegar
2 teaspoons soy sauce
1 teaspoon Worcestershire sauce
½ teaspoon pure chile powder
1 garlic clove, minced or pushed through a press
¼ teaspoon freshly ground black pepper

1. In a small saucepan mix the ingredients. Simmer for a few minutes over medium heat, and then remove the saucepan from the heat.

APPLE CIDER VINEGAR SAUCE

Vinegar sauce is usually thin enough that it can penetrate the meat while basting. Sugar, salt, and pepper usually offset its pronounced acidity. This version uses apple cider for sweetness, hot sauce and mustard for spiciness, and soy and Worcestershire sauces for umami.

MAKES: about 1¾ cups

1 cup apple cider
¼ cup cider vinegar
¼ cup Dijon mustard
2 tablespoons soy sauce
2 tablespoons Worcestershire sauce
1 teaspoon kosher salt
1 teaspoon hot pepper sauce

1. In a saucepan over high heat, whisk the ingredients and bring to a boil. Remove the pan from the heat.

PASILLA BARBECUE SAUCE

For this chile-based sauce, the preparation begins by browning onion and garlic to sweeten them a bit, but the more dominant effects come from the spiciness of roasted chile peppers, the acidity of tomatoes and vinegar, and the slight bitterness of beer. The oregano and the spices fill out the flavor profile with more complexity.

MAKES: about 2 cups

2 tablespoons extra-virgin olive oil
6 medium garlic cloves, peeled
⅓ cup finely chopped red onion
2 dried pasilla chile peppers, seeded and cut into strips
1 cup canned diced tomatoes in juice
1 cup amber Mexican beer
1 tablespoon cider vinegar
1 teaspoon kosher salt
½ teaspoon dried oregano
¼ teaspoon freshly ground black pepper

1. In a small, heavy-bottomed saucepan over medium heat, warm the oil and cook the garlic until lightly browned, 4 to 5 minutes, turning occasionally. Add the onion and the chiles and cook for about 3 minutes, stirring occasionally. Add the remaining ingredients, bring to a boil, and simmer for 15 minutes. Remove the saucepan from the heat and let the mixture stand for 15 minutes to soften the chiles and blend the flavors. Puree in a blender.

HERB SAUCES

Herb sauces are bold, coarsely chopped or pulsed condiments made in a variety of styles all over the world. Whether it's Argentinian *chimichurri*, Italian pesto, or Moroccan *chermoula*, all herb sauces feature soft leafy herbs, good oil, garlic, and salt. The flavor balance is not as sweet as it is in most barbecue sauces. Instead, there is an emphasis on sour, acidic ingredients, such as vinegar, citrus, or tomatillos, which help to preserve freshness and boost the herbal flavor. Some form of saltiness is universally important, as it supports each sauce's finished flavors. In addition to kosher or sea salt, anchovies, fish sauce, capers, or olives may be used.

CHIMICHURRI

Chimichurri is an Argentinian condiment served with grilled beef as a garnish or a dipping sauce. Classic *chimichurri* features parsley; however, oregano, cilantro, or basil is sometimes added for extra flavor.

MAKES: about 1½ cups

- 2 large garlic cloves
- 2 cups loosely packed fresh Italian parsley leaves and tender stems
- 2 tablespoons fresh oregano leaves
- ½ cup extra-virgin olive oil
- 2 tablespoons red wine vinegar
- 1 teaspoon kosher salt
- ½ teaspoon freshly ground black pepper
- ¼ teaspoon crushed red pepper flakes

1. In a food processor mince the garlic. Add the parsley and the oregano. Pulse to finely chop the herbs. Then slowly add the oil in a steady stream. Add the remaining ingredients and mix well.

CHERMOULA

Chermoula is a North African sauce typically used to garnish fish, but it's also delicious with meat, chicken, and vegetables.

MAKES: about 1¼ cups

- ⅓ cup extra-virgin olive oil
- ¼ cup fresh lemon juice
- ¼ cup chopped fresh Italian parsley leaves
- ¼ cup chopped fresh cilantro leaves
- 1 tablespoon minced garlic
- 1½ teaspoons paprika
- 1 teaspoon ground cumin
- 1 teaspoon kosher salt
- ½ teaspoon freshly ground black pepper
- ¼ teaspoon ground cayenne pepper

1. In a medium bowl combine all of the ingredients.

CILANTRO PESTO

Pesto is a well known and beloved herb sauce that hails from the Liguria region of northern Italy. It is traditionally prepared with fresh basil; however, in the United States we also use other leafy herbs, such as fresh cilantro or parsley (or even arugula). As with most herb sauces, the leaves are ground with olive oil, garlic, and nuts to achieve a coarse consistency. Parmesan or pecorino cheese can be added at the end for saltiness and umami.

MAKES: about 1 cup

- 2 tablespoons coarsely chopped walnuts
- 2 medium garlic cloves
- 1½ cups loosely packed fresh cilantro leaves and tender stems
- ½ cup loosely packed fresh Italian parsley leaves and tender stems
- ½ teaspoon kosher salt
- ¼ teaspoon freshly ground black pepper
- ¼ cup extra-virgin olive oil

1. In a food processor finely chop the walnuts and the garlic. Scrape down the sides of the bowl. Add the cilantro, parsley, salt, and pepper and process until finely chopped. With the motor running, slowly add the oil to create a smooth puree.

SALSAS

The conquistadores gave salsas their name when they came to the Americas, yet the origins of these sauces extend as far back as the days of the Aztecs. So let's just say salsas have stood the test of time. The best-known version today is a blend of tomatoes, onions, and chiles (salsa *roja*). It is distinguished by a chunky texture that shows off the main components.

When making your own salsa, bear in mind the idea that "what grows together, goes together." If you are making an island-style salsa, use tropical ingredients, such as mango and pineapple for sweetness and citrus juice for sourness. A southwestern-style salsa might include tomatoes and corn for sweetness and pickled jalapeños for sourness, not to mention spiciness. And no matter where you are going with your salsa, don't forget the salt.

ROASTED TOMATILLO SALSA

Salsa ingredients are not always raw. Grilling coaxes natural plant sugars out of many vegetables and introduces a nice smoky char to the mix.

MAKES: about 2 cups

- 1 medium yellow onion, cut crosswise into ½-inch slices
  Extra-virgin olive oil
- 10 medium tomatillos, about 8 ounces total, husked and rinsed
- 1 small jalapeño chile pepper, stem removed
- ¼ cup loosely packed fresh cilantro leaves and tender stems
- 1 medium garlic clove
- ½ teaspoon packed dark brown sugar
- ½ teaspoon kosher salt

1. Prepare the grill for direct cooking over high heat (450° to 550°F).

2. Lightly brush the onion slices on both sides with oil. Grill the onion slices, tomatillos, and jalapeño over *direct high heat*, with the lid closed, until lightly charred, 6 to 8 minutes, turning once or twice and swapping their positions as needed for even cooking. Be sure the tomatillos are completely soft as you remove them from the grill. In a food processor combine the onion slices, tomatillos, and jalapeño, along with all the remaining ingredients. Pulse until blended but still chunky.

BLACK BEAN AND AVOCADO SALSA

MAKES: about 4 cups

- 1 can (15 ounces) black beans, rinsed and drained
- 1 large Hass avocado, diced
- 1 medium red bell pepper, finely diced
- 1 cup fresh corn kernels
- 1 small red onion, finely diced
- ½ cup coarsely chopped fresh cilantro leaves
- ¼ cup fresh lime juice
- 2 tablespoons extra-virgin olive oil
- 1 teaspoon ground cumin
- 1 teaspoon kosher salt
- ½ teaspoon freshly ground black pepper
- ¼ teaspoon ground cayenne pepper

1. In a large bowl combine all of the ingredients.

NECTARINE, RED PEPPER, AND ONION SALSA

This sweeter-style salsa goes well with savory items like fish or chicken.

MAKES: about 2½ cups

- 2 firm but ripe nectarines, about 1 pound total, diced
- 1 small red bell pepper, diced
- ½ cup diced red onion
- 1 jalapeño chile pepper, seeded and minced
- 2 tablespoons finely chopped fresh mint leaves
- 2 tablespoons finely chopped fresh Italian parsley leaves
- 1 tablespoon fresh lime juice
- 1 tablespoon honey
- ¼ teaspoon crushed red pepper flakes
- ¼ teaspoon kosher salt

1. In a large bowl combine all of the ingredients.

VINAIGRETTES

If you think a vinaigrette is just for salads, then think again. In the world of grilling, it plays many roles, first as a fully loaded marinade for lean items like chicken breasts, shrimp, and vegetables. It also works nicely as a basting sauce or a moisturizer for almost anything on the grill, including pork chops and portabello mushrooms. Finally, you can spoon a vinaigrette over whatever has just come hot off the grill. It's a brilliant way to dress up a simple steak or a platter of grilled vegetables.

A vinaigrette is actually one of the original "mother sauces" of French cuisine, but that shouldn't intimidate you. Just whisk some vinegar with three or four times as much oil and season to taste. That temporary emulsion can go in any flavor direction you like.

FRENCH VINAIGRETTE

This is the classic version that you might serve with a salad. It shouldn't be too sweet. Cider vinegar and olive oil form its base. To that, shallots and mustard add sharpness, lemon zest adds brightness, and salt and pepper do what they always do well.

MAKES: about ¾ cup

- 3 tablespoons cider vinegar
- 1 tablespoon minced shallot
- 2 teaspoons finely grated lemon zest
- 1 teaspoon Dijon mustard
- ½ cup extra-virgin olive oil
- ½ teaspoon kosher salt
- ¼ teaspoon freshly ground black pepper

1. In a small bowl whisk the vinegar, shallot, lemon zest, and mustard. Slowly drizzle and whisk in the oil until it is emulsified. Season with the salt and pepper.

BALSAMIC VINAIGRETTE

Rich and sweet balsamic vinegar stands up well to more pronounced flavors including brown sugar (sweet), mustard (sharp), and garlic (spice).

MAKES: about 1 cup

- ¼ cup balsamic vinegar
- 2 teaspoons packed golden brown sugar
- 1 teaspoon mustard powder
- 1 small clove garlic, minced
- ½ teaspoon kosher salt
- ½ teaspoon freshly ground black pepper
- ¾ cup extra-virgin olive oil

1. In a small bowl whisk all of the ingredients except the oil. Then slowly drizzle and whisk in the oil until the vinaigrette is emulsified.

ASIAN VINAIGRETTE

A combination of rice vinegar and lime juice plus olive oil and toasted sesame oil team up to achieve a 3:1 ratio in this Asian-inspired vinaigrette. Honey adds sweetness. Cilantro, ginger, garlic, and Sriracha add spice. Soy sauce adds salt.

MAKES: about 1 cup

- 2 tablespoons rice vinegar
- 1 tablespoon fresh lime juice
- 1 tablespoon finely chopped fresh cilantro leaves
- 2 teaspoons honey
- 2 teaspoons soy sauce
- 2 teaspoons peeled, finely grated fresh ginger
- 1 teaspoon hot chili-garlic sauce, such as Sriracha
- 1 small garlic clove, minced
- ½ cup extra-virgin olive oil
- 2 teaspoons toasted sesame oil

1. In a medium bowl whisk all of the ingredients except the oils. Then slowly drizzle and whisk in the olive oil and sesame oil until the vinaigrette is emulsified.

WHITE SAUCES

The term "white sauces" is meant to capture all the creamy emulsions and dairy-based sauces used for dipping and garnishing grilled beef, lamb, pork, poultry, fish, vegetables, and bread. Besides a common color, they also usually share a generous kick of garlic. The base might include mayonnaise, egg and oil, yogurt, or sour cream. To increase sweetness, sweet pickles, red bell peppers, or a pinch of sugar may be added. Onions, lemon juice, cornichons, capers, mustard, and vinegar provide sharpness and sourness. They get their umami from things like Worcestershire sauce and anchovies.

RÉMOULADE

Mayonnaise-based rémoulade is inherently sweet. To balance that taste, it needs some vinegar, pickles, capers, and mustard. Spicy Louisiana-style rémoulade can include creole seasoning, mustard, paprika, parsley, and horseradish. French rémoulade is less sweet than its Louisiana cousin and often includes cornichons, capers, chives, and tarragon.

MAKES: about ¾ cup

½ cup mayonnaise
1 tablespoon capers, drained and minced
1 tablespoon sweet pickle relish
1 tablespoon finely chopped fresh tarragon leaves
2 teaspoons minced shallot
1 teaspoon tarragon vinegar or white wine vinegar
½ teaspoon Dijon mustard
1 small garlic clove, minced or pushed through a press
¼ teaspoon paprika
¼ teaspoon kosher salt

1. In a medium bowl whisk the ingredients. If not using right away, cover and refrigerate for as long as 24 hours.

LEMON-BASIL AIOLI

Aioli is a Provençal-style emulsion of oil, egg, and garlic. Purists will make it with raw egg yolks, but a high-quality mayonnaise makes a fine substitution.

MAKES: about ½ cup

¼ cup mayonnaise
1 tablespoon finely chopped fresh basil leaves
1½ teaspoons finely grated lemon zest
2 teaspoons fresh lemon juice
1 small garlic clove, minced or pushed through a press
¼ teaspoon kosher salt

1. In a small bowl combine the ingredients and mix thoroughly.

TZATZIKI

Tzatziki is the cooler, creamier version of white sauces. It's less sweet than mayo-rich rémoulade, and it gets a burst of acidity from yogurt and lemon juice. Chopped or grated cucumbers cool the yogurt's tang. Garlic, hot pepper sauce, or cayenne pepper is added for punch. Mint, dill, or parsley contributes traditional flavor and color. Variations include adding red peppers for a sweeter North African-style sauce, or blending bread or potatoes into the mix for Greek *Skordalia*.

MAKES: about 1½ cups

---

1 cup whole-milk Greek yogurt
½ English cucumber, finely diced
¼ cup chopped fresh mint leaves
1 tablespoon fresh lemon juice
2 garlic cloves, minced or pushed through a press
1 teaspoon kosher salt
½ teaspoon freshly ground black pepper
¼ teaspoon hot pepper sauce

1. In a medium bowl combine the ingredients. Refrigerate until ready to use.

INDEX

INDEX

METRIC EQUIVALENTS

METRIC EQUIVALENTS FOR DIFFERENT TYPES OF INGREDIENTS

A standard cup measure of a dry or solid ingredient will vary in weight depending on the type of ingredient. A standard cup of liquid is the same volume for any type of liquid. Use the following chart when converting standard cup measures to grams (weight) or milliliters (volume).

STANDARD CUP	FINE POWDER (e.g., flour)	GRAIN (e.g., rice)	GRANULAR (e.g., sugar)	LIQUID SOLIDS (e.g., butter)	LIQUID (e.g., milk)
1/8	18 g	19 g	24 g	25 g	30 ml
1/4	35 g	38 g	48 g	50 g	60 ml
1/3	47 g	50 g	63 g	67 g	80 ml
1/2	70 g	75 g	95 g	100 g	120 ml
2/3	93 g	100 g	125 g	133 g	160 ml
3/4	105 g	113 g	143 g	150 g	180 ml
1	140 g	150 g	190 g	200 g	240 ml

USEFUL EQUIVALENTS FOR LIQUID INGREDIENTS BY VOLUME

1/4 tsp						=	1 ml		
1/2 tsp						=	2 ml		
1 tsp						=	5 ml		
3 tsp	=	1 tbs			=	1/2 fl oz	=	15 ml	
		2 tbs	=	1/8 cup	=	1 fl oz	=	30 ml	
		4 tbs	=	1/4 cup	=	2 fl oz	=	60 ml	
		5 1/3 tbs	=	1/3 cup	=	3 fl oz	=	80 ml	
		8 tbs	=	1/2 cup	=	4 fl oz	=	120 ml	
		10 2/3 tbs	=	2/3 cup	=	5 fl oz	=	160 ml	
		12 tbs	=	3/4 cup	=	6 fl oz	=	180 ml	
		16 tbs	=	1 cup	=	8 fl oz	=	240 ml	
		1 pt	=	2 cups	=	16 fl oz	=	480 ml	
		1 qt	=	4 cups	=	32 fl oz	=	960 ml	
						33 fl oz	=	1000 ml	= 1 L

USEFUL EQUIVALENTS FOR COOKING/OVEN TEMPERATURES

	FAHRENHEIT	CELSIUS	GAS MARK
Freezing point	32°F	0°C	
Room temperature	68°F	20°C	
Boiling point	212°F	100°C	
Bake	325°F	160°C	3
	350°F	180°C	4
	375°F	190°C	5
	400°F	200°C	6
	425°F	220°C	7
	450°F	230°C	8

USEFUL EQUIVALENTS FOR DRY INGREDIENTS BY WEIGHT

To convert ounces to grams, multiply the number of ounces by 30.

1 oz	=	1/16 lb	=	30 g
4 oz	=	1/4 lb	=	120 g
8 oz	=	1/2 lb	=	240 g
12 oz	=	3/4 lb	=	360 g
16 oz	=	1 lb	=	480 g

USEFUL EQUIVALENTS FOR LENGTH

To convert inches to centimeters, multiply the number of inches by 2.5.

1 in			=	2.5 cm		
6 in	=	1/2 ft	=	15 cm		
12 in	=	1 ft	=	30 cm		
36 in	=	3 ft	=	1 yd	=	90 cm
40 in			=	100 cm	=	1 m

AUTHOR	Jamie Purviance
MANAGING EDITOR	Marsha Capen
EDITORIAL, DESIGN, AND PRODUCTION	rabble+rouser, inc.: Christina Schroeder, Chief Creative Marsha Capen, Editorial Director Shum Prats, Creative Director Abby Wilson, Assistant Editor
PHOTOGRAPHY	Tim Turner, Photographer and Photo Art Direction Christy Clow, Digital Guru Takamasa Ota, Photo Assistant Joe Bankmann, Photo Assistant
FOOD STYLING	Lynn Gagné, Food Stylist Nina Albazi, Assistant Food Stylist
COLOR IMAGING AND IN-HOUSE PREPRESS	Weber Creative Services: Amy Dorsch, Director of Creative Services Robert Page, Supervisor Digital Imaging Deanna Budnick, Senior Production Artist
CONTRIBUTORS	Lynda Balslev, Brigit Binns, Lena Birnbaum, David Bonom, Angela Brassinga, Tara Duggan, Sarah Epstein, Mary Goodbody, Gina Hodgson, Michael Kalhorn, Shannon Kinsella, Rick Rodgers, Cheryl Sternman Rule, Mark Scarbrough, Manuela Tar, Jess Thomson, Kerry Trotter, Amy Vogler, Bruce Weinstein, Sharron Wood, Terri Pischoff Wuerthner
INDEXER	Becky LaBrum
WEBER-STEPHEN PRODUCTS LLC	Mike Kempster, Chief Marketing Officer Brooke Jones, Director of Marketing
PUBLISHING CONSULTANT	Susan Maruyama, Round Mountain Media
OXMOOR HOUSE	Jim Childs, Publisher Leah McLaughlin, Editorial Director Felicity Keane, Creative Director Fonda Hitchcock, Brand Manager Sarah Putman Clegg, Senior Editor

10 9 8 7 6 5 4 3 2 1

ISBN-10: 0-376-02798-3
ISBN-13: 978-0-376-02798-6
Library of Congress Control Number: 2012947779

Weber Customer Service: 1.800.446.1071

www.weber.com®
www.sunset.com
www.oxmoorhouse.com
www.rabbleandrouser.com